7102935553 £5-50
A D77

✔ **KU-546-825**

MALTBY

This book is to be returned on or before

02.

Classification
in the
1970s

A SECOND LOOK

Contributors

D AUSTIN
R R FREEMAN
M A GOPINATH
J P IMMROTH
KAREN SPARCK JONES
E M KEEN
G A LLOYD
A MALTBY
J MILLS
SARAH K VANN
B C VICKERY

Classification
in the
1970s

A SECOND LOOK

Revised edition
edited by

ARTHUR MALTBY
MA FLA FRSA

CLIVE BINGLEY   &   LINNET BOOKS
LONDON   HAMDEN · CONN

FIRST PUBLISHED 1972. THIS REVISED EDITION
FIRST PUBLISHED 1976 BY CLIVE BINGLEY LTD
16 PEMBRIDGE ROAD LONDON W11
SIMULTANEOUSLY PUBLISHED IN THE USA
BY LINNET BOOKS AN IMPRINT OF THE SHOE STRING PRESS INC
995 SHERMAN AVENUE HAMDEN CONNECTICUT 06514
SET IN 10 ON 12 POINT PRESS ROMAN
AND PRINTED AND BOUND IN THE UK BY
REDWOOD BURN LTD TROWBRIDGE AND ESHER
COPYRIGHT © CLIVE BINGLEY LTD 1976
ALL RIGHTS RESERVED
BINGLEY ISBN: 0-85157-221-9
LINNET ISBN: 0-208-01533-7

Library of Congress Cataloging in Publication Data

Maltby, Arthur.
  Classification in the 1970s.

  Includes bibliographical references and index.
  1. Classification—Books—Addresses, essays, lectures.
2. Indexng—Addresses, essays, lectures.
3. Information storage and retrieval systems—
Addresses, essays, lectures. I. Title.
Z696.M25 1976   025.4   76-43965
ISBN 0-208-01533-7

Contents

5

General Introduction

This book first appeared in 1972 to review developments in classification and the prospects for the schemes. It is gratifying to learn from the publisher that a revised edition is now warranted and I am most grateful to my fellow-contributors for their cooperation in providing it. As a collection of papers by specialists in various areas of the classification arena, it offers a wide range of facts and opinions and should, I believe, continue to complement the work of standard textbooks on the subject. In addition to expressing my thanks to the contributors and to my wife, who assisted in a whole variety of ways, I wish to acknowledge the help of Eric Coates who took time and trouble to provide me with information on the UNISIST Broad System of Ordering. I have drawn some material from this source for the relevant portion of my own introductory paper.

Of the ten papers in the first edition, three appear unchanged apart from a few updatings and corrections. The others have been subject to alteration varying from very little change to large-scale rewriting. As the writers on the schemes naturally tend to be advocates of the system they are discussing, so too there are differences in the viewpoints of some other writers. This is natural in a work which tries to offer facts but also to stimulate ideas by providing a series of personal anticipations of what lies ahead. In addition, one or two contributors have clearly moved away, at least in part, from their own original stance. That too is as it should be in cases where on-going investigation of a truly scientific kind is concerned; we should be prepared, as T H Huxley said in the late nineteenth century, to follow if necessary 'to whatever abyss nature may lead'. Fortunately, there is no abyss here—merely the interesting revision and correction of forecasts and hopes that should accompany 'a second look'. I am pleased to have one additional 'viewer' with us, this being Karen Sparck Jones who has contributed a welcome chapter on automatic classification.

The papers of my ten fellow-contributors, considered together, represent a wide and deep survey of the best current thinking on classification with some anticipation of further developments. They still remind me, as I re-read them before publication, of a phrase used by Christopher Marlowe in a very different context—'infinite riches in a little room'.
I hope and believe that students and practitioners in librarianship and information science will find those papers which are appropriate to their interests as absorbing and informative as I found them all.

ARTHUR MALTBY

Burntisland
Fife Scotland
April 1976

8

Classification — logic limits, levels

A MALTBY

Research and development concerning the subject approach to the organization of books and other library materials, although for certain librarians a 'mentally intoxicating study' (to borrow Arundel Esdaile's memorable phrase) sometimes appears to those working in libraries other than specialized ones to be remote from practical situations in which they find themselves. This attitude is, at least occasionally, understandable and it is on this account that the introductory paper to the present volume concentrates upon the achievement, problems and possibilities of classification within the context of the general library. Perhaps the reason that changes in, or prospects for, classification seem irrelevant to some public, college, or even university librarians is that the heavily used general schemes seem to roll on as inexorably as time itself. Some internal growth and reconstruction there may be, but the well accepted systems show no sign of being supplanted and indeed have gathered strength from increasing mechanization amd MARC records. They seem destined to remain as fixtures—to survive as effective systems, to be accepted continually and meekly despite their defects, or to endure somewhere between these extremes as the case may be. Notwithstanding this situation, there remain some fundamental questions which profoundly concern the future of classification in general libraries particularly if, by 'classification' we really mean a rational sequence of the maximum utility and not simply a convenient pigeonholing system. Such questions are often inwardly pondered rather than clearly formulated and explicitly stated by the busy librarian, but they might well include the following:

Is a new scheme for shelf arrangement required for some general libraries? If it is, at least in certain circumstances, is it still feasible to test or to introduce one?

In classifying, how much emphasis should be placed on administrative or quasi-administrative factors—uniformity of classification practice throughout a library system, or the full use of a national centralized

9

classification service—and how much on the achievement of an order of maximum helfpulness which considers the distinctive requirements of the individual library?

Has classification become altogether too intricate? Are there situations in which some other equipment or service (for example, subject bibliographies) could take more of the load and carry out, in an equally satisfactory or superior manner, the work at present left to classification schemes?

Can any single classification truly serve both documentation and shelf arrangement, not to mention the intermediary position occupied (when adopted) by classified catalogues?

Answers to such questions must be based partly on opinion rather than facts and some queries of this kind undoubtedly lead us through tortuous paths of reasoning or persuasion. They nevertheless cry out for examination and further investigation if progress and prospects for the classifying process are to be realised in all areas of librarianship. It is hoped that this introductory paper may at least point the way towards answers for some of these questions, although the answers offered here would not be accepted by all contributors to the volume. A personal conviction regarding the major part of the final query can be stated at once. It is this writer's emphatic belief that there is an increasing gulf between the type of classification needed for shelf arrangement and that required by sophisticated retrieval systems.

Not so long ago, D J Foskett (1) admitting that classification theory and research have become complex and are causing controversy, wrote 'This would be surprising if classification were no more than a fairly convenient way of arranging books on shelves. Some librarians think it is . . . Yet today we can see clearly two relatively new spectacles on the library scene; on the one hand, some librarians are criticizing the Decimal Classification for being too detailed and unwieldy, on the other hand, some librarians and still more information officers, are busy revising the Universal Decimal Classification in order to make it more detailed'.

This apparent contradiction of librarians' requirements can be seen as sure evidence that classification has different roles to play in different situations and that there are at least two, and possibly more, 'levels' at which classificatory practice needs to operate. The dichotomy is now too certain for any one scheme to be viewed with real confidence as a classification for all seasons or situations. It is significant that the research project described by Austin in this volume began its embryonic

10

life as one seeking a total system aimed at serving both shelf order and information retrieval, but soon abandoned the attempt to satisfy the first function. Austin says elsewhere that his work is not designed to supersede the 'well-tried classifications in their tasks of ordering books on shelves and cards in catalogues. This job they appear to do reasonably well'. (2) He argues too that 'it is futile to expend time and effort classifying books by a faceted scheme which requires a high level of intellectual input, simply in order to shelve each work under some favoured facet, then scatter its subordinate facets in exactly the same way as any of the traditional enumerative schemes'. (3) While some may argue about the validity of the guarded praise given to the well-tried systems, the increasing division in the functions of classification today was made clear by the recognition that the proposed CRG/BNB scheme could not serve both shelf arrangement and mechanized information retrieval. However, before examining at greater length these 'levels of classification' it is valuable to reassess the logical justification for the process and its present day achievement and limitations.

The inherent logic of a classification, whatever form or depth it takes, appears self-evident to those who have worked in a variety of library situations. We owe a very great, if sometimes unobtrusive, debt to the process for, although alphabetical subject order certainly has its uses on various occasions, librarians—and many scholars or specialists too—recognise that we need primarily a sequence which expresses important relationships between subjects. Thus Luke Hansard, to select a single striking instance, when first producing an organized Catalogue and Breviate of British Parliamentary Papers, was led to observe that his objective 'appeared not likely to be obtained by a general or promiscuous (his word!) alphabetical arrangement, for by that method all relative connection of the subjects, and chronological dependence, would be lost, and a mass of undigested matters would forbiddingly present itself to the mind'. (4) Thus it can hardly be surprising that there is a long established link between the word 'classification' and logical division as followed by philosophers and others over many centuries. Classification within the context of librarianship and information science has, however, become increasingly embarrassed by such a linkage and it was because so fixed and binding an association is of dubious value for librarians that Douglas Foskett urged the substitution of the expression 'systematic arrangement' for the use of the term 'classification' as the description of the task of locating and relating subject information. It was once fashionable for librarians to refute the assertion of W S Jevons to the effect that the classification of books is logically absurd, but his remark clearly can be

11

vindicated if, by classification, we mean a process which follows strictly and closely the rules of logical division. The emergence of a distinctive method of subject analysis for knowledge as embodied in books and other library materials, heralded by the various writings of Ranganathan and by Palmer and Wells' *Fundamentals of library classification, 1951,* did much to emancipate our thinking from the strict genus to species progression advocated by the logicians. It is true that, to quote Foskett (5) again, 'reliance on logical classification can only confuse students and bring upon classifiers the reproach that they want to make a completely static universe . . . arrangement of subjects in libraries, therefore, cannot be based solely on 'classification' in the sense in which the term is used in logic and the classification sciences'. Faceted classification, through its flexibility in permitting the combination of basic concepts, provides the opportunity to classify precisely without the annoyance and inhibition of a schedule in which certain amalgamations of concepts are inevitably shut out because of the sequence in which the characteristics of division are applied. The classification scheme which lists subjects as such, exhausting each characteristic of division before utilizing the next in its gigantic task of enumeration is, however unconsciously, really striving to perpetuate in library classification the rules of formal logic. Yet, although the modern trend in our classifications is away from the rigidity of logical division, this is surely—in a very real if non-technical sense—more logical!

The apparent paradox stems from the fact that what seems most rational for library classification is a system which owes no allegiance, tenuous or otherwise, to the laws of logicians. Such independence is most clearly found in the faceted systems. Yet there is a temptation to which it is suspected that some students of library classification (and perhaps lecturers too) have succumbed, to be diverted by the detail and manipulative ability of the highly synthetic classifications at the expense of the equally important fundamental issue of helpful order. In Britain, for instance, enthusiasm for facet analysis was such some fifteen years ago that the young librarian might have been forgiven for thinking that the understanding of the development and principles of synthesis was the sole rock upon which classification studies should be based. It is not, of course, and the renewed efforts in recent years to seek out durable principles for the achievement of helpful order in an information science context—by semantic analysis, by the exploration of the theory of integrative levels of knowledge in the universe, and by other means—must be welcomed. Another significant and laudable trend is the growth of the study of the nature and structure of basic disciplines

12

as a theme in its own right and one which may precede a consideration of the library classifications. This development, well illustrated in the writings of Langridge (6), is certainly one of which Bliss would have approved and indeed the theory of gradation by speciality, as expounded in his 1929 book, seems a clear forerunner of the study of integrative levels. The interest in the structure of the universe of knowledge is also well illustrated in the brave, if exploratory attempts of Mayne (7).

With due attention now being paid to both flexibility in classification through synthesis and the fundamental issue of helpful order, important progress has been made. If the link with logic in a restrictive and narrow sense has been severed and the study of Porphyry's Tree and the Predicables superseded in a way which could scarcely be imagined twenty five years ago, the long qualified librarian can rest assured that his young counterpart now has a chance to study techniques more fundamental, relevant and, to that extent, much more rational or 'logical' for his professional training. Nor is the link with logical principles entirely lost. The subject, in fact, retains its capacity to assist in the development of an orderly mind. The student who encounters the theory of notation for the first time has been known to lament unnecessarily the fact that he may not be a mathematician. In fact to cope with and (dare it be said?) to enjoy library classification, we need not grieve over a possible lack of preliminary scientific training. The qualities needed are rather an interest in scientific method and the ability to think clearly and logically. Such qualities, as Langridge indicates in the work cited above, are helpful to us in all walks of life—although we sometimes need to overcome other aspects of our temperament to allow logic or classificatory method to hold sway. An example which might appeal to Mr Langridge was noticed recently on the sleeve of a jazz record, where the artist (Chris Barber) declares 'I am fairly excitable, yet (when playing) my sense of precision and order dominates'.

If the work put into library classification is justified and the process vindicated as a logical or wise one for the majority of libraries, then the defects of classification must be remembered also and weighed against its achievement. There are some special library situations where post-coordinate indexing, with or without classificatory leanings, is preferred to any pre-coordination of concepts as found in a classification scheme. Apart from these, and ignoring any possible incompetence on the part of the individual classifier, the chief actual or potential limitations of classification in the modern library may be viewed succinctly as follows:

1 The difference between libraries, even those of the same type, plus such irksome but very real pragmatic factors as the size and shape of a building or department, all have a very definite effect upon the

capabilities of any classification scheme. Reading and browsing can be influenced strongly by the shelf on which volumes are located, shelves which are too high or too near the floor being shunned. Readers still prefer material to be located in an area where it can be quickly seen and reached—which, in the United States some years ago, was aptly described as 'the zone of convenience'. Any Organization and Methods team too would have us plan our sequence to minimize congestion and 'traffic bottlenecks' rather than to maximise useful groupings of documents. It is virtually impossible to combat fully administrative, physical or psychological obstacles of this kind: they remain a possible foe to the best planned of systematic sequences.

2 Notation is sometimes too long if classification is specific, yet detailed classification is often needed. In fairness it should be added that there are factors other than the degree of detail—type of symbols used, allocation of notation to subjects, and whether the notation is hierarchical or not—which affect the question of notational brevity.

3 Classification needs to keep pace with the advancement of knowledge—the growth of subject areas, the decline of certain subject associations and the forging of new ones. Despite this the positive knowledge of many (perhaps thousands of) books already classified by an existing arrangement does act as a powerful deterrent to even conservative change in numerous libraries. This, like the point above, is a very real problem and certainly cannot be resolved by the rejection of classification, but only by the careful determination of both present and long-term priorities. The librarian who wants specificity with short notation and a system which never changes but it always up to date is like an ambitious but unrealistic investor who concurrently seeks extensive capital growth, a high income and the maximum security for his money!

4 The necessity of parallel arrangements for oversize books and non-book material makes the achievement of a single systematic sequence impossible, except in the catalogue. Some materials—current periodicals, for instance—scarcely justify a classified order.

5 Classification, both on the shelves and in the catalogue, presents its subjects in a long line or dimensional row, whereas the true pattern of knowledge is obviously multi-dimensional. The necessity of linear order is seen as a real handicap by some writers on classification.

6 Books or documents which deal with more than one subject cause problems. The detailed subject analysis permitted by some schemes provides a partial solution, but often at the cost of a certain
14

amount of notational distress. The catalogue (classified or otherwise) invariably has to come to the rescue of the shelf order in catering for the secondary subject theme or themes in a multi-topical work.

7 Conventional schemes subordinate topics to disciplines so that 'coffee' for example may, according to its context, be found under botany, food manufacture, or economics. Such distribution is quite correct, even essential, but may cause problems if an interdisciplinary study of a subject is taking place and information on *all* aspects of 'coffee', 'coal', 'the horse', or some other topic that has been distributed according to discipline are required together. The thematic approach now favoured by some educational institutions tends to boost the demand for such cross-disciplinary examination of topics.

8 The final limitation enumerated here is a very basic one. As the amoeba divides to multiply, so classification scatters in order to collect. Emphasis placed on some subject associations means that others must be neglected. The good classification endeavours constantly to bring out the groupings that are of utility to the majority, leaving the A-Z subject index to indicate the scattering of relatively unimportant subject associations. A faceted classification can be of considerable benefit here in making the librarian clearly aware of which relationships have been brought to the fore because, provided it follows a standard citation order, the combination order of the facets is the key both to the groupings which the system exhibits and those which it has not displayed. Yet some subject associations must continually be sacrificed. Thus, for example, if we consider the Bibliographic Classification at the main class level where its order has been the subject of praise, we find that ethics is placed with religion and applied social science and is thus removed from the cognate area of logic and philosophy. Bliss would point to the fact that he has drawn on a long and respected tradition in selecting the one association rather than the other and that there is an alternative for those who want it. Nevertheless the point emerges that even a good and well planned sequence must ignore some desirable subject groupings.

All the above facts, although we try to restrain their impact, are genuine problems and it is certain that there are others with which we must contend. Criticisms of classification and attempted radical solutions to its problems are legion and range from partly understandable attempts at modification or simplification of systems, through partial loss of confidence in open access methods and the consequent advocacy of a stack-room type of situation until, eventually, complete scepticism is reached. In the latter sphere, the provocative and sometimes amusing paper by

Moss (8) comes to mind. It is worthy of some consultation and thought, whatever our viewpoint, for its endeavour ruthlessly to expose pretension and to pinpoint real practical difficulties. Some of these difficulties are freely admitted, but are greatly minimized through the support afforded by catalogues, indexes, display, bibliographies, and personal assistance to readers. Even the most uncompromising supporter of classification, Ranganathan, is recorded as placing due emphasis on the fact that all 'our technology requires the genial personality of the librarian to interpret it to the reader'. (9) The real issue confronting Moss and all other critics is to find a constructive and viable alternative to classification that can serve most library situations so well—for, despite the difficulties, classification *is* a good servant. Many compromises and alternatives simply do not work or else they generate problems the magnitude of which greatly exceed the limitations of classification. The very fact that one *can* see and list classification's defects in addition to noting its achievement (plus the knowledge that classified order is by no means the sole device for subject retrieval) is a potent argument in its favour because, in the case of many alternatives, the extent of the waste, problems and inefficiency would be most difficult to measure. The advantages of the classified order—for browsing in the open access library, for reference service, for the possible arrangement of a subject catalogue, and for various administrative services in the general library—remain assured. Berwick Sayers (10), in a short word of apologia to students many years ago summed up the situation neatly when he admitted 'Classification is often tiresome', yet immediately and very rightly added 'but we can't do without it!'

Prospects for classification as a whole are thus bright, but account needs to be taken of the requirements of different library situations and the possible inability of any one system to satisfy all of these. Systematic arrangement is, therefore, required at various tiers or levels, the perhaps ambiguous but for our purpose alliterative term 'levels' being used, not in Ranganathan's sense, but in an attempt to draw attention to what might be called the ecology of library classification. The fact that a number of librarians, who ought to be interested in classification research, ignore the enormous amount of intellectual effort now being put into the subject at the information science level is not the result of it appearing esoteric, but is due largely to immediate environmental factors—an inability to see a clear application for the research within their own library situation. The problems of shelf classification at public and academic library level continue to be relatively ignored apart from the revision of the long established systems. There has been virtually no real innovation in this sphere, although there still seems to be scope for some experiment which would complement existing research. At present, those who are unhappy about the full or orthodox employment of the general schemes usually seek refuge either in adaptation or broad classification. Indeed it is interesting to note that when, just over a decade ago, several new university libraries were being established in the United Kingdom two pleas were published simultaneously; one in favour of adaptation via a modification of the Decimal Classification (11), the other advocating a simplified form of conventional classification as the norm for such libraries (12). It is feared that neither solution has provided the best answer for the modern university or large college library. Broad classification—in the sense of simplification within the framework of a system really designed to be applied in more detail— apart from the effect on cataloguing and the uncertainty of interpretation as to just what constitutes 'broad shelf arrangement' is at best often little more than a ruined shell of the scheme represented. At worst, when the hierarchy and sequence of the classification concerned are suspect, such broad arrangement can result in some very curious juxtapositions which a closer arrangement would largely eliminate.

The writer has more sympathy with the kind of adaptation used in an endeavour to improve shelf arrangement in two newer British university libraries—York and Stirling. There is a very understandable wish in many librarians to promote the more extensive and better use of the subject approach in the academic world, so that an attempt is sometimes made to mould a scheme so that it fits the shape or 'faculty pattern' of the university or college. On the grounds of helpful sequence this is highly commendable. But there are also powerful reasons for utilizing a general classification as it stands rather than with extensive modifications. The growth of national centralized cataloguing and the increasing availability of MARC tapes with the consequent need for a compatible local subject cataloguing data input indicate the folly of being out of step with uniform practice. Thus it would be wiser to accept Congress or Dewey than to improvise. If all academic institutions exhibited the same basic faculty structure, there might be a case for a new general scheme reflecting this, but alas they offer what seems largely to be a classic case of *tot homines quot sententiae*. The established general schemes, which have—it must be stressed— made increasing efforts in recent years to remedy their weaknesses ought (in the absence of further research and appropriate findings) to remain, with any modification being restricted to minor details.

17

What of the public library—is there scope for experiment rather than mere revision for classification there? There may still well be, if attention is placed on arrangement for the lending library and, most especially, for branch libraries. Lack of interest in problems of shelf arrangement, so conspicuous in this quarter nowadays, is doubtless partly due to the appeal and efficiency of the Decimal Classification. Perhaps it is also due to the fact that the problems are wrongly thought to offer all too little in the way of an intellectual challenge: that, like one of Jane Austen's heroines, they 'cannot speak to us well enough to be unintelligible'. If neglect is in part due to the latter supposition, it is unfortunate and one must hope that the tasks will eventually find recognition (as in her own context Miss Morland did) within the total framework of classificatory research.

Conventional broad classification and adaptation have been dismissed as unwise, but another possibility for the lending library is that of using reader interest arrangement, a United States public library experiment which, despite relatively little publicity, has spread with some limited success. The essence of reader interest order for the public library service is that it endeavours to arrange material in a bold and imaginative way which might well cut across the orthodox subject disciplines in order to produce groupings which coincide with the pattern of the reader's thinking, activities and habits. In the words of one of its advocates, Rutzen (13), it is 'not a classification of the fields of knowledge, but a shelving arrangement based on . . . the needs of the people'. Nor is it necessarily a broad arrangement on all occasions, although it would usually be so considered. A visitor to the library at Detroit is quoted by Ruth Rutzen as saying 'It is not less of classification that suits them (the readers) better. They need a different kind of classification and more of it'. At present reader interest arrangement, where practised, exists in many diverse forms. Several public libraries which do not consciously employ it as a matter of policy nevertheless adopt the kind of arrangement which essentially represents a groping towards this concept. It is conceivable that such a method could partly break down the often artificial barrier between fiction and non-fiction and satisfy those who want to abolish or reduce the huge alphabetical sequence of novels. It is also well suited to some of the more admirable and imaginative views of the role of the public lending library service and echoes the advice given by E A Savage in his work on classification and display, or elsewhere when he spoke of attempts at imaginative groupings 'adapted and modified group by group into a more harmonious order and stronger expository power'. (14)

It seems just possible that reader interest arrangement could combine an acceptable shelf order for branch libraries with an economical notation and that suitable research could generate a system based on the reader interest concept which could be applied, in fairly uniform manner, across a range of public lending libraries with the associated advantages which wide acceptance usually brings. As it has been remarked above that faculty reader interest differs from university to university, so also can the idea of a widely, perhaps internationally, acceptable reader interest order for public libraries be challenged. Although the proportion of material in each class would naturally differ considerably from library to library and would depend upon the nature of the community served, it is feasible that a single reader interest order, if soundly based, would have far more than a local appeal (and might help win a few non-users to the library?) since the responsibilities and interests of the adult individual—his home, his work, current affairs, his place in society, his recreational needs—are fundamentally alike in many regions. So, at best, it could fulfil the hope of an enthusiast who rightly wrote 'the scholar, the student or the systematic reader has always been well provided for. On the other hand, the planless reader and the browser, who in fact constitute the great percentage of the public library clientele . . . want and need above all a book arrangement which is non-technical, easily accessible and time-saving'. (15)

It would be futile, of course, to pretend that the reader interest idea is without its own problems. The quest for a reader interest grouping of wide appeal could prove an arduous one and—assuming that such an order could be found—there would also be the tasks of updating its divisions when required and devising a notation. In terms of library administration, there is the problem of justifying the use of one system for a public reference library or the central departments as a whole and another (reader interest) in branches. On the other hand, the question of utilizing different classifications for different tasks is one that should at least be considered. A person who certainly believed in it was Fremont Rider, biographer of Dewey and a man whose first classification credo and hint of intent followed hard on the heels of that of Bliss in the *Library journal* for 1910. When he eventually produced his *International classification* (IC) in 1961, he offered it purely as a shelving system, claiming that for such a deliberately restricted role synthesis should be rejected. Thus there are no 'add to' or 'divide like' instructions in Rider's scheme. He also offers a pure notation of letters and is able to cater for some 17,000 topics without exceeding class-marks of three letters. It is very easy to dismiss the system because of its lack of use and Rider's own apparent indifference to the setting up of a revision programme for it. Yet it recognises that, although recorded knowledge is multi-faceted, only the primary facet can be displayed in a linear order on the shelves and that if more finesse is needed for such arrangement then detail via synthesis may not necessarily be the best way to achieve it. The present writer has discussed the scheme at more length elsewhere (16), but it should at least be noted that it is speedy and simple to apply, offers a modern arrangement with short notation, and is unencumbered with apparatus too complex for organization at the shelf level.

These points in themselves will not give it any prospect of use at a time when the emphasis is more and more on the centralization, mechanization and thus the standardization of technical services. Yet the schemes which are standards ought to be scrutinized against the claims of a newcomer such as the IC. The widely used general schemes LC and DC, offer themselves for use at various levels or for different tasks and may thus have a tendency to fall a victim to compromise in their efforts to be a sufficiently good 'all-rounder'. Thus it is that Perreault, admittedly scarcely a good friend of the Congress system, claims that it fails to meet the needs of the browsing function and asks 'if it is not good for the classed catalog, nor for electronic searching, besides not being good for browsing, what is it good for?' (17) If the three areas mentioned in the quotation are accepted as distinct 'levels', it could—at least as a hypothesis—be argued that what might really score for shelf arrangement is a system like the IC that can be applied quickly and with little intellectual effort since classmarks are ready-made and listed together with the enumerated topics. Such speculation could be continued by arguing that it is possible that the ideal scheme for the relatively gross level of subject organization that can be achieved on the shelves would be a purpose-built system and would take full account of browsing needs. One real obstacle lies in the definition of browsing, as Hyman's (18) study shows. Phyllis Richmond (19) has made what could eventually prove a most useful distinction between browsing in specific pre-selected areas of a classification on the one hand, and serendipity browsing on the other. The latter involves picking titles off the shelves out of curiosity and at random. She suggests that the Congress system is poor for the former task but good for the serendipity browser. It might be possible, given more information on browsing and the classification requirements of browsers, to develop a system better for both types of browsing.

A realist might well raise the objection that there is now little hope of *any* new system for classification on the shelves and it is significant that the recent British Library report on its own classification needs (20) plumps for DC plus a PRECIS type subject index, especially if the British

20

library reference collections are, in future, to be viewed as an organic unity. It can also be said that complications would arise in employing a purpose-built system for the arrangement of the documents themselves and a different and more sophisticated purpose-developed system for the organization of their surrogates within a catalogue. For instance, the sequence of entries in the classified part of a catalogue would no longer be an indication of their shelf location and this would need to appear on the entries also. Yet, if one can be so heretical for a moment as to even postulate a new start, it might be thought that such difficulties could be overcome and that schemes would benefit by having a single level of subject organization clearly in view upon which they could concentrate without hindrance or distraction. Thus we might have a partly synthetic scheme with a complex but hospitable and mnemonic notation for the classified sequence of the catalogue, supported by an enumerative scheme with a simple notation for the shelves. The former could be applied through a national cataloguing agency. The latter could be done speedily and with minimum cost at the local level, thus meeting the innate wish to do some of their own classification which surprisingly persists in many librarians and partly answering the wry comment heard recently to the effect that national cataloguing organizations classify for everybody and for nobody at the same time.

Such theorizing as this may be criticized as being unfair to the well-established systems (which is not its intent) or for representing an impossible course of action at this stage in the history of library classification. Yet we ought not to embark upon the second century of the systematic arrangement of materials without at least querying, at all levels, our traditions and existing procedures. What is more, interest in the idea of classification at different levels has grown since this paper was drafted in its original form in 1971. An outstanding instance of this is the development by an FID Working Group of the Broad System of Ordering for the UNISIST programme. At the time of writing the whole funding and future of this concept seem to rest with UNESCO, but the idea itself stems from the recognition that an international scientific communications network requires a switching device, or intermediate indexing language, to enable communication to over-ride barriers arising from the fact that there are several indexing languages in use. The BSO has some 2,000 terms and a numerical notation. It has clearly been influenced by the work of Dahlberg (21) and is not dissimilar to the outline for the revised Bliss Classification. This BSO system may have a useful future as a roof classification or broad 'translation service' for the many and varied schemes of

21

much greater detail which are used internationally. It clearly accepts the idea of classification at different tiers, as indeed does Geoffrey Lloyd in his paper on UDC within the present volume.

To return to the question of classification for the shelves, it is now some time since Shera (22) declared that 'the study of habits of use is requisite to the act of classifying. At the present time our knowledge of the uses to which literature is put, and the demands made upon bibliographic resources by those who consult them are lamentably fragmentary'. Yet little progress has been made towards rectifying the position. One, admittedly very small and tentative, experiment (23) suggested that readers would accept most systems of organization on the shelves provided that the system was explained and guided adequately, but this does not rule out the possibility that a scheme could be developed specifically for the shelves to seek excellence at that level. Ranganathan, in what sadly proved to be his last substantial paper, commented on the first edition of this book and stated that the present writer's exhortation to seek out reader opinion on classification for the shelves is 'a tall order' adding 'if it can be carried out with the necessary safeguards it will be ideal'. (24) He suggested that we must continue to depend upon the insight and experience of librarians. Dr Hyman's work is of some use in the latter respect, but despite all the problems more work could be done on browsing needs within open access collections. It does not seem impossible either, since funds were found for the Cranfield experiments, that some laboratory situation testing of the efficiency of classification within the context of shelf arrangement for general collections could be devised—certainly its results would have relevance for thousands of working situations. Then we might see how a reader interest arrangement and the shelf-orientated International Classification, or even the revised Bibliographic Classification, fared in this area alongside Congress or Dewey in the consumers' eyes. There would be immense difficulties, but these are not insuperable and it would be worthwhile in cost terms, especially when we consider how many libraries use systems which have been with us for a long time but which have never been subjected to unbiased scrutiny in the form of testing customer reaction. Possibly DC and LC would do well in such a programme and vindicate their popularity in terms of performance rather than simply in terms of historical circumstance and the support given to them by national agencies. Even if testing led to an affirmation of the position of these schemes, it would still be justified and would help to give direction and impetus to their future revision. But if, to borrow the

22

words of Dylan Thomas, we go on for ever, 'emptying our churns into the Dewi river', it should be because it is the right procedure to follow and we should not be whispering 'regardless of expense'. So difficulties in framing an appropriate research programme should not prevent an attempt to discover how the accepted classifications might stand up to the challenge of other, perhaps single-purpose-systems.

Another area which merits more investigation and is particularly worthy of attention in times of economic cutback is the question of the relationship between catalogues, bibliographies and the classification. At what level does each work best and how can we make them truly complementary? Swank provided (25), many years ago, an excellent survey of the history of the controversy of classification and cataloguing versus bibliographic tools, but the great increase in both the quality and quantity of the latter since then ought to make us reappraise the various methods of retrieving subject information. Thought on how the total apparatus at our disposal could best blend to ensure effectiveness with economy might help general library classifications to shed part of their load. They could then dovetail more effectively with catalogues to provide a key to subject resources not covered in the published bibliographic services.

It should not be thought then that there is no scope for research and exploration regarding the future of shelf classification in general libraries. Both the idea of testing consumer reactions to established systems as opposed to others (perhaps unconventional or purpose-made for shelf arrangement), and the examination of the role of classification in relation to subject bibliographies might repay scrutiny and funding. Yet whatever is or is not achieved in these directions, there will remain a need for clear and plentiful guiding with attention given to the presentation of the finished system if limitations are to be minimized and if it is to be 'logical' in terms of being intelligible to the reader. Such guiding will remain absolutely necessary whether we recognise different levels of subject organization and use different schemes for them or prefer to rely on one multi-purpose system. Even more necessary is a library staff who appreciate both what the classification can and cannot do and how it reacts with other retrieval devices. This is where the 'insight and experience' of the librarian are invaluable: no research, mechanization or other advance at any level will supersede the need for personal ability and initiative, for 'the genial personality' behind the technical systems.

REFERENCES

1 Foskett, D J: *Classification for a general index language: a review of recent research by the CRG.* Library Association research publication no. 2, 1970.

2 Austin, D: 'Prospects for a new general classification', *Journal of librarianship,* 1(3), July 1969, p 149-169.

3 Austin, D: 'Two steps forward'. In Palmer, B I and Austin, D. *Itself an education.* 2nd edition, Library Association, 1971, p 71.

4 Hansard, L: *Catalogue and breviate of Parliamentary Papers 1696-1834,* edited by P and G Ford. Irish University Press, 1968, p 6.

5 Foskett, D J: *Library classification and the field of knowledge.* Library Association reference and special libraries section, North Western Group. Occasional paper no. 1, 1958.

6 Langridge, D: *Approach to classification for students of librarianship.* London: Bingley; Hamden, Conn, Linnet Books, 1973.

7 Mayne, A J: 'Progress report on a new scheme for the classification of knowledge'. *International classification* 1(1) 1974, p 27-32.

8 Moss, R: 'How do we classify?' *Aslib proceedings* 14(2) February 1962, p 33-45.

9 *S R Ranganathan 1892-1972.* Library Association, 1974, p 18.

10 Sayers, W C B: *The grammar of classification.* 4th edition, Association of Assistant Librarians, 1935.

11 Stirling, J F: 'The York University classification scheme', *Journal of documentation,* 19(3), September 1963, p 118-126.

12 Thompson, J: 'Book classification in new university libraries', *Library Association record* 65(9), September 1963, p 327-329.

13 Rutzen, R: 'A classification for the reader', in Allerton Park Institute, *The role of classification in the modern American library,* edited by T Eaton and D E Strout, 1959, p 53-61.

14 Savage, E A: *A librarian looks at readers.* 2nd edition, Library Association, 1950, p 252.

15 Orvig, M: 'The reader interest arrangement: an American shelving system with a future', *Libri,* 5(3) 1955, p 223-232.

16 Maltby, A: 'Rider revisited: speculations derived from an unused classification'. To be published in *Library resources & technical services.*

17 Perreault, J: 'Reclassification: rationale and problems.' *Proceedings of a conference . . . held at the Center of Adult Education, University of Maryland,* 1968, p 56.

18 Hyman, R J: *Access to library collections.* Scarecrow Press. 1972.

19 Richmond, P A: 'General advantages and disadvantages of using the Library of Congress Classification', in *The use of the Library of Congress classification,* American Library Association, 1968, p 211.

20 British Library Research & Development report No. 5233. *British Library Working Party on classification and indexing,* 1975.

21 Dahlberg, I: 'Possibilities for a new Universal Decimal Classification' *Journal of documentation,* 27(1) March 1971, p 18-36.

22 Shera, J H: *Libraries and the organisation of knowledge.* London: Crosby Lockwood; Hamden, Conn, Archon Books, 1965.

23 Maltby, A and Hunter E J: 'Readers and classification'. *New library world,* 73(868) October 1972, p 411-413.

24 Ranganathan, S R: 'Comparative classification', *Library science with a slant to documentation* 9(3) September 1972, p 289-315.

25 Swank, R: 'Subject catalogs, classifications or bibliographies?: a review of critical discussions'. *Library Quarterly* 14(4) October 1944, p 316-332.

Bibliographic Classification

J MILLS
School of librarianship,
Polytechnic of North London

EDITOR'S INTRODUCTION: This paper provides a clear account (the fullest available) of the continuing comprehensive revision of the Bibliographic Classification, by the Chairman of the Bliss Classification Association. It may also be read profitably, quite independently of the study of the BC, for the considerable light shed on many fundamental classificatory problems and as an indication of the task of applying facet analysis and consistent citation order in the building or restructuring of any general system.

1 Preface

1.1 Viewed as a library classification scheme *per se,* the prospect for Bliss' Bibliographic Classification (the BC) is clear and bright. A radically revised and greatly expanded new edition is in preparation, to be published in some 18 separate subject classes beginning in 1976 and with completion within two to three years of the publication of the first parts. This new version will both improve significantly the BC structure as an instrument for information control and retrieval, and at the same time greatly increase its range and detail.

1.2 From the point of view of its future use, the prospect is less predictable. The law of the market which hopefully forecasts that nothing will keep a good product down does not operate automatically in the world of library classification, where the forces of inertia, the cost-benefits of centralized indexing and the difficulties of reclassification tend strongly to perpetuate the system in occupation, even if a better one comes along.

1.3 Before considering these two views of the new Bliss Classification in detail it seems sensible to review briefly its present nature and use.

1.31 Nature of the first edition

Although conceived and broadly described as long ago as 1910, it was first published (in extended outline) in 1935 (1) and finally appeared

25

in full between 1940 and 1953. (2) Its outstanding features are as follows:

1.32 BC is based, as are the other four existing general schemes considered, on the 'disciplines' reflecting the specialization of work and study in modern society. Bliss consiously refined this widely held assumption into a theory of 'consensus' and this resulted in a comprehensive overall order which is generally acknowledged to be quite the best of them all. The basic sequence may be given succinctly as follows:

Philosophy, Logic, Mathematics

Physical sciences

    Physics

    Chemistry

    Astronomical system and bodies

      Earth

Biological sciences

    Botany

    Zoology

      Man: anthropology in the widest sense

         Physical (including medicine, psychology)

         Social: the human studies, social sciences and humanities, arts.

1.33 To put some flesh onto this skeleton, below is an amplification showing some of the additional features necessitated by the practical demands of a working bibliographic classification, including notation. The latter, it should be noted, does not necessarily reflect the relations (of subordination or coordination) between the classes.

1-9   Anterior numeral classes (for special collections of various kinds, eg, 6, Periodicals)
Class 2 here (Bibliography and libraries) is an alternative to its preferred position in Class Z.

A   Philosophy and general science
(including logic, mathematics, metrology, statistics)

B   Physics
(including special physical technology, eg, radio)

C   Chemistry
(including mineralogy, chemical technology)

D   Astronomy, Geology, Geography (general and physical)

E   Biology
(including palaeontology, biogeography)

F   Botany
(including bacteriology)

G Zoology
   (including zoogeography and economic zoology)
H Anthropology (General and physical)
   (including medicine, hygiene, physical training and recreation)
I Psychology
   (including psychiatry)
J Education
K Social sciences
      sociology, ethnology, anthropogeography (including travel
      and description in general)
L-O Social-political history
      M Europe, N America, O Australia, Asia, Africa
P Religion, theology, ethics
Q Applied social sciences, social welfare
R Political science
S Law
T Economics
U Arts in general, useful arts (including less scientific
      technologies)
V Aesthetic arts, recreative arts and pastimes
W-Y Philology: language and literature
      W Non-Indo-European, X Indo-European, Y English
Z Bibliography, bibliology, libraries

1.34 A dominant principle underlying this order is that of 'gradation by speciality': 'A very important instance is that of the nature sciences arranged in order of speciality, each science being in one sense individual and coordinate with its fellow sciences, yet in another sense subordinate to that on which it is mainly dependent for concepts and principles and from which it is largely derived by specialization'. (3) By this theory (advanced in various forms by a number of philosophers, particularly Comte, Ostwald, and Spencer) it is argued, for example, that Physics, dealing as it does with the fundamental nature of matter and energy itself, is more 'general' than Chemistry, which studies organizations of matter and energy at a more specialized level.

1.35 Another important principle is that of adaptability—'adaptation of of logical order to practical uses and to convenience through collocation . . ' (*A Bibliographic Classification,* Vols 1-2, p 23). It is reflected in extensive provision for alternative locations and treatments: eg, some technologies may be collocated with the others in the technology class U, or subordinated to the science on which they are based; or, International law may go with International relations or with Law.

1.36 The BC notation is remarkable for its brevity (which quality Bliss ranked highly), and this is secured to some extent by a disregard of expressiveness. Also, although not a fully faceted notation, it does allow extensive synthesis.

1.37 *The present use of BC*

About eighty libraries now use the scheme. These users are predominantly academic and learned libraries and government and special libraries. Most of them are in the British Commonwealth. In 1967 an abridged version of the scheme for use in schools was published by the (British) School Library Association. (4) Maintenance of the scheme is achieved via the *Bliss Classification bulletin;* this appears annually and in recent years has contained substantial additions to the BC, mainly in scientific and technical areas. By 1970 BC was providing, in a number of areas, the most detailed and up to date schedules (outside some full international editions of the UDC) of the major general classifications—eg, in electronics, oceanography, automatic control and control devices, nuclear reactor engineering, sound reproduction and recording, astronautics, microchemical analysis, physics and chemistry of the atmosphere, food preservation, operative surgery, child hygiene and care, gardening and fruitgrowing, solid state physics, physical and chemical metallurgy, printing, and so forth.

The *Bulletin* is published by the Bliss Classification Association (5). The H W Wilson Company, publishers of the BC, kindly made over the complete publishing rights to the Association, which has raised a special fund to enable a new and enlarged edition of the scheme to be prepared. The work is being done at the School of Librarianship, the Polytechnic of North London, by the writer, with the collaboration of full-time researchers Valerie Lang 1969-1972 and Vanda Broughton 1972 to date.

2 *The present revision of BC: policy on degree of change*

The considerations which led to the decision to make the revision a radical one rather than moderate are as follows:

2.1 In contrast with the excellence of its main structure, which will remain virtually untouched, the detailed order within some of the classes is unsatisfactory. In a nutshell, the facet analysis is not very well done; facets are confused, with the inevitable result that there is a lack of predictability in placing many compound subjects.

2.2 If this is to be remedied, there seems little point in making only a partial job of it. Editorially, a 'once for all' reclassification is a more attractive proposition than a protracted, piecemeal operation. Decisions in one class often affect decisions in others also, and the operation is more economically and efficiently performed as a single, integral revision.

2.3 Analogous to this, the practical problems of reclassification in a library can be planned more easily if the new scheme already exists as a total system. Also if a library has to reclassify a given class to any degree it is often the case that a *complete* revision will not take significantly longer.

2.4 A revised scheme enjoying a clear facet structure in each class and clear rules for consistent classifying is considerably easier to maintain and revise than an enumerative one not enjoying these features. Facet relations in a class are relatively stable ones. Although new concepts constantly arise, the great majority fall predictably into existing categories—they *must* be either *kinds* of the entity defining the class, or *parts* of it, or *processes* in it, or *operations* on it, or *agents* of these and so on.

The criticism often made of classification schemes—that they inevitably grow out of date—is not invalidated by developing a clear and comprehensive facet structure, but its practical implications are decidedly softened in their impact. The maintenance and development of such a system is correspondingly easier. (Further comment on the problem of development can be found at 4.231 and 4.55.)

2.5 The amount of detail in the first edition varies from subject to subject. In particular, some of the physical sciences and technologies are inadequate for a large modern collection. The whole history of bibliographical classification testifies to the desirability of a detailed vocabulary. The precision with which our shelf arrangements and our indexes can be searched rests entirely on this point. Its relevance to the use made of a scheme can be put very simply. If detail is provided, those who do not want it need not use it. If detail is *not* provided, those who want it have no such alternative—individual improvisation raises very serious practical problems and is inconsistent with the notion of a single common system.

2.51 Closely associated with the provision of (enumerated) detail is the provision of a fully synthetic notation. Although the present BC allows considerable synthesis, this is somewhat uneven and calls for extension and simplification.

2.6 BC will have gone some 25 years without a comprehensive revision. (Longer in the case of the science and technology classes *in toto*.)

2.61 We cannot expect BC to be revised as frequently as DC or LC; so this edition must look correspondingly further ahead. (By 'frequent revision' we mean publishing the complete system in a new edition, as distinct from the production of regular, but non-cumulated additions and amendments. So far as the latter goes, BC bulletins subsequent to the new edition will certainly keep BC as up to date as the others.)

2.7 It is assumed that present users of BC already employ a wide variety of the alternatives offered by the scheme as well as amendments and expansions of their own. As a result, whatever form the revision takes it will inevitably involve many users in varying degrees of reclassification. So we might as well make the best possible job of it.

2.8 A number of positive steps will be taken to minimize the work involved in reclassification. The scope and definition of classes will be met by clear and explicit rules for practical classification.

3 *Objectives and methods in the revision of BC*

3.1 The basic function of a library classification is to assist the retrieval of information by providing a helpful and predictable order for the arrangement of documents and/or their surrogates (descriptions of documents) in catalogues and bibliographies.

3.2 To be helpful it must allow a searcher for information to locate unambiguously a specific class (broad or narrow) and then, depending on whether too few or too many relevant documents are found, to expand or contract that class or to move to another alternative, but related, class.

3.3 A vital element here is the predictability of the order. In practice, this is mainly a problem of citation order—knowing which concepts are subordinated to which, eg, in a class Economics, to know whether *Mobility in service industries* is to be sought under *Service industries* or *Mobility*.

3.4 Once a class is located, the effective adjustment of the search by contraction and expansion is largely a function of the clarity of the hierarchy within which the class sits. The vital requirement here is that a given hierarchy should be pure and intact—ie, not mixed up with another. If we wish to contract the search within the class *Service industries* we need to be confident that all the various kinds of Industry are kept together and not mixed up, say, with Economic problems.

3.5 There is only one way in which a library classification can meet the above criteria and that is to give it a comprehensive and consistent facet structure and to provide at all points for the possibility of compounding between different classes. This is the first principle being observed in the revision of BC and its implementation is described in more detail below. For the great majority of classes, the method of revision is a straightforward examination of facet structure, citation and

30

filing order, adjustment of the class as it stands to the degree necessary to bring existing BC into line with this and a further adjustment of notation if necessary.

For some classes, however, analysis may disclose a need for relocation or partial relocation, or of redefinition involving classes in other areas of the scheme. The commoner (and simpler) situation will be dealt with first below and then some of the less usual but sometimes more far-reaching adjustments will be considered.

4 Simple revision of a class
4.1 Stage 1: Facet analysis

4.11 The terms appearing under the class in BC are analysed as to their broad relationship to the class and sorted into facets; eg, UVC Clothing industries discloses a *Materials* facet (Wool, cotton . . .), an *Operations* facet (Manufacturing, sewing, altering . . .), an *Agents* facet (Machine, personnel . . .), a *Wearers* facet (man, boy . . .), a *Garments* facet (underwear, jacket, hat . . .), a *Parts of garment* facet (Lining, trimming . . .).

4.12 The terms in each facet are then sorted into their subfacets (or arrays as Ranganathan calls them); eg, *Garment* may be divided by *Part of body covered* (head, trunk . . .), by *Season* winter . . .).

4.2 Stage 2: Literary warrant and degree of detail

4.21 The equivalent classes in the other major systems (DC, CC, LC, UDC), in any special classifications which may exist, in the cumulations of BNB since 1950 and other general catalogues of book literature are then examined. This serves two purposes:

4.22 It discloses any further principles of division operative in the literature; *eg,* entries in DC disclosed an array of Garments by *Function or occasion when worn* (Ceremonial, Ecclesiastical . . .) and entries in BNB reinforced this (*eg,* Safety clothing). These are added to the facet structure already established.

4.23 It ascertains the literary warrant which will determine the size of vocabulary (level of enumerative detail) in the new edition. It is well known that the vocabulary of one major scheme (DC) has proved inadequately detailed to meet the requirements of specific description in BNB. The level of detail aimed at in the new BC is one which will meet amply the demands of book literature in this respect.

4.231 Although not seeking to emulate the enumerated detail of the full international editions of the UDC or the 'depth' schedules of Colon it is hoped that good foundations will be laid for an extended use of BC in special collections by the enumeration of at least the *names* of a maximum number of arrays even if these names are followed by enumeration of only a limited number of specific subclasses. This means that the 'growing points' in each subject will have been anticipated to some extent and the expansion of a general class named by its principle of division (*eg,* Clothes by season when worn) by enumeration of its species (Winter, Summer . . .) should be straightforward. The notational problems of expansion are of course considerably eased by this procedure.

4.232 It should be remembered here that enumerative detail is not the only criterion by which the range or specificity of a scheme is judged; the provision of synthetic notation is just as important and this is considered in more detail below (4.5).

4.3 *Stage 3: Citation order*

With the full range of facets and arrays established, a decision on the citation order is made. BC already provides some evidence as to the desirable citation order; *eg,* by instructions to divide class x 'like class y': or, by Systematic Schedules which imply, say, that the *Product* of an industry is cited before other facets. But as in all other systems except Colon, these hints are by no means comprehensive, although some very large classes (*eg,* Social-Political history, Language and Literature) do in fact display quite thorough instructions.

4.31 In all cases where the issue is left open in existing BC, the 'standard' citation order will be adopted. This order (also referred to as the principle of Purpose, or 'Ends-before-means') was developed by Vickery and others in the Classification Research Group (London) in the 1950's and has some features in common with Ranganathan's PMEST. Briefly, the order is: Thing (representing the end-product in the subject, or the ultimate object of study in it)—its Kinds, Parts, Constituents, Properties, Processes, Operations, Agents, Space, Time, Form of presentation.

4.32 In most cases so far analysed this order is fully compatible with the order already implicit, if not explicit, in BC; the class UVC Clothing Industries (considered in some detail) is an example.

4.321 In those cases where standard citation order appears to be in conflict with literary warrant of the BC 'consensus' principle, the existing order is maintained unless it seems to be definitely inconsistent with its treatment in related classes. An example of the latter is Class Q Social welfare: here, the primary facet by the principle of Purpose is

32

the Recipient of welfare; the primary facet in existing BC is *Cause of need for social action* (which may take the form of assistance, punishment, etc). Consensus clearly favours the latter and a work on drug addiction in children is most likely to be regarded as a study of drug addiction rather than child welfare. So the revised Class Q will retain the existing BC citation order. However, this example is not as straightforward as it seems and it could be argued that the recipient of social action is still the primary facet— but is being characterized by his own action rather than the more obvious characteristics by which persons are classified (age, sex, etc).

The truth is that, so far, we have not met a clear example where standard citation order is unhelpful; but the possibility is held in mind and the revision principle being noted at this point is really that existing BC structure is always respected when it gives an obviously optimum arrangement.

4.33 Citation order between arrays is one of the major unresolved problems in library classification theory. This is not the place to indicate to what extent a consistent citation order has been developed, but it may be noted that the principle of Purpose continues to give assistance beyond the determination of citation order between facets; an example is the Buildings facet of Architecture; the primary array by the principle of Purpose is clearly the Building by function (Hospital, Library, Dwelling . . .) and other subfacets (Building by number of storeys, by Mode of construction, etc) are subordinated to it.

4.331 Another principle observed as far as possible is that arrays . derived by the use of other facet principles as specifiers (=species-makers) are cited *after* subfacets derived from other principles; *eg,* Buildings characterized by using *Operation* as specifier (Prefabricated buildings, Restored buildings . . .), or by using *Material* as specifier (Timber buildings, Brick buildings . . .) are subordinated to Buildings by *function.*

4.34 In those cases where BC provides alternatives, a preferred order (reflecting standard citation order as far as possible) will be indicated and the filing order will reflect this (see Section 4.4). But the facility for alternatives will be retained.

4.4 *Stage 4: Filing order*
The order of a classification is determined totally by three sets of decisions: as to *citation order* (beginning with the establishment of main classes and continuing through facets and arrays), *facet filing sequence,* and *orders in array.*

4.41 It is generally acknowledged that there should be a direct correspondence between the first two: *eg,* in the class Library Science, assuming the three major facets are Library Service, Library Material and Library Operation, to be cited in that order, then the *facet filing sequence* (the 'vertical' order of classes as listed in a bibliography as compared with the 'horizontal' order of the elements in a single compound class) should be

either Library science   *or* Library science

       Services   Operations

       Materials   Materials

       Operations   Services

4.42 The second has the advantage over the first of maintaining general-before-special consistency throughout. So far as is possible, the 'inverted' filing sequence in the second example will be observed in the new BC. Again, as in the case of citation order, the evidence so far is that this will not demand a great deal of amendment to existing BC schedules.

4.43 Order in array refers to the order of the mutually exclusive classes in an array. Generally speaking, there will be very little alteration of the existing BC orders in this respect.

4.5 *Stage 5: Notation*

The need for a fully synthetic notation (*ie,* one which allows compounding between any two classes, whether from different facets or arrays of the same class or from quite different classes) has already been noted as vital to the provision of specificity in description.

4.51 Existing BC has the basic equipment for this: the comma is a facet link within a class and the hyphen is a general-purpose link for phase relations or for facet relations for which the comma is not available. However, more is needed than the simple provision of connecting devices; the order in which the elements are to be combined and the resulting filing order must be carefully regulated and here existing provision is not always satisfactory.

4.52 The main disadvantages of synthetic as distinct from enumerative notation is that the use of connecting devices adds complexity to the notation. This will be minimized and virtually abolished in the new edition by the use of retroactive notation within each homogeneous class (but not between classes). Retroactive notation, demonstrated in Section 5, does not need different types of symbol to act as connecting devices.

4.53 Theoretically, it is quite feasible to dispense entirely with the use of a special connecting symbol like the comma or hyphen and to rely entirely on the use of the two basic types of character (letters and

34

numbers). An obvious example is the DC where the first character in the base character set (0/9) is reserved to introduce *Form of presentation* divisions (02/05, 08), *Common activities and agents* (01, 06/07), Periods (090) and Places (091, 093/099). This would have the considerable advantage of confining notation to symbols (letters and numbers) whose ordinal values are already known.

4.54 As revision has proceeded it has become clear that retroactive notation, flexibly used, can meet all the tasks demanded by synthesis and that the use of arbitrary symbols like comma or hyphen is unnecessary. However, there are two occasions when one of these may be useful. First, if the library uses a policy of multiple entry in its classified catalogue, the hyphen is a clear and simple device for separating the constituent facet terms, analogously to the use of the colon in UDC. Secondly, in a very few classes entailing use of alphabeting marks for names of persons combined with alternative citation orders, it may be easier to use the comma than a selected numeral. Apart from this, the new BC notation will consist entirely of capital letters and arabic numbers.

4.55 It may be noted here that the deliberately non-hierarchical character of the BC notation developed by Bliss in the interest of maximum brevity is a considerable boon in revision and maintenance since provision for expansion and insertion of classes is greatly facilitated. Hierarchical notations always break down eventually and BC avoids the dilemma.

4.56 It is hardly necessary to say that the fully faceted notation will make unnecessary in the schedules any enumeration of compound classes and this will compensate to some extent for the increase in the size of schedules due to the greater specificity in enumerated vocabulary.

4.6 *Stage 6: A/Z index to the schedules*
The logical corollary of a faceted classification and notation is a printed index to the schedules which lists only the simple terms in their facets without compounds, *eg,*

    Men
    Menswear: Clothing industries   UVD R
    Gloves: Clothing industries   UVF G
but not
    Menswear: Gloves: Clothing industries   UVF GR

Any attempt to index all such compounds is doomed to failure and will not be attempted in any degree. Such indexing will be left to the indexes of particular collections, which need, of course, to indicate which compounds, out of the many possible ones, the collection actually has represented. So far as indexing of the hierarchies within each facet goes, the principles of chain procedure will be observed, since it is systematic and predictable as well as being highly economical.

5 The procedures described above are applicable at any level of the BC, from a quite precise and limited class such as Clothing industry—or one of its subclasses (*eg,* Hat industry)—to a main class, whatever that means. To give some idea of what the detailed structure of the revision will look like, here is a full draft of a subclass in Class U Useful arts and Technology.

Clothing and apparel industries—Class UVC/UVE
　5.1 The *citation order* on which it is based is:
　　　Clothing industries—divided by
　　　　1　Product (whole garment) in this order:
　　　　1.1　By Part of body covered
　　　　1.2　By Age of wearer
　　　　1.3　By Sex
　　　　1.4　By Occasion (Place/Time) when born
　　　　1.5　By Material
　　　　1.6　By Mode of manufacture
　　　　2　Part
　　　　3　Material
　　　　4　Property-cum-process
　　　　5　Operation
　　　　6　Agent
　5.2 *The schedule* (reflecting the principle of inversion):

			Existing BC
UVC	Clothing industries		
		(Operations and Agents)	
UVC B	Buildings	(Agents)	UVC,E
UVC C	Equipment		UVC,E
UVC D	Personnel		UVC,G
UVC F	Economic activities	(Operations)	
UVC K	Manufacture=Production		UVC,E
UVC L	Design, drafting		
UVC M	Pattern making		
UVC PF	Style, fashion	(Properties-cum-Processes)	

36

✓C PQ	Quality		
✓C PW	Wear		
✓C S	Materials	(Materials)	UVC,D
✓C T	Textiles		
✓C UF	Furs		
✓C VP	Paper		
✓C XH	Haberdashery	(Parts)	UVC,P
✓C XJ	Fasteners		
✓C XT	Linings		UVC,Q
✓D	Products=Clothes	(Products)	
✓D C	Knitwear	(By mode of manufacture)	
✓D E	Textiles	(By material)	
✓D FF	Fur		
✓D GP	Paper		
		(By occasion when worn)	
✓D KC	Ceremonial	(By social function)	
✓D KL	Industrial		
✓D L	Evening	(By time of day)	
✓D M	Winter	(By time of year)	
✓D Q	Unisex	(By sex of wearer)	
✓D R	Men		UVD
✓D S	Women		UVF
✓D V	Children	(By age of wearer)	UVE
✓E J	(Trunk and arms): Jacket	(By part of body covered)	UVD and UVE
✓F G	(Extremities): Gloves		UVF;L
✓G	: Shoes		UVG

5.21 It may be assumed that the divisions B/X appearing under UVC are taken from a revised Schedule 21 in which the sequence of Agents, Operations, Properties-cum-Processes, Materials, Parts, is strictly maintained. So they would not in fact be enumerated in the UVC schedule.

37

5.22 The existing BC classmarks are only approximate equivalents. In some cases the concept in general does not appear and it is given only as a part of a compound—*eg*, Gloves appears only under Women's wear at UVF L.

5.23 Synthesis will be by retroactive notation; *eg*,

UVF G	Gloves
UVF GCM	Pattern making
UVF GCU F	Furs for glovemaking
UVF GDF F	Fur gloves
UVF GDK L	Industrial gloves

All divisions of UV which *precede* a given classmark (*eg*, UVF G in the above examples) may be added directly to that classmark, dropping the initial letters common to all the classmarks concerned (above UV).

5.231 Should any of these articles of clothing need further division into their kinds (*eg*, kinds of shoes, such as Slippers; kinds of trousers, such as Tights) this is allowed for by a section of notation deliberately not used in the division of UVD—*eg*,

UVE T	Trousers (say)
UVE TV	Children's
UVE TX	Tights

5.232 At the risk of frightening some potential users of BC, here is a rather fanciful example of the two forms of synthesis used together, at full blast:

Gloves—Children's—Winter—Fur—Pattern making—Machine

UVF GDV DMD FFC MCC

Although this is a most artificial and unlikely subject of a complexity seldom met in books, it does show how such specificity can in fact be represented exactly by a class symbol using only letters in retroactive combination. It is 15 characters long. This is well above what Bliss referred to as the 'feasible limit', although numerous classified catalogues of specialized collections have class numbers longer than this. But it compares favourably with what UDC, say, would need. Neither DC nor LC could, of course, even begin to provide such specificity if it were required.

6 Although the procedures described and exemplified above are adequate for the revision of the great majority of classes in the BC, the situation in some cases is complicated by further problems of analysis and collocation, usually with repercussions at a more general level.

38

6.1 Such situations are usually a reflection of the limitation of 'consensus' regarding the major specialized disciplinary fields, as a determinant of the level at which facet analysis can begin. The crucial role of facet analysis in modern library classification has already been indicated and should be borne in mind when reading what follows.

6.2 An outstanding point of difference between a general classification and a special classification is that the latter enjoys a reasonably well defined and limited scope whereas the former has the whole of human knowledge as its field. The theory of facet analysis was developed largely within the environment of defined and bounded areas. This was the case even in its major pioneer, the Colon Classification, in which the universe of knowledge is first divided conventionally into main classes.

6.3 If facet analysis is applied directly to the field of knowledge as a whole, the result is something like the two great categories of Entities and Attributes (further divided into Properties and Processes) developed by Tomlinson and Austin in their work for the Classification Research Group on a proposed new general classification (which never materialized). (6)

6.4 A legitimate question is whether the broad structure of BC, developed before a comprehensive theory of facet analysis had emerged, and imposing evident constraints on such analysis in the form of clusters and collocations determined by the principle of consensus, is *too* constrictive. The development of the principle of *basic subjects (classes)* in the new (7th) edition of Colon, whereby the number of starting points for facet analysis is vastly extended compared with the original set of main and canonical classes, is an indication of the strains which another general scheme is encountering in its search for a *modus vivendi* between facet analysis and the principle of beginning with an enumeration of *a priori* main classes reflecting consensus.

6.5 The evidence of the revision so far is reasonably encouraging for BC. The theory of gradation is, of course, closely related to the theory of integrative levels by which the Entities category in the CRG scheme is largely organized and a cursory glance at the sequence of main classes up to the Human Studies (Class H/K) shows just how close it is. Bliss's use of the principle of subordination (of the special to the general) is analogous in its application to the Systems theory which was a useful supplementary principle in the CRG work. It has the additional virtue of accommodating the notion of inclusive disciplines—*eg,* of prefacing the individual chemical substances by the disciplinary term 'Chemistry'. Any working library classification must incorporate these at some point

39

on the grounds of an irresistible literary warrant. BC does this on the whole in a workmanlike and acceptable manner and provides what for practical purposes is a well-organized sequence of fundamental entity terms with intercalated disciplinary terms.

6.51 This is not a perfect theoretical solution, however, in that pure entity term represents a wider class than any disciplinary view of that entity; *eg*, 'Gold' is wider than 'Chemistry of gold'. Ideally the entities should file before the discipline term (assuming an 'inverted' file sequence)— *eg*,

Atoms
Molecules

Gold

Physics
Chemistry
  Gold
Mineralogy
Geology
  Gold

This order (which maintains a consistent general-before-special sequence, in accord with a basic BC principle) is in fact, perfectly feasible in a revised BC. The situation reflects a common criticism levelled at all existing general schemes, which is that they fail to provide a general class for a wide range of distributed phenomena (which is how they are now usually referrred to). An 'aspect' classification like BC, DC, UDC, LC, etc takes as its primary facet the disciplines and subdisciplines through which the phenomena of the world are viewed. They are at one and the same time the different conceptual frameworks by which man views the world and specialisations in studying centred around particular types of phenomena (as Biology centres around organisms, for example, Chemistry around substances, Political science around institutions and action, Art around imaginative expression). Because specialisation in producing and consuming information is nearly always, and of necessity, within these disciplines and subdisciplines rather than on phenomena, the generally accepted basic structure for a general classification, and one seen in all these schemes, is one which subordinates the phenomena to the disciplines.

40

But these schemes all fail to provide for *general* studies of any given phenomenon—one free of any disciplinary context. Yet a literature which consists of multidisciplinary studies of particular phenomena is growing steadily, if slowly. Treatises appear on such phenomena as Form, Symmetry, Rhythm, Change, Food, Housing, Gold, Petroleum, the Shell, Woman, etc, etc. One reason why existing schemes give such poor service in children's libraries is that children's and schools literature is frequently thematic, centred on a phenomenon rather than in a discipline, and so much of it is strictly speaking unclassifiable by these schemes.

The new BC proposes to remedy this by providing a class at which general studies of these can get a precise and consistent location. (See Section 9 which indicates the proposed revision of the anterior numeral classes in BC.)

6.6 Nevertheless, as analysis proceeds over the whole range of the BC, some situations are disclosed (usually in the social sciences) where the collocations which Bliss derived from considerations of consensus and subordination are found to be doubtfully tenable in terms of facet relations.

6.61 BC shows similar fragmentation to that of other schemes, of course, since distributed relatives constitute a fundamental feature of any linear sequence. What the revised BC seeks to avoid is distribution due to doubtfully valid distinctions. For example, BC distinguishes Recreation in Class Q (Social and cultural aspects) from Class H (Physical and health aspects) from Class V (Representational arts) from Class KJ (Customs and folklore), KGU (Ethnic culture) and so on.

Similarly, Medical aid in Class Q (Welfare services) is distinguished from Medical aid in Class HI (Public health services) and HM/Z (Medicine proper).

6.62 Straight facet analysis of such headings quickly reveals the modifications imposed by the notion of consensus. For example, the analet (to use Farradane's excellent but neglected term)

Social welfare—Drug addicts—Medical aid

may reflect a general assumption that Social welfare is the containing class, but it certainly violates one of the oldest principles in indexing and one which is an important element in standard citation order—the principle that the recipient of an action is cited before the action; this would give an analet more like

Anthropology . . . Sick persons—Drug addicts—Medical aid—
through Social welfare

41

Nevertheless a clear need exists to scrutinize closely all such distinctions and to amend situations involving ambiguity and lack of predictability. For example, some of the distinctions which scatter the literature on Recreation will be abandoned.

7   Two related problems raised in the revision are those of inter-disciplinary classes and of 'new' comprehensively aggregating subjects. Both are the product of the very large growth of knowledge which the era of mass research and development has inevitably brought with it.

7.1 'Aggregating' subjects, exemplified in Space sciences, Soil sciences, etc, are aggregates of traditionally distinct subjects, accelerated by the intensive study of a given focal application. The contributory subjects do not cease to be their own 'thing' just because they are an important element in a big new aggregation; so a subject like Space sciences raises only the relatively straightforward problems of locating the new aggregate in its correct hierarchy and of indicating under the constituent specialities (which, in a general classification must remain distributed) the fact that they are studied in a particular application—*eg, Space* medicine. This is analogous to the situation met in the Colon classification by the provision of 'Specials' as a sort of super-personality array, and similar provision will be made in the new BC.

7.2 It may be noted here that in all these problems of growth, that of intercalating notationally—which absolutely bedevils a scheme like DC—is a minor problem in BC thanks to its largely non-hierarchical notation.

7.3 The term 'interdisciplinary' is used of a number of rather different situations:

7.31 Perhaps the commonest situation is where a subject which is at first assumed to 'belong' to a particular field is seen to apply to other fields as well, until eventually it is seen as a distinct subject in its own right, and demanding a separate class. 'Management' is a good example; originally thought of as a division of Business, it was then seen to refer to other organizations (schools, learned societies, governments, etc) and finally as a major part of the general activity Organizing.

The example of Soil sciences already quoted is analogous in that it originated as an implicit subclass of Earth but with the growth of know-ledge, was seen to require recognition as a possible subclass of any astronomical body—and hence, to need its own independent class as Soil systems (no particular astronomical body in mind). Similarly, we need to recognize a Biology independent of any particular life

42

support system such as Earth. The solution to this problem seems clear and has been indicated in Section 6.51.

7.32 Our own subject, Library and Information Science, illustrates a second situation. Here, a central core subject (organizing information stores for retrieval) draws heavily on a number of disparate disciplines and in turn feeds them. In the latter case, it is no different in principle from the situation in 7.31, except that the need to have an independent class has been accepted for many years and, in contrast with Management, say, it is usually cited *before* its application, so that a document on organizing information in Chemistry, for example, is subordinated to Library and information science rather than to Chemistry. We say 'the need . . . has been accepted'—but it is perhaps a special example and reflects simply a prejudice in favour of our own subject, which should in fact be distributed as Management usually is.

Insofar as the subject draws on others, however, it is necessary to distinguish two situations. Where a document considers simply the use of another subject as an agent in library work (*eg,* Computers in libraries) it is easily handled synthetically. But where other disciplines infiltrate into the intimate structure of the subjects (*eg,* to give a species of indexing, as in automatic indexing) this calls for enumeration as part of an internal facet.

7.33 The third situation is raised by an inconsistency in the existing BC—the treatment of Geography. By all the usual criteria this is a discipline in its own right, with its own profession, curriculi, professional bodies, etc. Yet BC distributes it, analogous to its distribution of Management in the first situation.

This again raises the problem of BC accepting a basic framework of *a priori* main classes as opposed to an initial facet analysis of the whole field of knowledge. If Management is regarded as an instrument serving various other human activities, a principle of citation order is implied which is no other than the 'standard' order of Purpose. By this criterion a subject like Library and information science also serves other, more fundamental, activities—and should be similarly distributed. And if political geography serves political science, and economic geography serves Economics then its present treatment in BC is justified.

7.34 Before admitting that this reflects a fundamental inconsistency in BC which no mere *revision* can remedy, the part played by consensus in BC must be remembered. Pursuing the argument in 7.33, it could be asserted that *communication,* being a fundamental human drive, should be served by its various contributing disciplines—that is to say, it should

43

be regarded as a main class and major disciplines such as linguistics (and even, perhaps, the Arts) subordinated to it. The problems this raises for a general classification are as great as those it solves and a very strong case remains for accepting the present fragmentation of communication under the various disciplines (whilst providing, of course, a *general* class for it as well). The present revision of BC accepts this view, which virtually reinstates consensus as giving us the legitimate starting points for facet analysis in a general classification.

8   Many of the wider theoretical problems considered above imply a need to augment existing BC by a series of basic categories to accommodate the *general* literature on a large number of distributed relatives which at present have no general class of their own, either in BC or any other general classification(apart from the moribund Subject Classification of J D Brown). The need for a comprehensive class of Phenomena to complement the existing classes of Disciplines and sub-disciplines, and the new BC's intention to provide this, has already been argued in Section 6.51. Consistent with the principle of inversion (to maintain general before special) this great Phenomena class will file before the Discipline classes (A/Z). It will contain all categories of phenomena— *ie,* properties and processes as well as entities.

  8.1   It will not give an exhaustive enumeration of all phenomena— this is not economically feasible, at least in the coming edition. Instead, it will provide clear rules whereby the indexer extracts from the most appropriate disciplinary context the 'isolate' phenomenon and gives it a unique position in the overall sequence of phenomena (*see* examples in Section 6.51).

  8.2   An alternative will be provided where multi-disciplinary treatment of a phenomena may be collocated with the most appropriate disciplinary class, rather than be located in the general Phenomena class.

  8.3   However, there is one phenomenon class in which multi-disciplinary treatments are already numerous and for which there seems to be a strong case for developing a large phenomena class now. Appropriately enough, this is the phenomenon of human knowledge and information itself. The first edition of the BC has already provided a substantial part of this class (documentation, publishing and bookselling, bibliography, library and information service, etc) at the very beginning of the scheme (Class 2), with an alternative for it at the very end (Class Z). As a matter of great practical convenience the new BC will extend this concept and provide a complete Information and

44

Communication class. It will provide alternatives for retaining under the discipline class any treatments of the phenomenon thought to be more helpfully collocated thus; an example here would be the retention of Epistemology as a major subclass in Philosophy.

8.4 By a piece of good fortune, the notational problem raised by these needs is solved almost perfectly by the situation attending the present anterior numeral classes 1/9. It is well known that these classes are very little used in many BC libraries, referring as they do to special collections of one sort and another (*eg,* Government publications, children's literature), which in most libraries are not notated by the scheme but—if at all— by local symbols. This virtually redundant numeral notation will be used to accommodate the new Phenomena classes in the new BC, as may be seen below.

9 *Outline of the new BC* (incorporating new numeral classes)

2	Generalia: physical forms (*eg,* cardsets, photographs)
3	Generalia: forms of presentation (*eg,* encyclopedias, serials)

(Phenomena)
> For multi-disciplinary treatments of particular phenomena. *Alternative* is to collocate with most appropriate disciplinary treatment

4	Attributes (*eg,* order, hierarchy . . .)
5	Activities (*eg,* motion, change . . .)
6	Entities (*eg,* particles, atoms, minerals, organisms, persons . . .)
7	Universe of knowledge

> Methods of enquiry, research
> Disciplines (as subjects)
>> *see also* special disciplines, *eg,* Philosophy, Science, Religion
> Communication and information
>> Communication theory
>> Media of communication
>>> Semiotics, codes
>>> Aural (speaking, etc), Visual (writing, etc), Audiovisual
>> Recorded information, information sciences and technologies
>> Generation of information: sources, authorship
>> Recording and reproduction
>>> Sound, reprography, photography, printing and typography

8	Data processing, computer science
	Records, documentation
	Types of records (*as* Generalia class)
	Distribution: Publishing, selling
	Collecting, listing, organising
	Bibliography, palaeography, epigraphy
	Library and information science
	Archives and records management
	Museology, exhibitions
9	Direct communication

Data processing, computer science
Records, documentation
    Types of records (*as* Generalia class)
    Distribution: Publishing, selling
    Collecting, listing, organising
        Bibliography, palaeography, epigraphy
        Library and information science
        Archives and records management
        Museology, exhibitions

9 Direct communication
    Individual communication: signalling, postal, telegraphy, telephony
        (Telecommunications engineering) *see*
    Mass communication: meetings, conferences, press, broadcasting
    Publicity and propaganda: public relations, advertising
    Public opinion: polls, user research

(Discipline—summary outline)
A   Philosophy, Logic, Mathematics
AY–I   Systemology, Science
J/Z   Social sciences and Humanities

9.1 The Generalia classes will be drawn from the revised and greatly enlarged Auxiliary Schedule 1. This contains two large facets of 'form' in which the numerous different arrays characterising documentary form are all distinguished explicitly and organised for retroactive combination. It also contains extensive 'common subdivisions of subject', developed partly from those in the *BNB Supplementary Schedules* (1960).

9.2 As an example of the greatly increased vocabulary to be found throughout the new BC, we may cite Auxiliary Schedule 2 for Place, which now includes arrays based on a wide range of characteristics (*eg,* Tropical, Temperate . . . Low altitude, high altitude . . .) as well as Places of the ancient and modern world. The vocabulary in the first edition is some 800 terms; in the new it is well over 4000.

10   *Summary conclusions on the nature of the new BC*
It may be claimed that the new BC will demonstrate the following features:

46

10.1 An overall order of major classes superior to any existing general scheme in the helpfulness of its order to the searcher for information;

10.2 Within these major classes, an order of maximum helpfulness based on consistent and predictable principles of citation and filing order;

10.3 A notation fully hospitable to current requirements of specificity as the scheme develops;

10.4 A notation of exceptional brevity and simplicity in view of its accomplishments.

10.5 A very thorough and consistent A/Z index, supplementing extensive and clear rules for practical application, which should make the scheme notably simple to use and apply.

10.6 A maintenance service to take full advantage of the consistency and predictability of structure enjoyed by a fully faceted, detailed and up-to-date system.

10.7 A system published in parts (like LC) where the user can purchase the whole scheme or merely those classes he needs.

11 *Prospects for the use of BC*

11.1 BC is being revised because some eighty libraries are using BC and need a revised edition, because it has the makings of an outstandingly good scheme and because the effort needed to revise, whilst substantial, is a relatively small investment in the perspective of the total investment these libraries have in retrieval languages.

11.2 Apart from this, what is seen in the crystal ball depends partly on the eye of the beholder and whether the latter tends to take a sanguine view of things.

11.3 The writer's view is that if a new general library, large or small, had the choice of existing general classifications, other things being equal it would be well advised to adopt the new BC.

But other things are not equal. If we take only the case of a new library (and there are plenty of these on the way!) or an existing library about to embark on an extensive expansion and development, and uneasy about its existing classification as a basis for such development, such a library will consider mainly the following questions.

11.31 The effectiveness (*ie*, helpfulness) of the order.

11.32 The economy with which the scheme can be applied; a major factor here is the possible availability of a centralized indexing service providing class-numbers for the scheme for a significant proportion of the likely stock of the library and operating speedily enough to make its use feasible.

11.321 At the moment, BC enjoys no such service, although it would undoubtedly be a very great advantage if BC users could look forward to the provision of BC numbers by a currently produced centralized cataloguing service. Readers of this book will be aware of the very rapid developments in centralized indexing of English and American bookform literature; a significant landmark was the use of MARC by the British National Bibliography beginning in January 1971. Whilst formidable problems still remain in the full use of MARC by individual library systems, the principle of a machine-readable record providing numerous fields of data in it which can be selectively printed out is a fundamental advance.

The BCA has already made informal approaches to BNB on the question of getting new BC class-numbers into the MARC record; there seemed to be no reason in principle why this should not come about eventually although serious problems of implementation would demand solution. In particular, a sufficient demand by users of BC would have to be demonstrated and financial provision made for the indexing effort involved in assigning BC numbers to current input. This might involve the development of a 'switching language' whereby the subject analysis and description implicit in the production of PRECIS index entries (which replaced the chain index in the alphabetical section of BNB in January 1971) could be translated quickly and economically into BC numbers. Although intriguing technical problems would be posed by this, the structure of the new BC, on the face of it at least, should be reasonably receptive to such processing.

11.322 The cost of classifying the document input to a library is made up of the time spent on concept analysis (examining the document and deciding how its information content might be summarized) and the translation of this summarisation string into the notation of the classification scheme used. If BC classmarks are assigned to the concept analyses provided by a centralised service this means that a substantial economy is still available via the centralised service.

11.323 If the centralised service uses an old classification with a very large programme of radical revision facing it for the next several decades and more, the reclassification which will be demanded of libraries using it will constitute a major cost which libraries using the new BC will avoid.

11.33 The reliability of the scheme as to its maintenance; although this is primarily a need to know that the scheme will be maintained by regular and comprehensive revision it also embodies the hope that new subjects will be incorporated speedily.

11.331 It has already been argued that the clear articulation of the system, which is a central advantage of faceted classification, should assist maintenance by indicating clearly the content and definition of existing facets and subfacets. At the same time the undeniable stability of the general structure of BC, reinforced by the thorough restructuring in detail which the new edition will give, should make the necessity for complete new editions at frequent intervals decidely less urgent than it is for other systems. In these circumstances it seems likely that the annual *Bulletin* (converted, perhaps, to a twice-yearly publication) can continue to provide regular updating and revision comparable in scope with that available to other general classifications.

11.332 Details of the organizational basis for these proposals will be found in the BC *Bulletin* of December 1970 (p 4/5).

11.4 So far as the possibility goes of libraries changing to the BC, the argument is much the same except that to the questions above would be added the critical one: would the change (to a presumably better scheme) be worth making—*ie,* would the superiority in performance (as to recall and precision) and in economy of application justify, over the years, the capital investment represented by the cost of change?

11.5 Here we run into the absence of any hard experimental evidence (of the kind Cranfield has supplied for certain situations involving special retrieval languages) to supplement the evidence of our senses and our everyday observation as librarians. The Cranfield evidence has admittedly diminished somewhat the weight which used to be attached to the retrieval language as an element in the total retrieval system. But the high incidence of human error as a cause of poor performance does suggest that a system whose consistency and predictability minimizes errors of application would score over systems lacking these qualities.

As to importance of the retrieval language in its basic function as an instrument for locating and relating classes of information, it is at the very least arguable that the self-service conditions which hold in the use of many general collections would put a much higher premium on this element of the retrieval system; *eg,* a reader examining the shelves of a DC library for information on Psychology (ostensibly at 150, in fact at 150, 130, 301 and 616.8) is obviously less well served than one seeking the same information from a similar collection arranged by BC.

REFERENCES
1 Bliss, H E: *A system of Bibliographical Classification,* Wilson, New York, 1935, 2nd ed, 1936.
2 Bliss, H E: *A bibliographic classification, extended by auxiliary schedules for composite specification and notation,* Wilson, New York, 1940-1953 (4 vols in 3):

vol 1 (Classes 1-9, A-G) 1940; vol 2 (Classes H-K)1947 (a 2nd edition of vols 1 and 2 appeared in 1952, in one volume); vol 3 (Classes L-Z), and vol 4 (General Index) 1953.

3 Bliss, H E: *The organization of knowledge and the system of the sciences,* Holt, New York, 1929.
4 *Abridged Bliss Classification,* School Library Association, London, 1967.
5 *Bliss Classification bulletin,* vols 1-3, Wilson, New York, 1954-1966; Bliss Classification Association, London (c/o Commonwealth Institute, Kensington High Street, London W8), vol 4, 1967-
6 *Classification and information control;* papers representing the work of the Classification Research Group during 1960-1968. Library Association, London, 1969.

Colon Classification

M A GOPINATH
Documentation Research and Training Centre,
Bangalore

EDITOR'S INTRODUCTION: Along with the preview article by Ranganathan himself (see reference 17 at end of paper) and the depth schedules and studies in Library science with a slant to documentation, *this is a primary source of information on the new edition of the Colon Classification and provides news of research and revision plans, the new emphasis given to Matter isolates and other details. It also provides much preliminary background theory which is not particularly easy reading and introduces technical terms, but can illuminate some things—for instance, we find that the Emptying Digit is CC's way of making notation temporarily non-expressive or non-hierarchical. The author tells me, incidentally, that the 1963 glossary of classification terms is being revised and that the new version may be completed by the end of 1976.*

0 BACKGROUND INFORMATION

0.1 *Correlated developments*

The Colon Classification (CC) is a theory-based scheme. Therefore, I shall first discuss the attributes of the universe of subjects that affect the theory of library classification as a whole. Thereafter, I shall attempt to give a bird's eye view of much of Ranganathan's general theory and shall then dwell on the impact of this theory on the design and development of CC, with an indication of its probable future.

0.2 *Need for coextensive representation of a subject*

The five laws of library science direct that the library should serve a reader exactly, exhaustively and expeditiously with the least cost and least wastage of human resources. In order to do this, a classification should be able to represent coextensively each and every subject.

A subject is an organized and systematized body of ideas. It may consist of one idea or a combination of several. The latter is the case with a majority of the subjects sought by readers. A coextensive representation

51

of a subject requires, as a prerequisite, the

    1 Recognition of each of the component ideas in the subject; and

    2 Determination of the degree of interrelation among the components.

0.3 *Attributes of the universe of subjects*

In order to give unique coextensive representation for each subject in the universe of subjects, the classificationist has to ascertain the various attributes in the universe of subjects that affect library classification. The attributes of the universe of subjects affecting the design of library classification include the following:

    1 The manifold multi-dimensional quality—that is, the tendency to grow in several directions;

    2 The different modes of formation of subjects;

    3 The variation in the strength of bond among the component facets;

    4 The interrelation among the subjects;

    5 The tendency of the universe of subjects to become turbulently dynamic;

    6 The variation in the frequency and pattern of incidence of different kinds of facets making up a subject; and

    7 The variation in the impact of the different kinds of ideas—that of the intuition-based seminal or near-seminal ideas and of the purely intellect-based phenomenal ones.

It is obvious then that there is a wide range of parameters of the universe of subjects that affect the design of a scheme for classification. The value of each of these parameters may vary over a wide range also.

0.4 *Impact on the design of schemes for classification*

There is evidence of considerable impact of these attributes of the universe of subjects on the design and development of schemes for classification. For example, the purely enumerative Dewey Decimal Classification had to be veneered with space and time facets in order to represent the manifold multi-dimensional quality of the universe of subjects. Thus the Universal Decimal Classification was designed. Its synthetic quality had to be augmented with the colon device (:). The Colon Classification was designed because the UDC could not give unique class numbers to each and every subject thrown forth by the universe of subjects. Even the Colon Classification had to be revised several times during the last forty years on account of the impact of the universe of subjects. (20)

52

0.5 *Guided development*
In order to meet effectively and productively the impact of the different
attributes of the universe of subjects, a classification should be such that
the scheme can conveniently accommodate the developments in the
universe of subjects without its basic structure being affected to any
appreciable extent. The freely-faceted analytico-synthetic scheme for
classification developed in India has this capacity to a much greater
degree than other models, such as the purely enumerative model (Rider's
International Classification), relatively enumerative model (*eg* Dewey
Decimal Classification), almost faceted model (*eg* Universal Decimal
Classification) and rigidly faceted model (Colon Classification, versions
1 and 2). To continue keeping up with the changes in the universe of
subjects in this way, even a freely faceted scheme should have built-in
capacity for self-perpetuation—that is, to accommodate the new developments in the universe of subjects as and when they occur, without making
considerable alterations in the basic structure and design of the scheme.
One method of achieving this is to provide a set of explicitly stated
normative principles to guide the development of the scheme and also the
methodology for the design of schemes for classification.

0.6 *Development of general theory of classification*
0.61 *Early attempts*
Early in the century, E C Richardson attempted to develop a few canons
to guide the development of library classification, and was followed by
W C Berwick Sayers with a further set. Then came H E Bliss with his
principles for classification, but these were largely descriptive and lacked
the quality of self-perpetuation. In 1931, Ranganathan proclaimed his
five laws of library science, which provided the much needed guiding
principles comprehending each and every activity of library service. The
function and essential purpose of library classification was thus specified.
This led Ranganathan to develop a few canons and principles which were
published in 1937. (28) However, these were not fully dynamic.

0.62 *Dynamic theory of classification*
Ranganathan was conscious of the limitations of the descriptive and static
theories of classification. Just like a painter who steps periodically back
from his canvas to gain perspective, Ranganathan occasionally viewed the
higher levels of thinking by divorcing his mind from the details of the
phenomenal level, and regarding classification theory in a purely objective
light. One such occasion led him, in 1950, to seize the idea of mentally

53

separating the work of classification—theory as well as practice—into three different planes of work; namely idea plane, verbal plane, and notational plane. This big leap in the classification led Ranganathan to develop a dynamic general theory of classification with the built-in capacity to meet the emergent developments in the universe of subjects.

0.63 *Demarcating the functions*
Ranganathan clearly demarcated the functions of the different planes of work.. Delineating the structure of the universe of subjects, studying the inter-relation among the subjects, and fixing the preferred sequence of subjects—past, present and future—are the distinctive functions of the idea plane, the work of which is paramount. Naming each subject by a synonym-free and homonym-free term is the distinctive function of the verbal plane. Implementing the findings of the idea plane is the function of the notational plane.

0.7 *Formulation of postulates and principles*
To guide the work in the three different planes, Ranganathan developed numerous canons, postulates and principles. (38) Some of the important postulates and principles are discussed in detail in the succeeding sections.

1 CONCEPT OF THE BASIC SUBJECT
1.1 *The postulate*
The first postulate is 'Every subject has a basic subject'. (15) 'Basic subject' is a generic term used to denote either a main or non-main subject.

1.2 *Identification of basic subject*
The classificationist and to some extent the classifier, may have to identify new basic subjects from among the new developments in the universe of subjects. Therefore, to secure consistency in identifying a new basic subject, a few criteria have been used during the last few years. These are:

    1 A subject which calls for schedules of special isolates forming facets of a set of compound subjects going with one and the same host subject;

    2 A subject which has to be taken as the central subject and in which one cannot distinctively recognize isolate facets; a subject not having any isolate facets. In other words, a subject which cannot be expressed as the compound subject; and

54

3 A subject which has some specialization in academic circles—such as degree courses, periodicals, etc.

These, though, are by no means definite and exhaustive. We have to gain more experience by our study about the structure, formation, and development of different subjects.

1.3 *Varieties of basic subjects*
The following two different varieties of basic subjects have been recognised (18):

1 Main subject—the basic subject resulting from the first order fission of the universe of subjects. These are enumerated in the schedule of main subjects.

2 Non-main basic subjects—basic subjects resulting from the fission of main subjects.

1.4 *Varieties of main subjects*
The following four different varieties of main subjects have been recognized (19):

1 Traditional main subjects—these are main subjects that have been traditionally taken for granted as the first order divisions of the universe of subjects. Mathematics, physics, chemistry, engineering, medicine, literature, linguistics, religion, and history are examples of traditional main subjects.

2 Distilled main subjects—a pure discipline is evolved out of the experiences in its appearance-in-action in diverse compound subjects going with different basic subjects. These are called 'distilled main subjects'. Management science and system analysis are examples of this kind.

3 Fused main subject—the trend of inter-disciplinary approach among specialists has created a number of fused main subjects. Biochemistry, chemical engineering, and geopolitics are examples of this kind; they stem from the fusion of two or more traditional disciplines.

4 Other kinds of main subjects—literary warrant on a few subjects satisfy certain criteria stipulated for deeming a subject as a main subject. These do not fall in any of the three varieties mentioned earlier. Journalism, public health, applied psychology, industrial economics, and social work are examples.

1.5 *Non-main basic subjects*
1.51 *Need for non-main basic subject*
The group of subjects going with some of the main subjects are again divided into a set of subjects called 'non-main basic subjects'. (14)

This sort of division is found helpful because of distinct trends recognizable in the classification of the universe of subjects.

1.52 *Canonical basic subject*
One example of non-main basic subjects is the group called 'Canonical Basic Subjects'. These are conventional divisions of a main subject and are not derived on the basis of any one characteristic. This kind of formation is somewhat analogous to the formation of traditional main subjects (*see* Section 1.4 of this paper). A canonical basic subject of a main subject generally has its own schedule of special isolates. The recognition of a canonical basic subject is somewhat nebulous and the classificationist has to prevail upon his own judgment in many cases. The set of criteria given for the recognition of a basic subject is very much applicable to the recognition of the canonical basic subjects. Other types of non-main basic subject identified include systems, environmental, special features and compound non-main basic subject.

2 COMPOUND SUBJECT
2.1 *Definition*
A compound subject is a subject with a basic subject and one or more component ideas called 'isolate ideas'. (18) For example, 'Fungus disease of rice plant in agriculture' is a compound subject. In this, 'agriculture' is the basic subject; 'fungus disease' and 'rice plant' are isolate ideas.

2.11 *Isolate idea*
An isolate idea cannot by itself become a subject; it can occur only as a component of a compound subject. (18) 'Anatomy' is an isolate idea.

2.12 *Compound isolate*
Two or more isolates or an isolate and a special component can combine to form a compound isolate. (22) 'Rural women' is a compound isolate, the 'rural group' and 'women' being two independent isolate ideas.

2.13 *Special component*
A special component is an idea, which is not by itself a subject or an isolate, but which can be used as a component to be attached to a host isolate as well as to its subdivisions, in order to form a compound isolate. (23) For example, the idea of 'Old English' is a compound isolate idea, having the isolate 'English' as the principal component; the
56

idea 'Old' is a special component formed on the basis of the characteristic 'by stage'.

2.2 *Large number of compound subjects*
Compound subjects can be formed by combining any number of isolate
ideas with a basic subject. Therefore, there will be a large number of
compound subjects within one basic subject. That is, the number of
compound subjects will be many times greater than the number of basic
subjects in the universe of subjects.

2.3 *Arrangement of Compound Subjects*
2.31 *Consistency in pattern of components*
The arrangement of compound subjects should be helpful to a majority
of readers. For this purpose, each component idea is to be recognized
and represented, as is the relative degree of inter-relationship between
the components in a compound subject. Further, there should be some
pattern of arrangement of components of
   1 One and the same compound subject;
   2 Different component subjects having one and the same basic subject;
   3 Compound subjects going with different basic subjects.
Such a consistency in arrangement helps the reader to anticipate precisely
the location of his specific subject. The classificationist and the classifier
should endeavour to secure this consistency.

2.32 *Facility for browsing*
Usually subjects sought by a specialist reader are of great depth or
intension. On account of the limitations of memory, he recalls his needs
only partially. Therefore the arrangement should be such as to help the
reader recall when he browses through it, the different components of
the subject of interest ot him at the moment, by a process similar to the
recall of ideas by association. (5) Further, it enables him to be aware,
as he browses, whether he is getting nearer to the subject of his interest,
or whether he is moving away from it. Such a display of subjects gives
an APUPA (Alien-Penumbral-Umbral-Penumbral-Alien) pattern. (41)

2.4 *Need for consistency in the sequence of components*
In other words, which component of the compound subject should be
at remove 1, which at remove 2, which at remove 3, and so on, with
respect to the basic subject in question, as point of reference, has to be
determined. This choice of invariants should be consistent, not only

57

with respect to one compound subject, but also with respect to different compound subjects going with one and the same basic subject, and also with all the compound subjects going with different basic subjects. Furthe the process of choosing invariants of different removes should be done in such a way that it minimizes the need for modification at a later stage of development in the universe of subjects. This poses a tantalizing problem.

2.5 *Work at near-seminal level*
2.51 *Generalization*
At the phenomenal level, arriving at a consistent sequence of components of compound subjects is a difficult task. On the other hand, this problem has been tackled by Ranganathan at a higher level of generalization—called 'near-seminal level'.

2.52 *Postulate of fundamental categories*
The postulate of fundamental categories states, 'Each isolate facet of a compound subject can be deemed to be a manifestation of one and only one of the five fundamental categories: personality; matter; energy; space, and time'—well known as PMEST. (32) The terms 'personality', 'matter', etc, are merely group names. They should not be taken to imply anything more than that.

2.521 *Identification of fundamental categories*
The classificationist, and sometimes the classifier, face the problem of identifying a new isolate as a manifestation of one or the other of the fundamental categories. Problems may arise particularly in recognizing 'energy', 'matter', and 'personality' isolates. However, with some experience and training, the manifestations can be determined in a majority of cases, without much difficulty.

2.53 *Postulates for sequence*
The sequence of different kinds of facets of a compound subject are governed by two postulates. (34)

   1 Postulate of first facet—'In a compound subject, the basic facet should be the first facet'. This postulate secures that all compound subjects going with a basic subject are arranged together.

   2 Postulate of concreteness—The five fundamental categories fall into the following sequence, when arranged according to their decreasing concreteness: 'personality', 'matter', 'energy', 'space', and 'time'.
These two postulates together secure the sequence (BS) [P] [M] [E] [S]

[T] in a compound subject made up of all these five kinds of isolate ideas.

2.54 *Postulate of rounds and levels*
Further work in the classification of subjects of great intension led to the recognition of the cycle of recurrence of the manifestation of the fundamental categories in compound subjects. This led to the postulate of rounds and levels. (33)

2.541 *Postulate of rounds*
The fundamental category 'energy' may manifest itself in one and the same subject more than once. The first manifestation is taken to end round 1 of the manifestation of the three fundamental categories 'personality', 'matter' and 'energy'; the second manifestation is taken to end round 2, and so on.

Each of the fundamental categories 'personality' and 'matter' manifests itself in round 1, round 2, and so on.

Ordinarily, any of the fundamental categories 'space' and 'time' may manifest itself only in the last of the rounds in a compound subject.

2.542 *Postulate of levels*
Any of the fundamental categories 'personality' and 'matter' manifests itself more than once in one and the same round within a subject; and similarly with 'space' and 'time' in the last round. 'Energy' can occur only once within a round and therefore has no level in its case.

The first manifestation of a fundamental category within a round will be said to be its 'level 1 facet' in that round. Its second manifestation within that round will be said to be its 'level 2 facet', and so on.

2.6 *Principles for facet sequence*
2.61 *Need for principles for facet sequence*
The postulates for sequence mentioned in section 2.53 help the determination of the sequence of isolate ideas in a compound subject only when one isolate idea deemed to be a manifestation of a fundamental category is incident in the compound subject. They do not help the determination of the sequence of two isolate ideas deemed to be a manifestation of one and the same fundamental category. In other words, the postulates of sequence do not help in the determination of the sequence between two 'personality' isolates or two 'matter' isolates or two 'energy' isolates, or two 'space' isolates, or two 'time'

isolates. Therefore, some guiding principles were needed to solve this problem.

2.62 *Wall-picture principle*
In 1962 Ranganathan formulated a principle called the 'wall-picture principle' for the determination of the sequence between isolate ideas deemed to be a manifestation of the one and the same fundamental categories. This wall-picture principle states, 'If the two isolate facets A and B of a compound subject going with a basic subject are such that the concept behind B will not be operative unless the concept behind A is conceded, even as a mural picture is not possible unless the wall exists to draw upon, then the facet A should precede the facet B'. (35)

2.63 *Example*
Consider the compound subject:
   Exercise of franchise by the Indian citizen in 1960's.
The analysed title is:
   History (basic subject)
   Indian community [personality round 1, level 1]
   Citizen [personality round 1, level 2]
   Franchise [matter round 1, level 2]
   Exercise [energy round 1]
   1960's [time level 1]
The sequence of the two personality isolates 'Indian community' and 'citizen' is determined on the basis of the wall-picture principle. The rounds of 'personality' and 'matter' isolates are also determined on the basis of the wall-picture principle. Other postulates can be derived from it. (35)

2.7 *Absolute syntax of ideas*
A subject is largely the product of human thinking. It presents an organized pattern of ideas created by the specialists in any field of enquiry. Working at the near-seminal level and postulating about the helpful sequence among the facets and isolates has led to the conjecture that there may be an 'absolute syntax' among the constituents of the subjects within a basic subject, perhaps parallel to the sequence of thought process itself, irrespective of the language in which the ideas may be expressed, and irrespective of the cultural background or other differences in the environments in which the specialists, as creators as well as the users of the subjects, may be placed. This is a field for

60

cooperative research and testing by specialists in psychology, statistics, linguistics, anthropology, and reference service. (26)

2.8 *Canons for work in the verbal plane*
In order to get a homonym-free and synonym-free terminology for the subjects and their component ideas, to be enumerated in a scheme for classification, Ranganathan has formulated four canons: canon of enumeration, canon of context, canon of currency, and canon of reticence. (38)

3 *Theory for notational plane*
3.1 *Function*
The relation of the notational plane to the idea plane is likened to that of a servant to his master. (29) The efficiency and the capability of the notational plane should be developed in such a way that it can efficiently implement the findings of the idea plane. For this purpose, the notational plane should have the quality of self-perpetuation. Therefore, the basic structure of the notational system should be based on a sound theoretical foundation.

3.2 *Coextensive representation*
In order to give a unique class number to each and every subject (past, present and future) in the universe of subjects, the notational system should represent each and every component coextensively. For this purpose, the notational system should have a hierarchical structure. It should represent the measure of intension of each component idea incident in the compound subject.

3.3 *Base of notation*
3.31 *Definition*
The totality of distinct digits used in a scheme for classification is denoted by the term 'base of the notational system'.

3.32 *Mixed base*
The longer the base, the shorter will be the average number of digits in a class number, or an isolate number. The digits used in a scheme for classification should be, as far as possible, simple, easy to write and read, and have a defined ordinal value. Brevity in the length of the class number is helpful. One way of achieving this is to increase the length of the base by taking digits from two or more species of digits. The ordinal value of

digits within each species should be according to the existing convention. Additional prescriptions are needed only to fix the relative ordinal values of the species themselves. Such use of two or more species of digits is denoted by the term 'mixed notation'.

3.4 *Empty digit*

The number of distinct digits available even in a mixed notation is relatively small when compared to a large number of ideas to be represented by the notational system. Therefore, provision for infinite extrapolation has to be made in the notational system. The decimal fraction notation of Dewey provides only for the unlimited succession of subdivisions. The empty digit device of Ranganathan provides for an unlimited addition of numbers to represent coordinate ideas. An empty digit is one which has no semantic content but does have its usual ordinal value. It can be used to derive any number of digits groups to represent coordinate ideas. An empty digit is used as a sectorizing digit. (27)

3.5 *Emptying digit*

Any new idea may crop up requiring a position as decided in the idea plane, between any two already existing consecutive ideas. There-fore, provision for interpolation between any two consecutive ordinal numbers is necessary. This interpolation cannot be adequately met by the gap device, because the interpolation may be needed where there is no gap. In 1963, Ranganathan postulated the 'emptying digit' to meet this problem. (27) An 'emptying digit' is a digit that deprives the semantic value of its preceding digit in a digit-group, but retains its ordinal value. For example, let us say, the digit 'K' represents 'zoology' and 'L' represents 'medicine', and that we have to introduce a new subject 'animal husbandry' between 'K-zoology' and 'L-medicine'. Then, if we postulate 'X' as an emptying digit, the digit-pair 'KX' can be used to represent 'animal husbandry'. In KX, X empties the semantic value of K, but retains its ordinal value. The digit-pair KX is coordinate with the digit K or digit L.

3.51 *Empty and emptying digits*

To provide for a large number of interpolations between any two consec-utive ordinal numbers in an array, the concept of empty-emptying digit was postulated. It is a digit simultaneously having empty as well as emptying value. Here, only a digit-triad could represent a coordinate idea.
62

For example, 'LY1-nursing' is a subject interpolated between two of its coordinates: 'L-medicine' and 'M-useful arts', and the digit Y is an empty-emptying digit.

3.6 *Indicator digits*
In order to coextensively represent the relation between the various components in compound subjects, different kinds of indicator digits are to be used. Incidentally, in the notational plane, this meets the challenge of the multi-dimensional attribute of the universe of subjects.

3.7 *Physiology of eye and psychology of memory*
The use of the indicator digits would serve an additional purpose of giving comfort to the eye and the memory of a reader. A block of ten digits will not be convenient to pick up in a single sweep of the eye; it is also difficult to carry it in the memory even for a short while. The optimum number of digits comfortable to the physiology of the eye and the psychology of the memory is deemed to be three, and the maximum six. Therefore, breaking a block of ten digits into sub-blocks of each of three digits or so, is helpful.

3.8 *Mnemonics*
In a scheme for classification, several different concepts have to be represented using one and the same set of digits in its notational system. Here, the mnemonics can be usefully employed. Several different kinds of mnemonics such as verbal mnemonics, scheduled mnemonics, systematic mnemonics and seminal mnemonics have been developed. (39)

4 GENESIS AND DEVELOPMENT OF COLON CLASSIFICATION
4.0 *Genesis*
In 1924, while attending the course at the School of Librarianship, University College, London, Ranganathan found that the Dewey Decimal Classification was not able to give coextensive class numbers to many newly emerging subjects embodied in the documents. As a result of this several subjects in the universe of subjects received the same number. Ranganathan found it to be due to the Decimal Classification being an enumerative classification, and he began searching for a solution to this anomaly in classification. While under this mental pressure, he happened to visit a Selfridge's store in London, and there he observed a demonstration of making different kinds of toys with a Meccano set. This released a trigger in Ranganathan's mind. He said to himself, 'Why can't I catch

63

this idea? With a few strips of iron pieces of different shapes and a few nuts and bolts, we can construct a variety of toys such as a house, bridge, rail-car, motor-car, or boat. Why can't we do the same with the subjects? Why can't we combine bits of ideas in several ways to represent a variety of subjects?' This trigger finally led Ranganathan to design the first completely analytico-synthetic classification—the Colon Classification. It was published in 1933, after eight years of experiment in the Madras University Library.

4.1 *Development of colon classification*
4.1 *Version 1 of CC*

The further developments of the Colon Classification from edition 1 (1933) onwards were based on a theory of library classification formulated by Ranganathan. The first consolidated account of Ranganathan's theory was published in 1937. On the basis of this theory, CC edition 1 was evaluated; the faults and inconsistencies found in it being removed in its second edition of 1939. This edition gave fairly coextensive numbers to a large number of subjects. The third edition of CC was published in 1950, and contained a few changes in the enumeration. During the period of development of these editions, CC was using only one facet indicator— namely ':' (colon). The stage of CC is denoted by Ranganathan by the term 'version 1 of CC'.

4.2 *Version 2 of CC*

The developments in the universe of subjects soon outgrew the capacity of version 1 of CC. The rigidity of facet structure imposed by the predetermined facet formula led to the need for the indication of absence of facets in some subjects. In other words, the predetermined facet-cormula imposed a facet structure on compound subjects, that was not inherent in compound subjects. This was due to the inhibition that the facets belonged to the basic subject and not to the compound subject of which it was a component. When once this problem was recognized in the idea plane, the theory in the notational plane realized that this was due to the lack of versatility in the notational plane. The developments in the general theory had identified that there are five fundamental categories. Version 2 of CC incorporated this and added, during 1950 to 1963, five different kinds of indicatior digits to indicate five different kinds of isolate ideas as shown below:

64

Indicator digit	*For*
' (Single inverted comma)	Time Isolate
. (Full stop)	Space Isolate
: (Colon)	Energy Isolate
; (Semi-colon)	Matter Isolate
, (Comma)	Personality Isolate

Another new feature of version 2 of CC is the acceptance in the idea plane of the interpolation of new main subjects and new partial comprehensions of main subjects in the array of main subjects. To implement this in the notational plane. Greek letters were used provisionally up to edition six (1960).

4.3 *Version 3 of CC*

Version 3 of Colon Classification is now under preparation for the press. It incorporates all the findings of the deeper and more dynamic theory of classification now being consciously developed. As a result it is tending to become a freely-faceted analytico-synthetic scheme for classification. It is now possible for the notational system of CC to place any new main subject, or non-main basic subject—simple or compound in any facet— in the helpful position determined by the idea plane. Any new compound subject will also be placed by the notational plane in the position determined by the idea plane as the most helpful position among the already existing subjects. Thus during the next decade the development in CC will be approximate to the ideal of a freely-faceted model of classification.

5 BASIC SUBJECTS, PARTIAL COMPREHENSIONS, AND SUBJECT BUNDLES

5.1 *Main subjects*

While presenting a preview of the forthcoming seventh edition of Colon Classification, Ranganathan had included eighty two main subjects in the schedule of main subjects. (17) CC edition six had included only thirty nine main subjects. Thus, there is an increase of more than a hundred per cent in the number of main subjects. What might be the reason for this large increase in the number of main subjects?

5.11 *Idea plane*

In the idea plane, the new modes of formation of main subjects such as 'distillation' and 'fusion' have added a large number of new main subjects.

There are sixteen distilled main subjects and ten fused main subjects. Besides these, there are twelve new main subjects which were earlier compound subjects and seven newly added main subjects.

5.12 *Development of a subject to the status of main subject*
The following table gives, as an illustration, the changes in the status of twelve different subjects during the years 1933 to 1970.

SN	Name of subject	Complex subject during	Compound subject during	Non-main basic subject during	Main subject since	Kind of main subject
1	Management science	. .	1933-1959	. .	1960	Distilled
2	Statistical analysis	. .	. .	1933 to 1968	1969	
3	Astronomy	. .	. .	1933 to 1968	1969	
4	Astrophysics	. .	1933 to 1968	. .	1969	Fused
5	Chemical engineering	1933 to 1967	. .	1968	1969	Fused
6	Microbiology	. .	1933 to 1968	. .	1969	
7	Biochemistry	1933 to 1952	1952 to 1956	1957 to 1967	1968	Fused
8	Forestry	. .	. .	1933 to 1968 ·	1969	
9	Public health	. .	1933 to 1968	. .	1969	
10	Nursing	. .	1933 to 1968	. .	1969	
11	Medical jurisprudence	1933 to 1968	. .	. .	1969	Fused
12	Geopolitics	1933 to 1968	. .	. .	1969	Fused

5.13 *Notational plane*
Accommodation of such a large number of main subjects in the notational plane was possible by:

1 Using all the three species of digits in the base of the notational system of CC namely Roman lower case, Indo-Arabic numerals, and Roman capitals; and

2 Using 9 as empty digit, T, V, X and Z as emptying digits, and U, W, and Y as empty-emptying digits.

With these devices, the notational system of CC has been endowed with the capacity to accommodate 5,520 main subjects!

5.14 *Likely developments in the schedule of main subjects*

The capacity of the CC notational system to accommodate more than 5,500 main subjects is an enormous capacity compared to the rate of growth of main subjects so far. However, this large capacity may tempt us to increase the number of main subjects. While one has to guard against this temptation, the cue given by the notational plane should be examined carefully before rejecting it. Because, the idea plane had restricted itself for a long-time saying that the number of main subjects should be few, mainly on account of the weakness of the notational plane. Team research and inter-disciplinary approaches are creating new subjects, a majority of which do not go as compound subjects with any one of the existing main subjects. Such subjects will necessarily have to be accommodated in the schedule of main subjects. Some subjects which initially occur as complex subjects or compound subjects are likely to develop their own set of fundamental laws and the situation needing reference to fundamental laws of the host main subject becomes less frequent. This is largely due to specialization leading to the atomization of subjects in the field of research. Such subjects are called 'adjunct main subject' and are placed near their parent main subject. Thus, at the rapid rate at which interdisciplinary approach is going on, the emergence of new main subjects will be large in number. Already the subjects such as biometry, biocybernetics, econometry, economico-cybernetics, socio-metry, and socio-cybernetics, have been claiming the status of main subject. (27) The Colon Classification has enough resilience to meet this challenge.

5.2 *Non-main basic subjects*
5.24 *Canonical basic subjects*

There are about 450 canonical basic subjects in CC edition 7 as against 327 in the CC edition 6. Thus, there is an increase of more than 100 canonical basic subjects. A review of the developments during the last three decades in some subjects, with the aid of the latest developments in the general theory of classification, showed that it is helpful to subdivide each of them in the first instance into canonical basic subjects. Particular mention is to be made of the main subjects 'D-engineering' and 'X-economics'.

5.241 *Engineering*
Until edition 6 appeared, 'engineering' had a special schedule of personality isolates. This fault was due to identifying 'work isolate' in 'D-engineering'. As a result of the review it was found that there was need for a different schedule of special isolates for each of the work isolates in 'D-engineering', such as 'civil engineering', 'mechanical engineering'. These schedules of special isolates were different from each other. There was no common set of personality isolates or sometimes even 'matter' (property) isolates. Further, the grouping of isolates on the basis of the 'work characteristics' was found to be a somewhat made-up group. This was hampering the design and construction of schedules for depth classification. In 1964, this was brought into conscious level and it was found that subdivision of 'engineering' into canonical basic subjects was found more helpful.

5.242 *Economics*
Similar was the case of 'X-economics'. Each special isolate grouped under the characteristic 'business' required a differentiated schedule of special isolates. Again, it has been found that the design of depth classification schedules would be greatly facilitated if the main subject 'X-economics' is divided first into canonical basic subjects. (25) This approach is giving encouraging results.

5.243 *Other main subjects*
The other main subjects, which are subdivided into canonical basic subjects, are '3-book science', 'B-mathematics', 'C-physics', 'E-chemistry', 'F-technology', 'H-geology', 'M-useful arts', 'N-fine arts', 'R-philosophy', and 'U-geography'.

5.244 *Advantage of fission into canonical basic subjects*
The number of canonical basic subjects in CC is likely to grow at a much faster rate in the 1970's and beyond than in the past. There is a continuous proliferation and speed in the growth of ideas due to the inevitable atomization of industry and sectors of research. Therefore, it is helpful

68

to the reader and convenient to the classifier and the classificationist, to closely approximate the trend of atomization in the universe of subjects, by building up schedules of special isolates, for each canonical basic subject which is recognized from time to time. This, in turn, would also help in making productive use of the capacity of the CC notational system. Similar work has taken place in the analysis of other kinds of non-main basic subjects.

5.3 *Partial Comprehension*
Several main subjects are sometimes treated integrally or disjunctively in the same book. (19) Edwin C Kemble's *Physical science: its structure and development* (MIT Press, 1966), is an example. Such a treatment of the subject is denoted by the term 'partial comprehension'. Some of the traditionally known partial comprehensions are natural sciences, humanities, and social sciences. In recent years partial comprehensions such as 'mathematical sciences', 'physical sciences', 'chemical sciences', 'biological sciences', 'plant sciences', 'animal sciences', 'medical sciences', and 'behavioural sciences' have been emerging. Most of these terms imply an integrated account of the subject. We also come across subjects such as 'natural and social sciences', 'pure and applied sciences', 'mathematics and physics', 'psychology and education'. Most of these subjects are embodied in textbooks, reference books, and periodical publications. They are largely disjunctive accounts. CC edition 7 has already provided for nearly thirty partial comprehensions based on the literary warrant of the 1960's. The partial comprehension can also occur at the level of basic subjects. For example, 'HOZ-physical geology' is a partial comprehension of the canonical basic subject 'H1 mineralogy, H2 petrology, H3 structural geology, and H4-geomorphology'. There is likely to be need for the partial comprehensions in the universe of isolate ideas. For example, consider '3Z5-Eurasia' comprehending the continents '4-Asia' and '5-Europe', '3Z6-Africa and Asia', and '3Z8-Australia and Asia'.

5.4 *Subject Bundle*
In recent years, some of the documents—largely about reference books, periodical publications, and research reports—embody subjects such as 'ocean sciences' and 'soil sciences'. These documents contain contributions from the specialists in the different fields. For example, 'soil sciences' may contain a contribution such as 'soil physics', 'soil engineering', 'soil chemistry', 'soil biology', and 'soil microbiology'. Each contribution is expounded and read independently of each other. Such

a collection of contributions, published in the form of a document for economic and organizational purpose, is called a 'subject bundle'. (36) The CC 7th edition has included the following subject bundle.

AC	Surface science	AP	Ocean science
AD	Soil science	AR	Atmosphere science
AE	Materials science	AS	Space science
AM	Earth science	AV	Defence science
AN	Hydro science		

6 ISOLATE IDEAS

6.1 *Personality isolates*

6.11 *Concept of personality*

A large number of compound subjects in the universe of subjects have personality isolate ideas. An isolate idea deemed to be a manifestation of the fundamental category Personality is largely the ultimate entity or phenomenon on which the theme of the compound subject centres round. Actually, besides basic subject, personality isolate forms the core of a compound subject. For example,

1 In the compound subject 'production of motor cars', 'production engineering' is the basic subject and 'motor car' is the personality isolate. Thus, 'personality' is easily identifiable in a majority of compound subjects. In the facet structure, 'personality' follows immediately after the basic subject. Its potency to individualize a compound subject is greatest among the universe of isolate ideas. Therefore, the strength of bond between personality isolate and a basic subject has been fixed to be greater than any other isolate ideas.

6.12 *Levels of personality and concept of whole and non-whole*

The personality isolates enumerated in the schedules of CC are generally made up to entities. It may be a whole entity or a non-whole entity. The concept of separating a whole entity from that of its non-wholes was sensed and brought into use in 1953. (42) The change of level among the personality isolates occurs when there is a whole entity and a non-whole of it occurring in one and the same round in the facet structure of a compound subject.

6.13 *Concept of compound personality isolate*

Among the universe of whole entities, there may be a variety of whole entities derived on the basis of different kinds of characteristics. For example, the schedule for round 1 and level 1 of personality isolates in

'Y-sociology' consists of the various kinds of groups derived on the basis of the different characteristics. A compound subject may have an isolate idea such as 'British Royalty class'. This is an isolate idea derived from the basis of two-characteristics, and denoting a typical whole entity. This can be represented by combining the isolate numbers for two isolate ideas in the schedule—namely, '856 British' and '51 Royalty'. Then the number for 'British Royalty' will be 856-51. This is called a compound isolate.

6.14 *Schedule of personality in CC*
In CC edition 7, the schedules of personality isolates will have a large variety of personality isolate ideas having different kinds of speciators. For example, in one of the depth versions of CC, there are about 220 speciators for 'motor cars' in the schedule for 'production engineering'. There are about 1,200 isolates enumerated in this schedule. (13) The same schedule can also be used for the classification of books.

6.2 *Matter isolates*
Until the publication of CC edition 6, the matter isolates were few. This was because, at that time, matter was said to consist 'usually of materials used for construction, consumption, etc'. (16) However, during the period 1960 to 1966, the developments in the general theory of classification led to the recognition of property isolates as manifest- ations of matter. A systematic examination of the CC edition 6 schedules for recognizing property isolates led to the realization that a majority of what were enumerated as 'energy *cum* personality isolates'— such as 'anatomy', 'physiology', 'disease'— were really property iso- lates. (1) Thus, a large number of property isolates were found to be incident in the schedules of CC. In 1968, the method isolates were also deemed to be a manifestation of matter. Thus, a large number of isolates in the CC edition 7 schedules are likely to be manifestations of the fundamental category matter.

6.3 *Energy isolates*
The recognition of the matter (property) isolates has led to a decrease in the incidence of energy isolates in CC schedules. Future CC schedules are likely to contain very few special energy isolates. A schedule of common energy isolates is being developed to meet the need for repre- sentation of energy isolates incident in different compound subjects. Here are examples of a few common energy isolates:

a1	Decrease	a5	Separation
a2	Increase	fD	Analysis
a3	Removal	g	Evaluation

6.4 *Space isolates*

The space isolates in the seventh edition are largely in the form of an expanded schedule. It contains isolates representing the various physiographical features (such as rivers, deserts, mountains), population clusters (villages, towns, cities), political divisions (China, India and Japan), all worked into the details of districts, counties, and also for the special kinds of speciators, such as orientation and near-Sovereign formations.

6.5 *Time isolates*

The schedule of time isolates, in addition to the usual time isolates, includes featured time—such as, day, sunrise, noon, afternoon, evening, night, mid-night, twilight, waxing moon, waning moon, seasons and meteorological periods. During the 'seventies, literary warrant may necessitate the enumeration of special time isolates to classify subjects, such as 'time for maturation of the cataract of the eye', 'fruition bearing period of mango tree'. The special time isolates can occur in any round, and its position will have to be determined on the basis of the wall-picture principle.

6.6 *Relative growth in the number of isolate ideas*

A Neelameghan (10) has suggested that it would be useful to study the relative growth of different kinds of isolate ideas, such as personality isolates, matter isolates, and energy isolates connected with a basic subject. This would help in the efficient use of the notational system. The relative rate of growth of isolate ideas differs for different kinds of basic subjects. For example, in the field of medicine the rate of growth of new ideas constituting the personality facet (that is, organs of the human body) is small compared to that of ideas constituting the matter facet (that is, about anatomy, physiology, disease, etc). This is so since there is relatively little change, over a period of time, in the number and kinds of human organs. As compared to this pattern we find the number of new ideas constituting the personality facet of subjects connected with the basic subject commodity production technology increases at a fast rate. These ideas in the personality facet are about man-made commodities. There are subjects such as chemistry, etc in which the

72

personality isolates represent ideas about natural objects and man-made objects. Thus the rate of growth in this field may be intermediate between the two fields mentioned earlier. In the personality isolates in 'education' and 'sociology', we find a rapid growth in the number and variety derived from the basis of the different characteristics.

6.7 *Schedules of common isolates*
The number of common property isolates are likely to increase in the next ten years. The inter-disciplinary approach has brought in different kinds of studies concerned with different objects. These are likely to constitute a common set of ideas. CC had attempted to draw up a schedule of common property isolates even in 1960 (21), though this was only a pilot project. A fairly comprehensive schedule of common property isolates is now under construction, and the schedule of matter material isolates is also under preparation. Edition 7 may include a schedule of common matter material isolates to meet the demands of book classification. As stated in section 6.3, a schedule of common energy isolates will also be included in the forthcoming edition. The schedule of common anteriorizing isolates includes a few more isolates to represent the new kind of approach to documents, such as glossary, standards, patents, review reports and trend reports. The use of the new indicator digit ' " ' (inverted comma) for indicating anteriorizing isolates has increased the expressiveness of the class number and the hospitality in the array in the notational plane. (12)

7 NOTATIONAL SYSTEM OF CC
7.1 *Mixed base*
CC uses a mixed base. It consists of Roman lower case letters, Indo-Arabic numerals, Roman capitals, and the Greek letter Δ (delta). When arranged in the sequence of increasing ordinal value, the digits will be as follows:

a	b	c	d	e	f	g	h	j	k	m	n	p	q	r	s	t	u	v	w
x	y	z	0	1	2	3	4	5	6	7	8	9	A	B	C	D	E	F	G
H	I	J	K	L	M	Δ	N	O	P	Q	R	S	T	U	V	W	X	Y	Z

For distinctiveness and to avoid confusion with digits 1(one) 0 (zero), the Roman lower case i, l, and o have been omitted. The digits 1 and 0 and the Greek letter Δ (delta) have been used only in the schedule of main subjects. Thus, the total number of digits in the base of the CC notational system is fifty seven.

7.2 *Total capacity of an array*

CC has deemed the digits z, o, 9, and Z as empty digits. These can be used to repeat the other fifty three digits four times. That is, we can have 212 two-digited numbers. We can also have the following sixteen pairs of empty digits to repeat the fifty three digited base sixteen times.

| zz | z0 | z9 | zZ | 0z | 00 | 09 | 0Z |
| 9z | 90 | 99 | 9Z | Zz | Z0 | Z9 | ZZ |

These give rise to 53 x 16=848 three-digited numbers. CC also uses packeted numbers, such as (a) . . . (1) . . . (Y). The '(' (starter bracket) is given the highest ordinal value—that is, greater than 'Z'. This gives an additional fifty three three-digit numbers. Thus, a total of 1,166 numbers, which include fifty three one-digited, 212 two-digited, 901 three-digited numbers, are available, for representation in an array. (19) For use in the schedule of main subjects, the digits T, V, and X have been deemed to be emptying digits, and the digits U, W, and Y as empty-emptying digits.

Before CC edition 6 appeared (1960), the Indo-Arabic numbers had been largely used for representing the special isolates. But the organization of the notational plane with the use of all the digits on the base and the newly postulated empty digits z, o, and Z has increased enormously the capacity of an array in the notational plane. This is likely to accommodate efficiently the new developments in the universe of subjects in 1970's. In order to minimize the need for interpolation among isolate ideas, CC uses different kinds of mnemonics while assigning the notation to new isolate ideas. In spite of this, if the need for interpolation arises, the digit Λ (inverted V) can be used as empty-emptying digit. This digit is given an ordinal value greater than '(' (starter bracket).

7.3 *Use of indicator digits*

CC edition 7 uses the following twelve different kinds of indicator digits. The following table shows the indicator digits arranged according to the increasing ordinal values. It also gives what each of these digits indicates.

Indicator

Digit	*Name*	*Indicates*
←	Backward arrow	Range (backward)
"	Inverted comma	Anteriorizing isolate
&	Ampersand	Phase relation
'	Single inverted comma	Time facet
.	Dot	Space facet

74

Indicator		
Digit	Name	Indicates
:	Colon	Energy facet
;	Semi-colon	Matter facet
,	Comma	Personality facet
-	Hyphen	Component of compound isolate or compound non-main basic subject
=	Equal to	Special component of compound isolate
+	Plus	Second and later components of an internationally known multinomial
→	Forward arrow	Range (forward)

The absolute value of any indicator digit is less than 'a'.

8 PRACTICAL CLASSIFICATION

8.1 CC is approximating towards a freely-faceted classification. This means that the sequence of component ideas in a compound subject should be analysed according to a set of postulates and principles and not on the basis of a pre-determined facet formula.

8.2 *Example*

Eight successive steps are suggested by Ranganathan to translate the name of a subject into the 'language' of notation:

Step 0   Raw title

        Emotional developments in adolescent girls.

        Perusal of the contents of the book suggested that the raw title is expressive, but for the term 'Psychology'.

Step 1   Expressive title

        In Psychology, emotional development of adolescent girls.

Step 2   Title in kernel terms

        Psychology. Emotion. Development. Adolescent girls.

Step 3   Analysed title

        Psychology (BS). Emotion [1M1]. Development [1M2]. Adolescent girls [1P1].

Step 4   Transformed title

        Psychology (BS). Adolescent girls [1P1]. Emotion [1M1]. Development [1M2].

Step 5   Title in standard terms
             Psychology (BS). Adolescent girls [1P1]. Emotion [1M1].
             Development [1M2].
Step 6   Title in focal numbers
             S(BS). 25 [1P1]. 52 [1M1]. g7 [1M2].
Step 7   Class number
             s,25; 52;g7.

91   USE AND ACCEPTABILITY OF CC

91.1   *Use as a practical scheme of classification*

There is a general notion among some writers and critics that CC is
merely a theoretical classification; an ideal model used only for teaching
and demonstration of the principles of classification. This is a wrong
notion for the scheme has been used in about 2,500 libraries in India.
These include libraries of many kinds and it is also employed in a few
libraries elsewhere, *eg,* in Sudan at the College of Agriculture Library at
Khartoum. Many libraries comment favourably and say that CC gives
them autonomy to classify new subjects quickly and consistently.

91.2   *Complexity in notation*

Another comment is on the complexity of the notational system used,
but mixed notation is now a feature of almost all schemes and has come
to stay. Concepts such as empty and emptying digits may seem complex
but the facility they give to the notational system is enormous compared
to the input by those learning them. In fact, the new generation of
librarians and documentalists studying CC on courses in India learn the
notational system without any great difficulty.

91.3   *Frequent changes*

'Frequent changes in class number disregarding the practical difficulties'
is another widely prevalent complaint against CC. Yet, if anyone exam-
ines successive editions of CC from 1933 onwards, it will be found that
the changes introduced in each edition are few, compared to the large
scale changes taking place in DC. Most CC developments do not alter
the relative position of documents already classified, despite notational
change. Ranganathan was very cautious in introducing new notations
as such (40), although inevitable situations arising out of developments
in the universe of subjects have necessarily forced the introduction of
new digits and concepts.

76

91.4 *Use of CC in electronic doc-finding*

The analytico-synthetic and freely faceted model has been found to be a virtue in electronic document finding systems and the Documentation Research and Training Centre in Bangalore has developed appropriate programs. (4,8) This research doubtless heralds a new era for the CC.

92 REVISION OF CC: KEEPING SCHEDULES UP TO DATE
92.1 *Edition 7*

This is planned in several volumes. It is at present anticipated that the first volume will contain the schedule of basic subjects plus schedules for common personality isolates, common property isolates, common energy isolates, space isolates, time isolates, environment and language divisions. This may be published in 1977. Later volumes will appear not earlier than 1978 and will cover subject fields in groupings—natural sciences, humanities, social sciences. Each volume will contain an alphabetical index to schedules and the rules needed for classifying.

92.2 *Book classification*

The method of revising CC schedules and keeping them up to date is as follows: a large number of bibliographies, particularly subject bibliographies, are scanned; an assortment of entries are classified using the current CC edition; the new concepts which are not enumerated in the schedule are picked up; their position in the respective arrays is determined with the aid of the principles for helpful sequence; suitable notation is assigned. Results are reported in the periodical, *Library science with a slant to documentation* and in the *Papers and Proceedings of the DRTC annual seminar.*

92.3 *Depth classification*

Over 130 depth schedules have now been developed, the largest numbers by far being in the technology and engineering fields. This should refute another criticism of CC to the effect that the schedules in such areas are undeveloped. Depth schedules in the fields of commodity production are provided for the close classification of subjects or commodities described in trade catalogues, standards and specifications, whereas in other fields the detail is for reports, technical papers in journals and, if necessary, for monographs. Depth classification schedules have been utilized by a number of specialist librarians in their documentation service and some schedules have been developed specifically for use in a specialist library and subject experts have assisted in their making. Judgement can be exercised in application with regard to the detail needed, as isolate ideas relevant to a particular purpose or situation can be picked up. For example, commercial information or product descriptions may require the representation of many attributes (3,6), whereas research documents may require the specification of one particular attribute of a subject only. (9)

92.4 *Team work in research*

The programme for research outlined by Ranganathan (24, 37) provides for systematic feedback and envisages the global participation of persons engaged in pragmatic research in the subject. Team research at various levels in designing and testing schedules has evolved and methodology has been continuously refined in the light of new findings. The incidence of flair and subjectivity will get progressively reduced in favour of objective scientific method. This in turn will increase controlled development and thus the reliability of the findings at each stage. The DRTC is actively promoting different levels of research in classification.

92.5 *Versatility claimed*

The Colon Classification is a versatile scheme. It has the resilience and capacity to meet the demands of minute classification. But its essential feature is that it is a classification for books and it gives primary importance to shelf arrangement. Edition 7 aims at maintaining simplicity and brevity of notation relative to the complexity of ideas expressed in class numbers. It can be used as a base for the derivation of subject headings and thesaurus construction using a computer. Precision in the notational plane, via the use of indicator digits particularly, makes it easily adaptable to synthesis by computer in the formulation of class numbers. In spite of its traditional discipline-oriented structure, it can accommodate many new ideas or phenomena because of its resilient notational structure. As CC is a freely-faceted scheme based on sound and thoroughly explored theory, it is possible to revise the schedules for subjects going with particular basic subjects in the light of new developments and this can be done with the minimum structural disturbance of the classification. In particular, any reassignment of isolates involves change only within a short range of the sequence of subjects. It will not involve tidal changes such as transferring a compound subject from the core of one basic subject to another. The scheme is able to keep step with changes in the universe of subjects and thus its expectation of productive life is greatly increased.

It would only be in the event of exceptional periods of turbulence in that universe that there may be a total shake up of the foundation itself, and a new methodology would then have to be worked out perhaps leading to major changes in the design of CC.

REFERENCES
1 Section 6.2 Gopinath, M A: DRTC Research Cell: *Report for 1966* (Annual seminar (DRTC) 4, 1966, paper ZA, section 31).
2 Section 5.14 Gopinath, M A: Reception of cybernetics in Colon Classification (Lib sc. 7, 1970, paper K).
3 Section 92.3 Gupta, A K: letter to editor (reply to G H Hutton's paper on 'Product analysis by coordinate index') (*Aslib proceeding* 20, 1968, 509-ll).
4 Section 91.4 Gupta, B S S: Program-package for a system for document finding (Lib sc. 7, 1970, paper H).
5 Section 2.32 Hanna, J F: 'New approach to the formulation and testing of learning models' (Synthese. 16, 1966, 347).
6 Section 92.3 Hutton, G H: 'Product analysis by coordinate index' (*Aslib proceedings* 20, 1968, 172).
7 Section 5.14 Jayarajan, P: 'New basic subjects, partial comprehensions, and subject bundles' (Annual seminar (DRTC), 8, 1970, paper BC).
8 Section 91.4 Library science with a slant to documentation. Special issue on Doc-Finder. 5, 4; 1968, December.
9 Section 92.3 Mills, J: 'Library classification (Progress in documentation)' *Journal of documentation,* 26, 1970, 150).
10 Section 6.6 Neelameghan, A: Comparison of 'Subject' with 'System' (Annual seminar (DRTC), 7, 1970, paper BB, section 63).
11 Section 7.2 Neelameghan, A: Use of zero in the notational system of CC (Annual seminar (DRTC), 6, 1968, paper BL, appendix).
12 Section 6.7 Neelameghan, A and Bhattacharyya, G: Extrapolation at the beginning of an array in Colon Classification. (Annual seminar DRTC), 6, 1968, paper BK, section 6).
13 Sections 6.14 and 92.4 Neelameghan, A, Gopinath, M A and Denton, Patricia: Motor vehicle production engineering–Depth classification (demonstration) (Lib sc. 4, 1967, paper H).
14 Section 1.51 Ranganathan, S R: Basic subjects and their kinds (Lib sc. 5, 1968, paper C).
15 Sections 1.1 and 1.51 Ranganathan, S R: Basic subjects and their kinds (Lib sc. 5, 1968, paper C, section 03).
16 Section 6.2 Ranganathan, S R: *Colon classification* (edition 6). 1960, part 1, Rule 0554.
17 Section 5.1 Ranganathan, S R: Colon classification (edition 7) 1971: A preview. (Lib sc. 6,1969, paper M, section 1).
18 Sections 1.3, 2.1 and 2.11 *Ibid* (section 051).
19 Sections 1.4 and 5.3 *Ibid* (section 053).
20 Section 0.4 *Ibid* (section 08).
21 Section 6.7 Ranganathan, S R: Common property isolates (An lib sc. 7, 1960, paper A).
22 Section 2.12 Ranganathan, S R: Compound isolate and compound basic subject: evolution of the concept through forty years. (Lib sc. 7, 1970, paper A, section 6).
23 Section 2.13 *Ibid* (section 8).

24 Section 92.4 Ranganathan, S R: *Descriptive account of Colon classification.* 1967, US edition 1965, Section zs2.

25 Section 5.242 Ranganathan, S R: Formation of basic subjects and isolates in social sciences (Annual seminar (DRTC), 8 1970, paper BA, section 3).

26 Section 2.7 Ranganathan, S R: Hidden roots of classification (Lib sc. 4, 1967, paper A, sections 84 and 85).

27 Sections 3.4 and 3.5 Ranganathan S R: Notational plane: Interpolation and extrapolation (An lib sc. 10, 1963, paper A).

28 Section 0.61 Ranganathan, S R: *Prolegomena to library classification.* 1937, page 281.

29 Section 3.1 *Ibid.* (edition 3) 1967, chap MC and part H.

30 Section 0.63 *Ibid,* chap ME.

31 Section 1 *Ibid,* chap RC.

32 Section 2.52 *Ibid,* chap RD.

33 Section 2.54 *Ibid,* chap RH and RJ.

34 Section 2.53 *Ibid,* chap RK.

35 Sections 2.62 and 2.63 *Ibid,* chap RM.

36 Section 5.4 *Ibid,* chap TE.

37 Section 92.4 *Ibid,* chap XK.

38 Sections 0.7 and 2.8 *Ibid,* part B.

39 Section 3.8 *Ibid,* part K.

40 Section 91.3 *Ibid,* Section HA7.

41 Section 2.32 *Ibid,* Section QB 7.

42 Section 6.12 Ranganathan, S R: W Universe: Portion, Constituent, Organ (Annals, Ind Lib Assoc. 3, 1953, 1-6).

Library of Congress Classification

J P IMMROTH
Graduate School of Library and Information Sciences,
University of Pittsburgh

EDITOR'S INTRODUCTION: Professor Immroth is well known for his writing and research on the Congress Classification and his long contribution on this theme to Kent and Lancour's Encyclopaedia of Library and Information Science was published only last year. The present paper reappears in this edition, however, as it provides a unique opportunity to see the scheme defended on the grounds of theoretical as well as empirical virtues.

The future of the Library of Congress Classification and in fact the future of all Library of Congress cataloguing, and its basically related subject analysis can be viewed both theoretically and empirically. It is the purpose of this paper to examine in general both the theoretical aspects of LC Classification as well as the empirical aspects.

THEORETICAL APPROACH

In examining Library of Congress Classification from a theoretical point of view it must be acknowledged that LC Classification is an enumerative classification and not an analytico-synthetic scheme. However, much of the basic theoretical structures developed by Ranganathan and further codified by such writers as Mills may be applied to LC Classification. The reason for considering LC Classification from a theoretical point of view in regard to the future is that often LC Classification has been criticized for its failure to have a sound theoretical base. It is my purpose to attempt to demonstrate that LC Classification's theoretical base, at least in regard to the emerging and prevalent theories of classification, is valid. I do not believe one should discount LC theoretically and thus ignore this major scheme as all too often is done when discussions of classification theory are presented. If LC Classification is to continue to prosper in the future a justification of its theoretical base is most significant.

81

From a theoretical point of view I will apply the concepts of Ranganathan in regard to the three planes of classification—the idea plane, the verbal plane, and the notational plane—as well as certain of his canons, laws, and postulates. In performing this function I have relied heavily upon the principles of classification scheme construction as developed by Mills in his *Modern outline of library classification* (1) and as discussed by A C Foskett in his *Subject approach to information,* (2) as well as a recent article in the fifth volume of the *Encyclopedia of library and information science* (3) by A Neelameghan.

Sequence within each class

Initially we must determine if the individual LC classes do contain the essential characteristics of a helpful order allowing subjects to be divided by appropriate characteristics and based upon literary warrant. In most instances it seems that LC Classification meets this criteria very well. Certainly LC Classification is based on literary warrant, although much of it may be based on the literary warrant of the late nineteenth and early twentieth century. With the continuous revisions of the system, current literary warrant is taken into consideration and causes new areas to develop.

In considering the order of application of characteristics, LC's basic pattern throughout is based upon the literary warrant and the material concerned and not on an 'analysis of ideas' such as the Universal Decimal Classification. This simply demonstrates that LC Classification is, in essence, what we may call a *book* classification as opposed to the Decimal Classification and the Universal Decimal Classification which stem from philosophical systems. Within the literary warrant much of the order is based upon an educational and scientific consensus; not purely from a theoretical point of view, but directly from the point of view of the products of the educational and scientific consensus as may be represented in their writings. As the then Librarian of Congress, Herbert Putnam, stated in 1901: 'The system devised has not sought to follow strictly the scientific order of subjects. It has sought rather convenient sequence of the various groups, considering them as groups of *books,* not as groups of mere subjects.' (4)

The rules for logical division which are presented by Mills create no major problem when examining LC Classification in regard to the sequence within each class. Probably most of the individual classes are as mutually exclusive as any system of classification can afford or allow; certainly there are some possibilities of cross classification but these can

82

be removed by proper use of phase relations. In my work in chain indexing LC Classification I have found that the principle of modulation is present in most cases. The steps are proximate. This is a feature that is often far better developed in LC Classification than it is in the Decimal Classification; in fact it is probably a feature of any classification which is not dependent upon its notation to demonstrate certain elements of the hierarchy. Finally in regard to rules of logical division, the division within LC Classification is probably as exhaustive as any system of classification with the exception of certain areas in schedules Q for Science and T for Technology. These definitely are not as exhaustive as the unabridged version of the UDC. However, without doubt, the division within the humanities in general, and within literature in particular, is far more exhaustive than any of the other systems. The order of facets, that is to say the order in chain, is basically followed throughout LC Classification in regard to the order of increasing complexity—hence in order of decreasing extension. There is a basic pattern of generic before specific works, hence the principle of inversion has been successfully (and probably intuitively) applied to LC Classification. The order within facets, the order in array, uses practically all of the potential devices that may be isolated such as chronological order, evolutionary order, increasing complexity, size, geographical order, preferred category, canonical order, and alphabetical order. The last of these, alphabetical order, is very regularly employed in LC Classification by the use of the first Cutter number of the notation in an A-Z sequence. This particular feature (which I will discuss further under 'notation') is one of the major advantages of LC Classification. The lack of consistency of order within facets is often criticized and certainly this is a valid criticism. LC Classification is not consistent with the individual facets, particularly the common facets in different contexts. Basically, the consistency has been over-ruled to allow the literary warrant of any individual subject to become the basic criterion for the order in array of the individual facets.

Sequence and coordination of main classes
The sequence and coordination of main classes in LC Classification basically follows the concepts of the late nineteenth century educational and scientific consensus as represented within the major treatises that dealt with main classes of that period. Much of the source of the order of LC Classification follows the order of Charles Ammi Cutter's Expansive Classification. In fact the outline of Cutter's Expansive Classification was used as a basis for the order of LC Classification with a few minor adjustments. (5)

The collocation of related classes within LC Classification in some instances is done in far better fashion than in the Decimal Classification. This is particularly true in the collocation of language and literature into the single class P. Often because of the vast amount of enumeration of individual material within the classes and facets, this collocation does not allow a great benefit to occur. The distance between English language PE and English literature PR can be quite large in any representative collection of literature in a middle-sized to large library. The concept from Bliss of gradation in speciality often occurs within LC Classification. Phase relations within LC Classification are also fairly well handled, although only by the principles of specific enumeration. This certainly can be seen in regard to the bias phase, the influence phase, and the tool phase. All of these may be covered in LC Classification by the often ambiguous heading 'General Special'. This refers to special aspects of a general subject.

CN	EPIGRAPHY
	General works. Introductions and manuals.
74	Early works to 1800.
75	Later works, 1801-
	General special. Special aspects, relations, etc.
77	Relation to archeology, history, etc.
80	Relation to religion.
85	Other

The comparison phase is also handled by the entry 'General Special' which can in some instances cause cross classification. This then, from a theoretical point of view, may be a weakness in LC Classification in that specific instructions are not given for the choice in a comparison or conjunctive phase in regard to phase relations. However this weakness is far less, let us say, than the weakness we have in UDC, where often the phase relations are not clearly specified, not to mention the fact that strict citation order is not specified in UDC.

Provision for form classes

LC Classification makes provision for form classes that meet the theoretical criteria. First of all, there are generalia classes; one might say there are two generalia classes in LC Classification. There is class A which deals with the typical generalia material such as encyclopedias, dictionaries, publications of societies, and even a 'catch all' class called AZ which deals with those instances where scholarship or learning in general occurs, *ie,* cases where material is written on the humanities, sciences, and social

84

sciences. Class Z creates a generalia class for bibliography and library science. There are major form classes in regard to literature, music, art, as are necessary in the treating of the humanistic disciplines, as opposed to the subject classes which are treated within the sciences and social sciences. Further it is my sincere opinion that there are common facets in LC Classification. First there are common facets for form of presentation. These are represented by what are called Martel's seven points, or by their proper name 'The general principle of arrangement within the classes'. This is a unifying element in the internal form of arrangement within the classes, subclasses, subjects or facets. This internal form was provided by Martel to the individual subject specialists who were preparing the individual classes of LC Classification. These seven points are: 1) general form divisions, such as periodicals, societies, collections, dictionaries, etc; 2) theory, philosophy; 3) history; 4) treatises, general works; 5) law, relation, state relations; 6) study and teaching; 7) special subjects and subdivision of subjects progressing from the more general to specific and as far as possible following the principles of literary warrant. Under individual classes, subclasses, facets, this general principle of arrangement occurs throughout LC Classification although the exact sequence may differ in individual cases. The following examples demonstrate how this sequence is not consistent in its order though the common facets are consistent in their appearance (if they are needed in the individual subject class that is being treated).

CR	HERALDRY
1	Periodicals. Societies.
	Collected works.
4	Several authors.
5	Individual authors.
7	Congress, conventions, etc.
9	Exhibitions.
11	Directories.
13	Dictionaries. Encyclopedias.
	Science, technique, theory, etc.
	General works.
19	To 1800.
	1801-
21	Treatises.
23	Manuals.
27	Minor. Pamphlets, etc.
	General special. Special aspects, relations, etc.

29	Symbolism.
31	Heraldry and art, architecture, etc.

CR   **HERALDRY**
Science, technique, theory, etc.

33	Heraldry and literature.
	Special.
41	Special branches, charges, etc. A-Z.

JV   **EMIGRATION AND IMMIGRATION**
Periodicals.

6001	American.
6002	English.
6003	French.
6004	German.
6005	Italian.
6006	Other.
6008	*Associations* (International).
6011	*Congresses* (International).
	Collections.
6014	Monographs.
6018	Documents. General only.
	History.
6021	General.
	By period.
	Under each:
	(1) General.
	(2) Special.
6023-4	Ancient.
6026-7	Medieval to 1800.
6029-30	Nineteenth century.
6032-3	Twentieth century.
	Treatises
6035	General.
	Special.
6038	Relations to the state.
6041	Minor works. Pamphlets, etc.
	Law.
6045	General collections.
6049	International law.

AM	MUSEOGRAPHY AND MUSEOLOGY
1	Periodicals, societies, collections, etc.
4	Early works (to 1800).
5	General treatises.
7	General special.
8	Children's museums.
9	Minor. Pamphlets, etc.
	Museography.
10-99	By country.

The form of presentation allows for both inner and outer form facets to occur. There are facets of a bibliographical and of a philosophical nature. In addition to the 'form of presentation common facets', as represented by Martel's seven points, throughout LC Classification there are uses of subdivision by time, although once again these are not employed consistently. The time periods have been deliberately developed as seemed appropriate from the literary warrant of the discipline involved. The examples on the preceding pages demonstrate this. There are also place facets used throughout LC Classification. These are presented in one of two fashions: in a so-called logical, that is to say, an order based on the preferred category of an American user, and the other order being the use of the alphabetical device. It may also be noted at this point that the place facets in LC Classification have certain advantages over the place facets in the Decimal Classifications. By and large the place facets have been entered into the enumeration at the point deemed most useful for the literary warrant of the individual area. In an enumerative system such as LC this may be called subject division under country. Often in LC Classification, especially in the social sciences, subject division under country is used instead of country division under subject. In the Decimal Classification the subject is usually subdivided fully before adding any geographic division. In LC however, a class or subclass may be divided geographically and then have further subdivisions. An example of this is the division of 'Constitutional history' and 'Administration' in class J 'Political science'. Subdivisions by country occur before further subdivisions of the subject, *ie,* subclasses, JK United States, JL British America, Latin America, JN Europe and JQ Asia, Africa, Australia, etc. This process of subdividing a subject first by country and then using specific subdivisions appropriate to the country improves the citation order of the individual facets. A consistent place facet may be discerned in the use of certain tables within LC Classification which are often called floating tables. These tables, which occur primarily in class H, create a place facet which may be used in a consistent order whenever the instruction is given to subdivide geographically by A-Z. One such table is the table of countries in one alphabet which occurs in class H and which may be used whenever the instructions within the schedule call for geographic division alphabetically. This table is simply a list of countries likely to occur in any geographic division. Each country arranged alphabetically has been assigned one or two Cutter numbers. Additional tables of this nature within class H are notation for states and other subdivisions under countries which may be used to extend this table as well as a table of states in the United States and a table of cities in the United States. All of these may be seen as a use of a synthetic device within LC Classification which allows a common application of the place facet.

Notation

From a theoretical viewpoint, LC's notation is certainly adequate. It is not a decimal or radix base notation. It reflects the order of a system rather than determining it in practically all cases. A possible criticism here is that at some point when the numeric base of one to 9,999 has been reached, this would limit the notation. However, in no cases within the system has this limit yet occurred. This is due to the possible expansions of the notation by the use of decimals or by the use of Cutter numbers. LC Classification's notation passes the simplicity test in that only the upper case Roman alphabet and the Indo-Arabic numericals are used, as well as a few instances of the use of lower case Roman alphabet symbols, and the use of dates. From the point of view of brevity the length of the base is very sound, giving a much broader structure than a straight decimal base such as the Decimal Classification allows. It should be pointed out in this sense, however, that in three classes, class E, class F, and class Z, which were developed at the very beginning of the system, the length of the base was limited to one upper case Roman alphabet letter rather than two and thus the base for those individual classes is not sound. It has had to be extended by the use of decimal extensions to the numeric numbers as well as by tables. LC's notation is not expressive other than the most simple expressiveness that might be given by the single and double letters. There are many internal synthetic devices within the notation to facilitate number building, particularly in the social sciences and humanities. A sense of flexibility is present in the use of shelf list numbers within LC Classification. These are numbers presented in parenthesis within the printed schedules which are not used on LC printed cards, but which do exist as added entries in the LC shelf list and can be used by

88

libraries that would prefer to class the material in the so-called shelf list numbers. There are no systematic mnemonics used in LC Classification although some of the double letters do represent literal mnemonics as in the case of divisions of class A, and class M or T. We may now look at LC and ask is it hospitable, does its notation allow for compound, complex and new subjects? In examining its notation in regard to hospitality in chain, LC's notation is a non-faceted, non-retroactive notation; it is basically and simply a code. Hospitality in array, however, is far better treated in LC Classification than hospitality in chain. New symbols may be introduced if desirable as is often the case. This is done in Cutter numbers; it is also done in regard to actual extensions of the notation by a date.

The index

There is no general index to LC Classification. In the *Encyclopedia of library and information science,* Professor Immroth noted two general indexes issued in 1974 by the Canadian Library Association and the US Historical Documents Institute. There are separate indexes to twenty one of the twenty nine individual schedules. Theoretically this should be a major weakness of the system but in practice it is not. The problem of the index will be dealt with in detail in the following sections of this paper.

Although LC Classification does not meet all the requirements of the theory of classification and classification scheme construction, it is clear that it does have some sound theoretical principles with which to face the future and in many instances is superior to either the Decimal Classification or the Universal Decimal Classification.

AN EMPIRICAL APPROACH

In turning to the future of LC Classification from the empirical point of view, there are certain basic premises of general classification to be considered. These include the process of subject analysis performed by classifiers, the existence of a permanent organization for perpetuating the system and the actual uses of the system. Of these premises, the second is fulfilled by the Congress Classification through LC call numbers on the printed cards, on the proof slips of the printed cards, and on the magnetic MARC tapes. In addition, the individual schedules are regularly published by the Library of Congress as well as the publication of quarterly *Additions and changes* to the classification. The third basic premise deals with the use of LC Classification. At present, in most instances, libraries use LC Classification as simply a shelf classification for subject location—a marking and parking system. This greatly reduces the potential of this very detailed enumerative system. As LC Classification seems to have the largest general vocabulary base of any general classification scheme, the use of this vocabulary base in a chain index to a classified catalogue would seem most helpful. The failure of many libraries in the United States to take advantage of classified catalogues certainly reduces the effectiveness of subject analysis at the precoordinate, and possibly even at postcoordinate level. The possibilities of applying chain procedure to LC are discussed in the following section dealing with the first basic premise.

The process of subject analysis
The process of subject analysis is basically concerned with the assignment of classification numbers and subject headings. The classification numbers are assigned in accordance with the predetermined enumerative classification schedules and the subject headings are assigned in accordance with the predetermined enumerative LC list of subject headings. All too often, alas, this dual process is done in an intuitive fashion not following a precise methodology such as the eight steps recommended by Ranganathan. (6) Inherent in the use of schedules and lists is the language used as descriptors, whether in classified or alphabetical array. Each specific subject may have two or even three different descriptors as a result. There is the vocabulary of the classification schedules, the vocabulary of the subject headings and in some cases the vocabulary of the indexes to the classification schedules. A very basic example of this problem has been investigated by the writer. (7) I have attempted to analyse the vocabulary control in LC Classification indexes and subject headings.

The index
Students are generally taught to classify directly from the classification tables and not the indexes. (8) In fact one of the foremost twentieth century scholars and teachers of classification, the late W C Berwick Sayers, recommends only using the index as a 'mere check' after consulting the tables. (9) Further classifiers usually become so familiar with the main tables that they do not use the index except with 'great caution' as the historian of American classification, Leo LaMontagne, states. (10) It may be observed further that some of the Library of Congress schedules have no index and yet are regularly used. (11) In addition there is no general index to LC Classification (though a general index is in preparation at Columbia University). There are, of course, at least three possible substitutions for a general index. (12) Thus I investigated descriptively the relationship between the schedules and their indexes. Sayers states in his canons and criteria of classification that a classification system needs to
90

have 'An index which shall provide a means of rapid reference to the place of any term in the schedules of the scheme'. (13) He writes in regard specifically to the LC indexes, 'It is scarcely possible to imagine an index carried to greater fulness'. (14) A similar view is presented by Margaret Mann: 'The indexes are very full, including geographical entries, personal names when used as subjects, names of battles, and other topics frequently omitted from such lists. References are made from different forms of names and attention is sometimes directed to related subjects'. (15)

LaMontagne, however, points out that the individual indexes are of 'varying fullness' (16) and Mills discerns that some indexes 'fail to show the "distributed relatives" as clearly as a good relative index should' and that there are 'often surprising omissions'. (17) The wide variation of these comments seems to justify not only the need to discern the internal function of these indexes. It may be of further importance in relation to the proposed cumulation of all these indexes into one grand general index. In fact the question may be posed—can these separate indexes be simply interfiled to generate a general index? In 1961, LaMontagne stated: 'One of the most frequent, non-theoretical criticisms of the LC Classification is that it has no general, or combined, Index. A start toward the compilation of one was made in 1947, when all existing indexes were cut and mounted on cards. Although lack of funds prevented the cutting of sub-entries the mounted cards fill sixty trays. Excluding "Law" index entries, which will not be available for some time, a combined index would constitute a volume of approximately 1,000 pages containing 100,000 entries. In view of the present work-load no date of publication can be given.' (18)

Sayers refers to this proposed general index as 'an instrument of value' (19) and Richard S Angell, on the staff of the Library of Congress, infers that a general index will be completed after the compilation of class K: 'Law'. (20) In May of 1967, the first subclass KF, 'Law of the United States', was issued. My own research has shown that the individual indexes vary in fullness and do not represent a consistent pattern of development. In my samples I found forty four per cent of the schedule terms indexed, fifty three per cent of the class numbers indexed, and thirty five per cent of the Cutter numbers indexed. (21)

Further the question of whether or not the index to a classification schedule could be used as a list of subject headings was raised in a speech given by Jay E Daily in 1957: 'Would it be possible to make the entries in the relative index to a classification and the subject headings the same? The traditions of cataloguers have been quite different. There is now no complete code of practice which will make clear to subject cataloguers what Merrill's Code does for classifiers of books. Perhaps, since both classification and subject cataloguing are usually done by the same person, we need one for both.

'Let us assume that we try to devise a method that would enable us to discover whether there is a possibility of constructing a classification the relative index of which would be a list of subject headings. We must first discover what point of similarity there is between classification and lists of subject headings. The answer, it seems to me, is that both deal with language in its broadest, general sense. A list of subject headings is a special use of vernacular language. A classification employs a highly specialized language—notation, and in the schedules provides it with a translation, which also shows the grammar of the notation.' (22)
Such an arrangement would allow a genuine sense of subject integrity to be present. If a subject heading list were truly an index to a related subject classification, then one could assume that the terms in the index came from the classification schedule; or that the classification schedule itself was a list of classified subject headings or descriptors; or that the list of subject headings was simply the classification headings arranged in an alphabetical array. The classified approach to a list of subject headings or descriptors such as does exist in various forms of category lists and hierarchical trees could be extended to a related classification scheme by this arrangement.

One of the reasons for the need of my research was to estimate how close the LC subject headings and LC classification comes to this reversible concept. Normally it seems that separate forms of vocabulary control are applied to alphabetical subject indexes and to headings in a classification schedule. A heading in a classification schedule may use fewer words than an isolated heading in a simple alphabetical array because of the context of other headings. (23) Another parameter is the transformation of the classification heading from its classified form to its form in the index to the classification scheme. The vocabulary control which is used on lists of subject headings usually involves the 'translation from natural (source) language to "key word" (index entries for purpose of facilitating alphabetization of a subject index)'. (24)

If one turns directly to rules for the control of vocabulary in the development of subject headings, there are several possible codes or approaches. One of the most important for library science is the approach of Charles Ammi Cutter in his *Rules for a dictionary catalog*. There are eighteen specific rules presented for the formation of subject
92

headings. (25) These rules are the basis for the current list of subject headings issued by the Library of Congress. The value and precision of these rules are open to question. Jay E Daily in his *Grammar of subject headings* seriously questions Cutter's rules and presents some fifteen rules of his own. (26) John Metcalfe attempts to bring Cutter's rules up-to-date with 'Tentative code of rules for alphabetico-specific entry'. (27) In addition there are other possible rules for vocabulary control such as the work of Ranganathan in his *Dictionary catalogue code* and his *Classed catalogue code* (28), Otto Kaiser and his *Systematic indexing* (29), Julia Pettee, Marie Prevost, Mortimer Taube, A Thompson, etc. In fact one may turn to any system for information retrieval and find some sort of vocabulary control in force.

The foregoing discussion demonstrates the possible important relationships between subject headings and classification. My own recent studies have shown that there are many levels of inconsistency in the vocabulary of the LC subject heading list. These inconsistencies are graphemic, morphological, syntactical, lexical, and contextual. Categories of near synonyms have been isolated by the methodology employed by this writer, as have ambiguous and redundant headings. Graphemic inconsistencies include such basic problems as spelling and hyphenization. For instance in the subject heading list the spelling of 'Archaeology' retains the internal digraph 'ae' while in the classification schedules the digraph is reduced to 'e' 'Archeology'. Similarly hyphenization inconsistencies may be seen in the difference between the subject heading 'Military religious orders' and the classification heading 'Military-religious orders'. Morphological and syntactical inconsistencies may be seen in the subject heading 'Decorations of honor' and the classification heading simply 'Decorations'. An example of lexical inconsistency may be demonstrated in the following example: there are separate subject headings for 'Badges' and 'Devices' both with classificatory references to the class 'Heraldry'. The classification heading combines these two near synonyms into a single focus 'Devices and badges'. Near synonyms are defined by this writer as terms with the same or closely related lexical meanings. Contextual inconsistencies occur in such cases as the subject heading 'Achievements (heraldry)' being contextually qualified by 'Heraldry' while the previously mentioned 'Badges' or 'Devices' is not so qualified. Ambiguous headings are subject headings with more than one classificatory reference. The subject heading 'Emblems' is an ambiguous heading by this definition as it has the following classificatory references: '(Art, N7740; Christianity, BV 150-155; Comparative religion, BL 603; Heraldry, CR; Literature, PN 6349-6358)'. Redundant

93

headings are subject headings which receive the same classificatory references. 'Badges' and 'Devices' are redundant headings as they both receive
the same classificatory reference 'CR 67-69'. In continuing research on
this problem James Williams and I have generated a classified list of LC
subject headings as joint project of the Graduate School of Library and
Information Sciences, the Knowledge Availability Systems Center and
Office of Communications Programs of the University of Pittsburgh.

As previously noted, one solution to the problems of inconsistency of
LC subject analysis is the possibility of chain indexing. A chain index is
based on the extracted vocabulary of a classification system retaining all
necessary context but deleting all that which is deemed unnecessary. For
example, the following term from schedule T 'Technology' of LC Classification, 'TP 605 Whiskey' refers to the distilling of whiskey by the fermentation industries.

T	Technology
TP	Chemical technology.
TP 500-659	Fermentation industries.
TP 589-617	Distilling.
TP 597-617	Distilled liquors.
TP 605	Whiskey.

The following index terms could result:

Whiskey: Fermentation industries, TP 605
Distilled liquors: Fermentation industries, TP 597-617
Distilling: Fermentation industries, TP 589-617
Fermentation industries: Chemical technology, TP 500-659
Chemical technology, TP
Technology, T

The term 'whiskey' may be found in a different context in schedule H,
'Social Sciences', under the number 'HD 9395'. In this context, the
index entry would be 'Whiskey: economic history, HD 9395'. It should
be observed that the chain indexing of classification schedules often
varies in relation to the necessary revision of the schedule terminology
as a result of the notation of the classification. As long as the notation
is perfectly hierarchical or sequential only a minimum of elements will be
of little value. It may also be seen at this point that if the vocabulary control necessary for chain indexing could be previously applied to the construction of the classification schedule, then no major modification of
schedule terms would be necessary. This possibility could directly lead
to the use of the chain index in place of subject headings.

94

On the other hand the development of the chain index can be most helpful even if terminology changes are necessary. Coates observes that 'Whereas in chain procedural indexing to the Colon scheme, the subject indexer can virtually limit the field of his concern to the digits of the notation, in applying the technique to the Decimal Classification he must maintain a close watch on the classification schedule of terms as well. This critical appraisal of the classification schedule may, at first sight, seem to involve a great deal of work for the subject indexer: but it is actually the work which the classifier must perform in order to classify. So that if classification and subject indexing are carried out as a unitary operation, there will be no superfluity of effort. In fact, chain procedure is an excellent and necessary check on the possibility of the classifier's jumping of mental fences out of turn.' (30) From this last quotation we may discern the fullest possible subject integration. By the use of a chain index, classification and subject indexing do become a unitary coordinated process. Continuing in this vein Coates says, 'We may now make an attempt to draw some general conclusions on the exploitation of classification on behalf of the alphabetico-specific catalogue. In the first place, chain procedural analysis of the position of a subject within a classification scheme can provide the verbal raw material for the subject heading and for the chain of references leading down to it. In order to extract this material competently, the subject cataloguer must refer directly to the real hierarchical structure of the classification schedule, and not merely to the ingredients of the notation: he must also be able to elaborate the published schedule in order to specify subjects not provided for by the classification maker, but he need not elaborate the notation.' (31)

It may be emphasized that chain indexing is still the obvious key to complete subject analysis containing integrated descriptors for both index and classification, both subject heading and classification, both classification index and subject heading. However, it must be observed that the converse of the last part of Coates concept may also occur. That is to say that the classification schedule may go to a greater depth of specificity than the list of subjects or descriptors involved. This is often the case with LC Classification. Finally it is most important to exercise vocabulary control with great care at this point. In any elaboration of terms or resolution of different terms to consistency, there is always a danger of creating an artificial language on the verbal plane. The prospect is so tempting in isolation. Coates presents a basic rule for vocabulary control in this regard: 'Research in classification is making an attempt to forge an instrument of communication without the crudities of natural language; but we should not overlook the fact that natural language is the soil out of which classification has grown. In the future development of classification it would be most unwise to disregard the hints and intimations which ordinary language offers on concept relationships. Neither in its theory nor in its practice can classification detach itself completely from its affiliations with language.' (32)

Recent research of this writer has generated twenty six rules for the chain indexing of LC classification. The chain index headings generated by these rules show ninety per cent direct indexing and a predictable number of sub-headings. Furthermore a predictable morphology resulted in these headings. The removal of ambiguous headings and redundant headings may also be accomplished by the application of these rules. In addition chain index headings reduce and isolate near synonyms as well as removing incorrect classificatory references. The chain index proves to be a more complete index than the existing LC indexes. It has a consistent morphology, and retains the context of the classification schedule in an alphabetical array.

One of the implications of my research is that the classifiers who use the indexes sparingly, and become more familiar with the individual schedules, may be more successful than those who rely solely on the index to give them access to the schedule. Secondly, library school students should be taught that the indexes are inconsistent and incomplete. They must be prepared to become familiar with the schedules and not rely on the indexes. Thirdly, it seems justified to suggest strongly that no general index to the classification be issued if it is simply a cumulation of these individual indexes. Fourthly, it is obvious that these indexes cannot be used as a tentative or initial index to a classified catalogue.

Fifthly, apparently the classification of a list of subject headings should to be consistent, be carried out as the list is being developed. Only as a classification has been defined and superimposed on a plan for developing a list of subject heading can the inherent classificatory properties of language be controlled. The nominal structure of the existing headings will only allow inherent class names of the nominal structure to create the main categories. The lexical inconsistencies of nominal classificatory language will not and cannot allow hierarchies of any specificity to develop, but only allow categorized lists of near synonyms to result.

It also appears that much of the assumed context or deep structure of the LC subject headings is contained in both the classificatory

96

references and the syndetic structure. This context normally disappears when the heading is applied.

Last it is the investigator's hope that a chain index removes most of these inconsistencies. Such a model follows strict structural and semantic rules to integrate the terminology of the chain index, the classification schedule, the classification index and the subject headings. Furthermore, this model also allows the classification schedules to be fully indexed. This constructive approach resulting from the third phase of my study creates a generative vocabulary subject analysis. The use of this vocabulary will not be limited to the future of Library of Congress subject cataloguing but can have implications for all classification schemes, subject heading lists, and (perhaps most important) specialized information science thesauri. In addition this vocabulary may serve as a natural access point to the classification numbers and subject headings stored on MARC tapes. Research in this aspect is being continued at the University of Pittsburgh.

The prospects for LC Classification are most hopeful, and its huge vocabulary base and massive enumeration still represent a unique challenge to future researchers.

REFERENCES
1 Mills, J: *A modern outline of library classification.* London, Chapman and Hall, 1960. p 54-56.
2 Foskett, A C: *The subject approach to information,* 2nd edition. London, Bingley; Hamden, Conn, Linnet Books, 1971, pp 13-203.
3 Neelameghan, A: 'Classification Theory of,' *Encyclopedia of library and information science,* vol 5, p 147-174.
4 Putnam, H: 'Manual: constitution, organization, methods, etc,' in *Report of the librarian of Congress* for the fiscal year ending June 30, 1901. Washington: Govt Print Off, 1901. p 23.
5 Immroth, John Phillip: *A guide to Library of Congress Classification.* Rochester, NY: Libraries Unlimited, 1968. p 16-21. (Page references here are all to the original edition of the *Guide,* but a third edition is now in course of preparation.)
6 Ranganathan, S R: *Colon Classification.* Bombay, Asia Publishing House, 1963. p 1.7-1.8.
7 Immroth, John Phillip: *An analysis of vocabulary control in Library of Congress Classification and Subject Headings.* Littleton, Colo: Libraries Unlimited, 1971.
8 Maltby, A: *Sayers' manual of classification for librarians.* 5th ed. London, Andre Deutsch, 1975. p 69; Margaret Mann, *Introduction to cataloging and the classification of books.* 2nd ed. Chicago: American Library Association, 1943. p 54; Bohdan S. Wynar, *Introduction to cataloguing and classification.* 3rd ed. 'Library science text series'. Rochester, NY: Libraries Unlimited, 1967. p 194.
9 Sayers, *loc cit.*
10 LaMontagne, Leo E: *American library classification with special reference to the Library of Congress.* Hamden, Conn: Shoe String Press, 1961. p 22.
11 Immroth: *Guide, op cit,* p 33.
12 *Ibid,* p 84-85.

13 Sayers, *op cit,* 3rd edition p 81.
14 *Ibid,* p 170.
15 Mann, *op cit,* p 82.
16 LaMontagne, *op cit,* p 213.
17 Mills, *op cit,* p 98-99.
18 LaMontagne, *op cit,* p 339.
19 Maltby, *Sayers' Manual* . . . 5th edition p 185.
20 Angell, Richard S: 'Development of class K at the Library of Congress', *Law library journal, LVII* November 1964. p 355.
21 Immroth: *Vocabulary control.* p 222-225.
22 Daily, Jay E: 'Subject headings and the theory of classification', *American documentation,* 7, 1957, p 270.
23 Kent, Allen: *Textbook on mechanized information retrieval.* 2nd ed, Library science and documentation, a series of texts and monographs, vol 111, New York, Interscience Publishers, 1966. p 238.
24 *Idem.*
25 Cutter, Charles Ammi: *Rules for a dictionary catalog.* 4th edition. US Bureau of Education, special report on public libraries—Part 11, Washington: Government Printing Office, 1904. p 66-77.
26 Daily, Jay E: 'The grammar of subject headings: a formulation of rules for subject headings based on a syntactical and morphological analysis of the Library of Congress list'. Unpublished DLS dissertation, School of Library Service, Columbia University, 1957. p 152-161.
27 Metcalfe, John: 'Tentative code of rules for alphabetico-specific entry', *Subject classifying and indexing of libraries and literature.* New York, The Scarecrow Press Inc, 1959. p 262-292.
28 Ranganathan, S R: *Dictionary catalogue code.* London, Grafton, 1945; *Classified catalogue code with additional rules for dictionary catalogue code.* New York, Asia Publishing House, 1963.
29 Kaiser, J O: 'Systematic indexing', *Readings in library cataloging,* ed and introd by R K Olding. Hamden, Conn: The Shoe String Press Inc, 1966. p 145-162.
30 Coates, E J: *Subject catalogues; headings and structure.* London, Library Association, 1960. p 116.
31 *Ibid,* p 145-146.
32 *Ibid,* p 175.

Universal Decimal Classification

G A LLOYD
formerly FID Classification Department,
The Hague

*EDITOR'S INTRODUCTION: The author, who retired from FID in
Spring 1976, writes: 'a number of changes have been made in this revised
version—mainly additions on the Basic Medium Edition and on UDC in
relation to the Broad System of Ordering for UNISIST with . . . a brief
last paragraph on the new UDC reform/rejuvenation programme'. In an
earlier letter to me, he had, too modestly, expressed some dismay over a
few earlier prophecies which had not materialized, but no observer—even
if closely associated with a system—can always 'win' on these and there
are special complex problems making for uncertainty in any speculations
on the future of UDC. The updated paper remains an excellent view of
the challenges facing the scheme and the root task of introducing necessary change without too much inconvenience for established users.*

Prologue

Whereas in a limited subject-field, the users of an information retrieval
(IR), selected dissemination of information (SDI) or other system can
often be well served by a relatively simple special classification and/or
descriptor-list, the advantages of this may be more than offset when the
need arises for a referral or switching centre to interconnect services with
common or overlapping interest profiles wishing to pool their resources,
as happens increasingly today. It then becomes necessary to find a suitable switching language (3) or scheme for reconciling thesauri (26), or to
adapt some existing general scheme: here, it will be assumed that, for the
organization of any information indexing, storage and retrieval system
covering all or many fields of knowledge, a comprehensive control subsystem based on a general classification or encyclopedic thesaurus, or on
a combination of both, is indispensable.

The first and most striking effect of the information explosion is the
sheer quantity of information generated, threatening to convert the conventionally controlled flow into an uncontrolled flood unless we make

full and urgent use of computers and all mechanization facilities now at our disposal: which raises, of course, the problem of systems compatibility between different types of computer hardware and software, as well as the underlying human skills and brainwork.

Secondly, there is the question of the language barrier, which is greatly aggravated by the ever-increasing volume of literature generated and is particularly evident in multilingual regions where a single natural language is neither the mother tongue nor the informational *lingua franca:* In such situations, optimal communication between the givers and the users of information must depend upon acceptance of one of the following possibilities:

1 employment of a battery of translators for every major system;
2 arbitrary adoption of one natural language (*eg* English) or world auxiliary (*eg* Esperanto) as the unifying indexing/retrieval language
3 arbitrary adoption of a 'neutral' (number of symbol) scheme, available in many natural-language editions, but not dependent on any one for notation.

The first would be uneconomic and likely to cause excessive delays in the flow of information; the second is politically debatable, even if a major world language like English were the sole *lingua franca.* The third would seem by far the most economic and practical basis for an interlingual switching scheme, given corresponding editions in at least all the major languages of the world.

Thirdly, and no less important, is the problem of subject specialization resulting from the diversity of progress in scattered (though often related) fields, and the corresponding proliferation of special indexing schemes to match the needs of these diverse interests: which raises at once problems of incompatibility between special-subject classifications and thesauri inevitably found in multi-subject information systems and networks. Concordance could obviously be established most easily by adopting as unifying or switching language a widely used general classification, which may also happen to be used by some of the branches in the network, given the existence of editions of suitable level and scope.

If it is to play the part of an international switching language in the major information networks and referral centres of the future, and at the same time retain its traditional indexing/filing role in libraries and documentation centres, any classification or indexing scheme must satisfy certain basic requirements, and be:

1 generally viable with other major classifications and serviceable to information dealers and users in all parts of the world;

100

2 widely adopted on the basis of internationally acceptable notation and editions available in many languages and of varied level and scope;

3 usable (with few adaptations) in mechanized information retrieval systems;

4 provided with organized maintenance, updating and revision facilities so as to be adaptable to new ideas, discoveries and innovations in all fields of science and technology, the humanities and arts.

No single existing classification can perfectly answer all these requirements, but serious claims are advanced for the Universal Decimal Classification (UDC) by its international sponsoring body, the Fédération Internationale de Documentation (FID) and its Central Classification Committee (FID/CCC), whose aim it is, not only to maintain the scheme in its traditional role in libraries and documentation centres, but so to improve it that is becomes an internationally accepted retrieval language for all types of information systems of the future.

1 *UDC and other general classifications*
The UDC, delivered in 1895 of its then young American parent Dewey (DC) by the Belgian pioneers Otlet and LaFontaine, has never in the United States enjoyed the same popularity as in Europe, Latin America and Japan. European enthusiasm—and such it was—mounting steadily during the first few decades of this century, was consolidated in the French (1927-33) and German (1934-53) full editions, and led in the forties and fifties to a veritable vogue in Britain—witness the numerous papers (by Bradford, Lancaster, Jones, Pollard and others) especially in the Proceedings of the British Society for International Bibliography, the launching of the English full edition (only now nearing completion) and the range of UDC editing/revision committees established by the British Standards Institution. In the USSR and East European countries, where adoption was virtually mandatory, UDC editions began to bourgeon in the postwar years, while in Germany (largely through Walther, Frank, Fill, (8, 9) and Schuchmann) and in the Netherlands and Belgium (thanks to Donker Duyvis, Lorphèvre, and others) advocacy of the UDC became a byword, almost a fetish. France and Italy remained for long aloof, but a similar wave swept Scandinavian documentation circles, and the popularity of the UDC spread from Spain and Portugal to the countries of Latin America, where it has vied successfully with the DC. Recently the wheel has come full circle, and there has been a certain awakening of interest in the United States (and Canada), with an eye to possible adoption in mechanized information systems (10-12, 29-33) and as an

alternative to the Library of Congress LC in reclassifying from the Dewey DC. (27a)

That the UDC can vie with the other main general classifications today—Dewey (DC), Library of Congress (LC), Ranganathan's Colon Classification (CC) and Bliss' Bibliographic Classification (BC)—is usually admitted, albeit grudgingly, by those whose enthusiasm is reserved for the 'new' faceted classification, and even the 'no-classification' attitude of many computer-hawks, whose disdain for all general classifications has earned the enmity of the faceteers, cannot much longer be maintained. Each of the five schemes has its own peculiar advantages and disadvantages, but neither the CC nor BC, nor even the LC (with its wide-flung catalogue-card distribution and now its MARC records) is as much used throughout the world as the UDC and its parent DC.

Until mid-century, the DC and UDC remained so akin in their main structures that DC-classed libraries could often use the UDC details as extensions, and even up to the last decade it was not wholly unrealistic, in a comparison of the two schemes, to suggest a two-level combined use. (15) The need is still there today, if the 'roof' classification recently proposed is to have the maximum chance of success, but earlier hopes of a unified DC/UDC have dwindled, especially since the transfer of linguistics from class 4 to 8 and other major relocations in the UDC.

'Ce monstre préhistorique', as the UDC is quotably described, 'has continued to adapt itself, slowly and unsteadily, but with surprising persistence, to the new demands imposed on it'; these are the words of J Mills (23) in the brief UDC part of his recent comprehensive review of progress in library classification in the *Journal of documentation*. Surprising or not, the persistent adaptability of the UDC is likely to manifest itself even more vigorously in the late seventies and beyond and may well refute the Rangan-avant-garde contention that 'the expectation of life of the UDC has expired'. Obviously the UDC is part of the prehistory of contemporary faceted classification, much as the piston engine is of the jet, tonal music of twelve-note, and Newton of Einstein. While Newton's ideas are not yet totally superseded by Einstein's, and the piston-driven vehicle and tonal music still retain some popularity, so the general run of librarians, documentalists and information-seekers will surely still find use, in the foreseeable future at any rate, for hierarchic classifications like UDC. This is not to devalue the sterling work of members of the Classification Research Group (CRG), the British National Bibliography (BNB), the FID's Classification Research Committee (FID/CR) and other devoted groups in their arduous search for the fully articulated general faceted

102

classification, nor is it to deny that some perfected version of the CRG/ BNB-based PRECIS may well prove the *deus ex machina* of the next generation. The pangs of parturition of the new scheme are by no means over though, and there is certainly a long period of transition with mutually beneficial influences ahead of us.

There are prospects indeed, as should become apparent, that the UDC— once it sheds the more archaic structural features— will sufficiently develop its functional capacities to meet the demands imposed during the eighties.

2 Wider adoption, increasing availability and promotion: role of an improved UDC Basic Medium Edition

Estimates obtained from only a dozen countries by the FID Classification Department (19) indicate that there are now well over 100,000 institutional users of the UDC, albeit mainly in the USSR, Poland and other East European countries, with a substantial number more in Latin America and Japan. In France, Italy, Spain and Portugal UDC is making headway, especially in technical university libraries: in other West and North European countries, as well as in the English-speaking countries generally (where the development of new faceted schemes is a strong counter-attraction), it is not easy to assess the present trend, but some 20,000 copies of the *Abridged English edition* (BS 1000A) have been distributed in the last ten or fifteen years and recent work on the feasibility of using UDC in mechanized systems gives grounds for belief that even in these more developed areas of the world the UDC will find a new lease of life! In the developing countries of Asia and Africa, especially the Arabic-speaking lands, there is steadily growing interest, though the influence of the Library of Congress and its associated facilities often militates against the adoption, and even the retention, of the UDC.

Among international organizations, the UDC has not yet received the support hoped for. Several (including ISO, UIT, WHO as well as UNESCO) are or were users, but the ISO Central Secretariat has not followed up the well-elaborated proposals of Wellisch (39) for an international centre for standards documentation, and the International Nuclear Information Service (INIS), despite the IAEA's co-sponsorship with FID of the *UDC special edition FID 351* in 1964 has preferred a keyword system. This has not, however, discouraged FID/CCC who still believe the UDC usable for major information networks and, noting from a recent Aslib report to UNISIST (the joint ICSU/UNESCO project for a worldwide information system) that the UDC is the least unsatisfactory of the existing schemes, plan to make it the most satisfactory!

The mass UDC usership of 100,000 can still be partly attributed— surprisingly enough, considering the wide use of Latin letters as scientific symbols—to the internationally accepted notation of arabic numerals (with a few extra signs); hence the reluctance to incorporate letters as UDC auxiliary symbols, except for computer programming and certain special relationships or extra-UDC categories.

A far more important factor than the numeral notation, however, is the availability of UDC editions in so many natural languages and of such varied levels and scope of subject. FID-authorized and other UDC editions are published in at least twenty natural languages in full, abridged, medium (intermediate) and special-subject versions, as may be seen from the FID publications catalogue (annually, free) and the brochure *Key to information-UDC* (FID 466, 1970):

> full editions, comprising 150,000-200,000 items (numbers with descriptors);
> abridged editions, with about ten per cent of the full;
> medium-length editions, with about 50,000 items, or 30 per cent of the full.

There is also an expanding range of special-subject editions in which the central theme or subject is represented by the full-edition schedule and subsidiary topics by medium-length, abridged or further reduced schedules. The much needed English Medium Edition, planned as companion to the 1967 *DK-Handausgabe* and the *Edition Moyenne,* could have played an important role in promoting UDC use in the USA and other English speaking countries, but completion of the preparation was so far delayed that a major revision of the 1967 editions was already necessary. Thus began in the mid-1970s the project for an improved UDC medium edition, which has been called the Basic Medium Edition (BME) (41) because intended as a basic standard version of the UDC (essential in English as well as in the other major languages). It aims to be centrally manageable and updatable by the FID Secretariat (with its limited staff), sufficiently detailed for university and other large general-scope libraries, but also usable as a background scheme for fringe-fields in more specialized centres (requiring the full edition for their core subjects), not to mention its possible use in conjunction with thesauri. (See section 7.)

To fulfil its important role of UDC popularization, the BME needed even more thorough preparation than the 1967 editions: the FID/CCC/

BME Panel of three members (for the English, French and German versions) has been helped by painstaking selections for many major fields by relevant committees for UDC revision, notably for the social sciences and several branches of science and technology. The German, French and English BME editions are expected to be available by the end of the 1970s, and should be followed quickly by Spanish and other major-language versions.

Lastly there are the important groups of UDC guides (available in several languages) and programmed instruction texts by Dubuc (7) in French and by Wellisch (40) in English—both likely to multiply during the coming years. What now seems desirable is the preparation (in several languages) of a comprehensive guide to the UDC, setting out clear recommendations for UDC classificationists with practical instructions for classifiers—perhaps incorporating a 'standard' programmed instruction course.

3 *UDC in mechanized information systems*

The mechanized processing of UDC revision proposals and updating of schedules, so far as it is mainly a matter of FID housekeeping, is touched on in the next section, but the use of UDC in the mechanized production of indexes and as an indexing language in computerized information retrieval systems is of much more interest to the classification community at large, and may be considered here in as much as it concerns the development of the UDC during the seventies.

As far back as 1934 (in the *General introduction* to the *Full English edition of UDC,* BS 1000, vol I, pt 1), it was argued that the UDC was suitable for mechanical sorting, and in 1948 the Royal Society Scientific Information Conference noted the need to explore the potentialities of the UDC in mechanized retrieval, but the few contributions during the forties and fifties were mainly concerned with item-punched cards (for which fixed-length index-codings were essential) and so was born—despite the introduction of feature-punched cards (which require no such limitation)—the *idée fixe* that variable-field codes like the UDC were unsuitable for mechanized information systems. (38) The idea persisted, and indeed is still not quite dead. Only in the middle and later sixties, thanks to pioneering work, mainly in the United States by Rigby, (29-32), Freeman (10, 11) and others, but also in Germany by Schneider and Koch (13, 34), in Denmark (2), Britain (4), Switzerland (36) and elsewhere, could the UDC be shown to be usable as an indexing language for computerized control and processing of information in all fields of knowledge.

Perhaps the most notable landmark in this respect was the American Institute of Physics UDC project under Freeman and Atherton (12), the important results of which formed the main theme of the first (1968 Copenhagen) seminar on UDC in a mechanized retrieval system—*Proceedings* issued 1969 (25), and still underlay much of the discussion during the second (1970 Frankfurt) seminar. If Copenhagen opened new perspectives and confirmed the conclusions of Freeman and Atherton that 'there is no longer any doubt that the UDC can be used as the indexing language in a mechanized system . . . in either batch-processing or interactive mode', Frankfurt usefully amplified these findings with reports on the use of UDC in several operational mechanized IR/SDI systems (*eg* in the General Steels Division of the British Steel Corporation) and on the computer-aided production of bibliographies, catalogues and indexes (*eg* for *Documentatio geographica*), at the same time breaking new ground with reports of two important future projects—the automation of the UDC-based Boreal Institute Library in Edmonton, Canada, and the planned new Bibliotheque des Halles in Paris.

Other contributions during the later sixties have explored or mooted special mechanized applications of the UDC, for example: the indexing of *Geo-science abstracts* with UNIDEK (33); and maintenance of user-profiles in the metallurgical field. (21) From all these, it seems clear that the use of the UDC, if not as efficient always as special-purpose machine codes, does offer prospects as an exchange device for switching between mutually incompatible schemes in larger pools or networks, especially if some of the pool participants already use the UDC for their own documentation.

Rigby (44) has admirably reviewed these developments during the 1960s in a recent report (FID 523) which contains summary descriptions of some sixty projects and operating systems using UDC in a mechanized mode.

4 *Organized UDC maintenance and revision facilities*

Compared with the organization of the DC, and still more of the LC, the international UDC centre in the FID Classification Department (FID-ClD) seems small indeed, with its staff at no time being more than two or three full-time personnel. Though this is partly compensated by the voluntary activities of numerous persons, working mainly as members of the score or more UDC special-subject revision committees (FID/C . . .), there is still a heavy burden of coordination and routine processing for the FID-ClD, since these committees and individual experts in specific fields, under the general guidance of FID/CCC, channel all proposals for improving the UDC through the FID/CIC office in the Hague. Here they are edited and, in consultation with the UDC Proposals editing sub-committee FID/CCC/P when necessary, widely circulated as P-notes for regular cumulation into yearly (formerly half-yearly) issue-numbers and three-year series of the *Extensions & Corrections to UDC* (EC-UDC). Intermittent efforts have also been made over the years to maintain at the FID General Secretariat a 'master copy' of the complete UDC, based on the French (1927-33) and German (1934-53) full editions, as updated or revised by the EC-UDC, but the much needed, up to date master edition has never materialized and remains one of the tasks of the next few years, conceivably with computer aid from the ETH Zurich Library, whose Director Dr. J-P Sydler, as Chairman of FID's UDC Mechanization Subcommittee FID/CCC/M, has raised the possibility within the FID/CCC since the mid 1970s.

Fortunately the routine revision processing and this quite major operation need not be so arduous now that an automatic punch-typewriter is installed in the FID office. At present the routine preparation of *Draft P-notes* and *P-notes,* any necessary amendments (in the light of comments received), and the final production of the yearly EC are done with simple punched-tape retyping, but the growing bulk of revision work, the compilation of an updated UDC 'master edition' and various other tasks may well depend on computer aid in the near future.

The automatic writing machine could have one other important UDC application, namely the automated production of concordances with other classifications, descriptor lists and thesauri, using simply programmed master punched cards rearrangeable by UDC number—or A/Z term-order and automatically retyping hard-copy in these different sequences:

UDC-ordered list, with corresponding English/French/-terms

English descriptors A/Z, followed by relevant UDC numbers

French-descriptors A/Z, followed by relevant UDC numbers, and so on.

Whilst in no way eliminating the intellectual work of compilation, this may prove invaluable during the late seventies, if concordances are to be established as part of the new UDC programme. (See Section 9.)

5 *The UDC development programme for the 1970s*
Some important arguments having been advanced for general, as opposed to special, classifications—especially for the UDC, it seems fitting to examine the main features of the new UDC Development Programme for the 1970s and try to assess the prospects for achieving its aims. Recently launched by FID/CCC with the support of the FID/ClD and several FID/C . . . special committees, and funds partly made available by the

107

FID but partly sought through UNESCO and other contracts, this programme is aimed not so much at routine revision (which of course will proceed through the FID/C . . . and other groups) but rather intended to implement the more urgent and radical plans of the CCC. Several aspects have already been noted. For example: increased publicity and information on the UDC, through articles and lectures, seminars and symposia, etc, including a late 1976 Seminar in Brussels as part of the Dewey DC Centenary Celebrations by FID/CCC; clearer rules and instructions for the development and use of the UDC, both in conventional and mechanized information systems; a wider range of UDC editions in more natural languages; and further automation and mechanization development, both for the information community at large and for FID housekeeping procedures in connection with UDC maintenance.

The new UDC Development Programme may be conveniently considered in four more or less concurrent phases outside the normal routine revision:

(1) elaboration of a UDC 'roof scheme' capable of fulfilling the role of international switching language (43) in multilingual and multidisciplinary information retrieval systems, especially of an international or large-scale nature;

(2) extended studies on the use of UDC combined with coordinate-indexing schemes, thesauri or special-subject classifications, and the compilation of appropriate concordances, as means to improving information retrieval systems generally;

(3) short-term priority projects, mainly FID-funded, to improve or remedy defective or deficient parts of the existing UDC schedules;

(4) further perspectives of structural and notational improvements of a more far-reaching nature.

Adaptable as the UDC has proved itself in the past, more radical changes will almost certainly be called for in the next decades. Yet with ever-increasing availability and still wider adoption, the UDC will also need—more than ever—some degree of stability to minimize inconvenience to existing users. No compromise between stability and adaptability can fully satisfy the requirements of both traditional libraries or documentation centres and the modern computerized retrieval systems of the future, so it may be useful to examine the possibilities of using the reasonably stable UDC with more quickly adaptable special-purpose schemes (of faceted or thesaurus type) at suitable levels or to accept as inevitable two quite separate forms of the UDC—one for libraries, the other for documentalists (28), an argument not far removed from

108

that of Otlet and LaFontaine in developing the UDC from DC and subsequent arguments for aligning the main divisions of both. (15)

6 The UDC as a 'roof scheme' for UNISIST and the Broad System of Ordering (BSO)

As a first step towards establishing a 'standard' hierarchic scheme (with
extensive general categories as auxiliary devices) in which to fit the
numerous specialized schemes used today, there arose in FID circles the
idea of making a large-span UDC 'roof scheme', under which could be
hung, at different ceilings or rafter levels and in various positions on each,
the relevant special classifications, thesauri or descriptor-lists, as well as
the more detailed UDC divisions themselves for those who prefer a homogeneous UDC-based system. This conception is not new—indeed the
'principle of complementarity' was already proposed a decade or more
ago (24) in connection with the SfB system for building documentation—
but it received a new impetus in the efforts to see UDC adopted as the
switching language for UNISIST, the joint ICSU/UNESCO project for a
world scientific information system. Introduction of the 'Dachklassifi-
kation' concept by an FID vice-president who also pleaded for development of the UDC as a 'multi-facet' scheme (1), has been welcomed and
followed up by the FID/CCC.

It was stated in an Aslib study for UNISIST that the UDC was found
the 'least unsatisfactory' of the major existing schemes, but there is
still reluctance among UNISIST interests to commit themselves to the
UDC, unless it can be presented as a concise, updated and well-balanced
schedule manifestly more satisfactory than the others. This was a major
reason why, during the 1972 FID Conference in Budapest, it was decided
to enlarge an FID/CCC panel formed in 1971 into a more representative
Working Group as FID/SRC to elaborate a Subject-field Reference Code
that could serve as the Broad System of Ordering (BSO) required for
UNISIST, ie, an independent 'roof classification' to control the transfer
of large blocks of information between constituent centres and services
using different indexing languages, special classifications, thesauri, etc.

After two or three years work, FID/SRC was able to offer two alternative and rather different schemes. Following a special meeting with
UNISIST experts in September 1974 to consider these, a small three-
man panel FID/BSO was appointed from among the FID/SRC members
to prepare and complete a single (merged) BSO for UNISIST which
should be ready for practical testing and finalization by 1977-78. But
the development of the BSO is another story! If it is adopted by

UNISIST and becomes widely used, it might be possible to use the UDC with it for depth retrieval, but any attempt to restructure the UDC fully in line with the BSO could only lead to a virtually new universal classification very different from the UDC of today (See Section 9).

7   *UDC combined use and concordances with other indexing languages*
The UDC is basically an aspect classification, whose scattering of related elements (distributed relatives) must be controlled by A-Z indexes, often inadequate, or by means of colon-related multiple entries, which recent relator refinements (27b) have not yet proved as precise and simple as thesaurus terms. Conversely, it is becoming clear that the success of a thesaurus, especially if its scope is at all wide, depends very much on the optimal combination of coordinate and hierarchic structuring, and that to reconcile different compatible thesauri in a given information retrieval system some common system of code numbers or symbols is needed (26), which may then just as well be those of a hierarchic scheme like the UDC. 'In information retrieval', to quote no less a proponent of faceted classification than D J Foskett in his fine review of Informatics in the *Journal of documentation* (1970, no 4), 'the inclusion of generic hierarchies is absolutely essential if we are to make the maximum use of mechanized retrieval systems . . . because information about the basic . . . entities in any field of knowledge makes the foundation of the inductive method of reasoning which . . . [is] characteristic of the classificatory sciences'. Thus it would seem that the use of well-constructed thesauri in conjunction with hierarchic (UDC) schedules could offer better search/ retrieval control than either used alone, though there are problems still to be studied of their respective differentiating and integrating functions. Encouraging results were reported from the Soreq nuclear information service (Israel) by Marosi (22), and the whole problem of combined UDC and thesaurus use was one of the main themes of the 1971 International Symposium on 'UDC in relation to other indexing languages' at Herceg Novi, Yugoslavia.

The compilation of concordances between the UDC and thesauri or other special schemes, apart from throwing more light on their combined use, should eventually help to establish optimal methods of subject organization and control, especially in mechanized retrieval systems. Several concordance projects have met with little or limited success, among them: UDC with two UNESCO/ICSSD thesauri for sociology and economics (about 500 terms in all); UDC with UNESCO/CDS computerized documentation service (2,600 terms); and a pilot project on concordance between the UDC and the EJC-TEST thesaurus of Engineering and
110

Scientific terms, involving samples of about 150-200 terms, to be used as part of a report to seek substantial funding (outside the FID) for a concordance with the full range of 22,000 terms in TEST. Regrettably, this UDC/TEST concordance project, which seemed reasonably promising, had to be abandoned for want of EJC interest and funding.

8 *Short term priority projects to improve the UDC*

In order to help update, revise and remedy the most defective and deficient sections of the UDC schedules more rapidly than is possible through the routine (FID/C . . .)committee procedure, the FID Council in 1969 agreed to allocate limited funds from its reserves for a series of priority projects to be undertaken, in the 1970s, by paid experts in liaison with the relevant committee or, failing such, with FID/CCC itself, mostly on an annual basis. Among the first priorities were the following projects:

001/009 revision to develop 03/04 or 002 for information sciences (but not theory), involving relocations of the contents of 01/02, 04/05 and 07/09 (see also Section 9) with 003 retained, a new 006 Standardization scheme adopted, (and the remaining parts of 00 developed as suggested in Section 9 below).

538 or 539 Solid state physics, a totally new scheme;

574/577 General, cellular and subcellular biology, with new schemes for molecular biology and cytogenetics—all these three projects undertaken by the USSR member of FID, Viniti, in Moscow;

in class 3, several major improvements, including Economics have been completed by FID/C3 and work is progressing on Sociology, Demography and other Social science sections;

in class 6, projects for 616 Pathology and 619 Veterinary medicine have still not been completed but several 63 (Agriculture) sections have been revised, while a new scheme 681.5 Automatic control engineering has been elaborated;

in the Common auxiliaries, several new or revised schedules including- -03 Materials facet, -05 Persons facet, and (4/9) Geo-political divisions.

A second group of priorities due for completion in the mid 1970s included the following projects:

preparation of a UDC roof scheme (as described above);

rationalization of the UDC auxiliaries, with scope notes and examples for each, and recommended filing order perhaps giving symbol substitutes for computer systems;

new project for Psychology, seriously out of date and misplaced at 159.9, to be elaborated by French experts;

improvement of the present range of 621.3.0 . . . special auxiliaries, to

111

be undertaken by a German expert working in liaison with the committee FID/C 621.3;

a completely new scheme for Organics, no longer adequate in the 547 schedules, as part of an ongoing project by Netherlands experts in liaison with the Chemistry revision committee 54+66.

Not all these priorities, it is feared, could or can be completed successfully by their appointed deadlines, but much depends on the fulfilment of reasonable quotas each year, and FID/CCC will try to ensure that the programme does not lag during the coming years, whatever the fate of the new UDC reform and renovation programme.

9 Prospects for renovating the UDC structure with more faceting

Although developments and prospects so far discussed have reasonably conformed to the watchword 'dynamic development with maximum stability', there is a considerable ferment of ideas in UDC circles for introducing not only new subjects but also major relocations to achieve better balance in the main class structure, and above all for greatly improving and extending the facet potentialities of the UDC (auxiliaries, both general and special). Separation of the humanities, social sciences and arts, distributed over six of the ten main classes in 1/3 and 7/9, by science and technology concentrated in 5 and 6 is a legacy from the DC parent and objectionable more on logical-aesthetic than pragmatic grounds. Nevertheless, that only two main UDC classes have to house well over half the world's documentary output of information is a serious practical disadvantage. Despite this, it is worth noting that the main UDC structure, as opposed to length of notation, presents a profile corresponding quite closely to that of the literature published in all fields of knowledge (14), which seems to justify the CCC policy of resisting the more radical pleas for transmogrification (1, 5) at least so far as libraries and permanent collections are concerned. On the other hand, a certain drastic renovation of the UDC house is essential to meet the needs of such major information systems as UNISIST, as was envisaged as far back as 1963 in a statement on the 'Future of the UDC' (6, 17, 20, 35), and the CCC will have to tackle the dilemma either by implementing the idea of the two- or more level 'roof scheme' hospitable to a range of other indexing languages, or by recognizing such a sharp division of interests between the librarian and the documentalist as to necessitate the co-existence of two distinct forms of the UDC (28), of which the 'library UDC' could then well be developed in closer line with the DC. In any case, the needs of large-scale information systems and networks make it essential to renovate parts of the main UDC structure and auxiliary notation, as well

112

as to carry on the normal updating and routine revision. There follows a brief survey of prospects for some of the improvements that might be made.

In class 0, several major improvements should stem from the priorities briefly described in Section 8, following the relocation of the contents of 01/02, 05 and 07/09 on some such pattern as:

001 Science and knowledge generally
002 Information sciences
003 Semiology, writing notation (unchanged)
004 Communication sciences
005 Organization, method and system
006 Standardization
007 Investigation, research etc
008 Civilization, culture, progress
009 Free (Humanities → 008?)

All 01/09 could thus be freed for future use, with 06 Organizations transferred to -06 alongside -05 Persons.

Classes 1 and 2 (Philosophy and Religion) may eventually be merged, but the immediate requirement is to establish better schedules for such major religions as Islam, Hinduism and Buddhism as has been done for the Jewish faith—and so help to remedy the present imbalance between Christianity and the other religions. Several two figure divisions of Class 1 (with little current literary warrant) could easily be telescoped, *eg*, in free three figure divisions of 13 or 14, to permit an eventual relocation of Theology and religion, perhaps in the vacated 18/19, should this prove desirable and practicable.

In Class 3 Social sciences, the ferment of ideas is much more vigorous, which is appropriate enough in view of the present state of human society. Important new schedules sometimes have to be developed or relocated with lengthy notations because of insufficient two or three figure divisions free, but there are some prospects for clearing 38 (Trade and communications) and most divisions of 36 (Welfare, movements, etc) are being cleared and could provide better placings for certain behavioural sciences like Management (from 65) and Psychology (from 159.9) alongside 35 Administration and 37 Education. Meanwhile, efforts are likely to be focused, now that the revision of 33 Economics is completed, on radically improving the Sociology schedule (perhaps by merging most of the contents of 39 in 30 or 31).

Classes 7, 8 and 9 are unlikely to undergo many radical relocations, though many improvements are likely in 77 Photography and 78 Music with the help of interested international or national organizations, while

113

an earlier scheme to merge sections 624/628 Civil engineering with 69/72 Building, planning & architecture (18) could, if ever implemented, fill vacant 3-figure divisions mainly in 713/718. However tempting it may be to envisage History as a behavioural/social science in class 3, or even more generalized in the vacated 09 mnemonic with (09), and Geography as one of the earth sciences alongside 55, a much more likely relocation (reverting to (0) would be the redevelopment of modern linguistics in a 2-figure division of class 0, closer to the sciences of communication and information.

Class 4 itself is indeed of as much concern as class 0 to the CCC, and wider UDC circles, whose initial inertia has given place to a growing interest in its possible redevelopment to cover broadly the huge area of man, life and environment, including life control sciences, communication, bionics and cybernetics; the eco- bio- sphere and environment control (resources, conservation, pollution) for life maintenance; and perhaps the life (bio-) sciences, biomedical and agricultural, though not necessarily the classical disciplines of biology, botany and zoology, which might remain in 57/59. Just as important, though very speculative, would be the effects on the grossly overburdened class 6, for if medicine and agriculture could be relocated from 61 and 63, and the management sciences from 64/65, class 6 would at last be devoted entirely to Technology, so that electrical, nuclear and other newer technologies could at last be assigned major 2- or 3-figure divisions, with at least one 2-figure division left free for future development.

Concurrently, the whole UDC auxiliary apparatus will of course be subjected to intensive study in a serious, planned and concerted effort by FID/CCC with the aims to:

develop and consolidate a systematic range of general categories, including common attributes (extending the recently elaborated -03 Materials and -05 Persons);

rationalize and augment the special auxiliaries -1/-9, . 0 . . . and ' . . . which are at present inadequate, difficult or impossible to revise in many major areas of class 3, in 53 (Physics) and elsewhere; and

simplify, and as far as possible standardize, the auxiliary symbols and their use throughout the whole UDC.

The new drive for UDC reform and renovation may well develop during the later 1970s (see Schmidt (45))—the enthusiasm is there, though funding may prove a serious stumbling block—but the task is huge and will last through the 1980s or longer, even with adequate expert support from the special UDC committees and individuals, for it involves virtually the remaking of the whole UDC as discussed briefly below.

Epilogue

A glance back through the 1970s and a quick appraisal of this article's earlier high hopes when written in 1971 could well remind us that 'the best laid schemes of mice and men gang aft a-gley'. Few of those hopes have yet been fulfilled, partly because the uneasy economic situation has seriously affected the FID's annual UDC budget and partly because FID/CCC and Classification Department have been slow to agree and implement a detailed programme of UDC development. Even if the essential funding and expertise can be found, it is an enormous task that now faces the CCC and FID central management, yet the UDC will become quickly obsolete and disused unless a way is found to reconcile the desire for stability among many thousands of users with the urgent need for real modernization.

In this the UDC sponsors will be greatly helped by A C Foskett's recent book (42), one of the most comprehensive studies on UDC yet published, authoritative (on the basis of 15 years as UDC user, reviser and teacher) but forward looking and constructive in its recognition of the need for wider availability of the schedules, clearer policy and better control over revision. Can a reasonable solution be found for a *two-level UDC of the future*?

This might comprise

(a) a broad basic schedule, partially restructured on the lines of (if not the same as) the SRC or BSO (see section 6) and of not more than about 5,000 divisions, to serve as a standard switching/transfer device, as a broad library shelving/filing scheme and as the framework for:

(b) a detailed schedule for depth retrieval and information exchange, with a greatly elaborated array of general entity facets (also usable independently) and multifarious special facets complementing the broad framework of (a).

If some such solution proves feasible with the broad basic schedule (a) as a much-pruned version of existing Abridged editions and the detailed schedule (b) of about the same scope as the British Medium Edition (BME) but with full facet arrays, UDC central management and updating would be much facilitated and the UDC certainly made more viable.

May this brief epilogue be not an epitaph but the prelude to a real UDC rejuvenation and resurgence!

REFERENCES

1 Arntz, H: 'Die DK–eine Vielfacetteklassifikation'. *Nachr Dok, 21,* 1970, s 139-142.

2 Barnholdt, B: 'A computer-based system for production of a UDC-classed library catalog at the Technological University Library of Denmark'. *Proc First Sem on UDC in a Mech Retr System, FID/CR Rept No 9,* (FID 405), Copenhagen, Danish Centre for Documentation, 1969.

3 Coates, E J: 'Switching languages for indexing'. *J doc, 26,* 1970, p 102-110.

4 Corbett, L: 'Computer-based information services, including the use of UDC at UKAEA Aldermaston'. In *Proc First Sem UDC in a Mech Retr System, FID/CR Rept No 9* (FID 405), Copenhagen, Dan Centre for Documentation, 1969.

5 Dahlberg, I: 'Möglichkeiten einer Neugestaltung der DK'. *Nachr Dok, 21,* 1970, s 141-153.

Dubuc, R: 'Les 'Sciences de l'Homme' dans la CDU', (dans 'L'avenir de la CDU'). *Rev int doc 30,* 1963, p 137-140.

7 Dubuc, R: *Exercises programmés sur la Classification décimale universelle* (FID 452). Paris, Gauthier-Villars, 1970.

8 Fill, K: 'Kritische Gedanken zur Revision der Dezimalklassifikation'. *Rev doc, 28,* 1961, p 148-168.

9 Fill, K: 'Sorgen um die Zukunft der Dezimalklassifikation'. *DK-Mitt, 9,* 1964, s 21-24.

10 Freeman, R R: 'Computers and classification systems'. *J doc 20,* 1964, p 137-145.

11 Freeman, R R: 'Actual and potential role of the Universal Decimal Classification in Language-sciences Documentation'. *Proc Conf held at Airlie House, March 4-6, 1966, under the sponsorship of the Center for Applied Linguistics.* New York, American Elsevier, 1968.

12 Freeman, R R and Atherton, P: *Amer Inst Physics: UDC Project, Rept Nos 1-9,* 1965-1968. Esp *AIP/UDC–5,* 'File organization and search strategy using the UDC in Mechanized Reference Retrieval Systems; *AIP/UDC–7,* 'AUDACIOUS (*A*utomatic *D*irect *A*ccess to *I*nformation with the *O*n-line UDC *S*ystem)–an experiment with an On-line, Inter-active Reference Retrieval System, using the UDC as the Index Language in the Field of Nuclear Sciences'; *AIP/UDC–9,* 'Final Report of the AIP/UDC Research Project for the Evaluation of the UDC as the Indexing Language for a Mechanized Reference Retrieval System (listing all nine reports).'

13 Koch, K-H: *Internationale Dezimalklassifikation (DK) und elektronische Datenverarbeitung.* Frankfurt/Main, Zentralstelle für maschinelle Dokumentation, ZMD-A-14, 1967.

14 Kofnovec, L and Simandl, D: *Comparison of UDC structure with the structure of world scientific and special literature.* Prague, UVTEI (mimeographed), 1970.

15 Lloyd, G A: 'Comparison of the Dewey and Universal Decimal Classifications at a minium 3-figure level'. *Rev doc, 27,* 1960, p 45-80; also as separate publication FID 329 of the series 'Etudes de classification'.

16 Lloyd, G A: 'A "new deal" for universal classification'. *Rev doc, 27,* 1960, p 149-153.

17 Lloyd, G A: 'Science and technology in the future UDC revision' (in 'Future of UDC'). *Rev int doc, 30,* 1963, p 132-137.

18 Lloyd, G A: 'What lies ahead for the UDC and ABC?' *25 Jahre Dokumentationsstelle für Bautechnik, Stuttgart 1941-1966,* p 101-105, Fraunhofer-Ges z Forderung d angew Forsch e V München Selbstverlag, 1966, 220s.

116

19 Lloyd, G A: 'The UDC in its international aspects' (paper pres at Evening Meeting, 25th February 1969), *Aslib proc, 21,* 1969, p 204-208.

20 Lorphèvre, G: 'L'action de la Commission Centrale de la Classification', (dans 'L'avenir de la CDU'). *Rev int doc, 30,* 1963, p 129-131.

21 McCash, W H and Carmichael, J J: 'UDC user profiles as developed for a computer-based SDI service in the iron and steel industry'. *J doc, 26,* 1970, p 295-312.

22 Marosi, A: 'EURATOM Thesaurus and UDC: combined use for the subject organization of a small information service'. *J doc, 25,* 1969, p 197-213.

23 Mills, J: 'Library classification' (in 'Progress in Documentation'). *J doc,26,* 1970, p 120-160, p 141-143.

24 Mölgaard-Hansen, R: 'A study on building filing systems'. IBCC Report No 2 (in the series 'Recent developments in Building Classification' reported to the CIB Congress in Rotterdam and the FID Conf Warsaw), 1959.

25 Mölgaard-Hansen, R and Rigby, M: *'Proc First Seminar on UDC in a Mechanized Retrieval System'* (Copenhagen, 1968). Dan Cent Doc, 1969, FID/CR Rept No 9 (FID 405).

26 Neville, H H: 'Feasibility study of a scheme for reconciling thesauri covering a common subject'. *J doc, 26,* 1970, p 313-336.

27 Perreault, J M: *Towards a theory for UDC.* London, Bingley; Hamden, Conn, Linnet Books, 1969; a) reclassification, p 181-241; b) relators, p 119-148, also *Rev int doc, 32,* 1965, p 136-144.

28 Petersen, C W:'Weiterentwicklung der DK'. *DK-Mitt,* 15 Jrg, 1970; 'Grundsätzliches . . .' Nr 3, Mai 1970, s 9-10; 'Vorschlage . . .' Nr 4, Juli 1970, s 13-14.

29 Rigby, M: 'Experiments in mechanized control of meteorological and geoastrophysical literature and the UDC schedules in these fields'. *Rev int doc, 31,* 1964, p 103-106.

30 Rigby, M: 'Standardization for classification in computerized documentation systems'. In Atherton, P (ed), *Classification research: Proc 2nd Int Study Conf, Elsinore 1964,* p 524-538, Copenhagen, Munksgaard (FID 370).

31 Rigby, M: 'A mechanized multi-access documentation system for the atmospheric sciences and water resources'. *Proc 2nd Ann Amer Water Res Conf,* 1967, p 415-431.

32 Rigby, M: 'A worldwide meso-documentation system for collection, storage, retrieval and dissemination of water literature'. *Int Conf on Water for Peace,* 1969, p 542-555.

33 Russell, M and Freeman, R R: 'Computer-aided indexing of a scientific abstracts journal by the UDC with UNIDEK: a case study'. *AIP/UDC Rept No 4,* 1967.

34 Schneider, K and Koch, K-H: *The use of the UDC in the production of mechanized indexes*–ZMD-A-21 (English edition of ZMD-A-10, 1967). Frankfurt/Main, Zentralstelle f masch Dok & Beuth-Vertrieb GmbH Berlin 30, 1970.

35 Schuchmann, M *et al:* 'Die Zukunft der DK–The future of the UDC–L'Avenir de la CDU'. *Rev int doc, 30,* 1963, p 129-140.

36 Stüdeli, B: 'Automatische Dokumentation–Prinzip und Anwendung. *In 23 Informationstagung der Schweiz Ges f Automatik,* 1968, Geneva NT,A4/1969, s 221.

37 Sviridov, F A and Lloyd, G A: 'Medical documentation and the UDC'. *Proc 3rd int cong med librarianship, Amsterdam, 5-9 May 1969,* repr in 'Excerpta Medica Int Congress series no 208'.

38 Vickery, B: 'The UDC and technical information indexing'. *Unesco Bull Libraries,* vol *15,* 1961, p 126-138.

39 Wellisch, H: 'An International Centre for Standards Documentation . . .' *Israel Soc Spec Libr & Info Cent (ISLIC) Contrib to Info Sci, No 3,* 20p Tel Aviv, 1969.

40 Wellisch, H: *The Universal Decimal Classification: a programmed instruction course* (FID 467). Univ Maryland, School of Libr & Info Services, 1970.

Additional references for this revised version of the paper
41 Arntz, H: 'Basic Medium Edition of the UDC (BME)', in German in *DK-Mitt,* 18, 1974, Nr 2, S 7-10.
42 Foskett, A C: '*The Universal Decimal Classification: history, present status and future prospects . . .*' London, Bingley, 1973, 171 pp.
43 Lloyd, Geoffrey, A: 'The Universal Decimal Classification as an international switching language' in *Subject retrieval in the seventies: new directions* (Proc. International Symposium at the . . . University of Maryland . . . May 14-15, 1971), pp 116-125.
44 Rigby, M: '*Computers and the UDC: a decade of progress 1963-1973'.* (FID 523), The Hague, 1974.
45 Schmidt, A-F: 'Gedanken zur reform der Dezimalklassifikation', *Nachr Dok,* 23, 1972, s 105-113. Further 'Die langfristige umwandlung der DK in eine universalle facettenklassifikation', *DK-Mitt.,* 17, 1973, Nr 5, s 11-20 and Nr 6, s 21-24.

Classificatory principles in natural language indexing systems

B C VICKERY
School of Library, Archive and Information Studies,
University College, London

EDITOR'S INTRODUCTION: Professor Vickery's contributions to the literature of bibliographical classification are many, but this particular paper remains a concise and lucid defence of classificatory activity together with an illustration of various forms which such activity can take. It is interesting to contrast this with the following paper by E M Keen and to note that there continues to be a general paucity of conversions from either viewpoint.

The justification for alphabetical sequence in information retrieval was trenchantly stated by John Metcalfe in a superbly polemical, though often wrong-headed book: 'All indexing depends directly or indirectly on alphabetical order, because whatever numbers, notations, symbols or codings it goes on to, it must begin with names written with the letters called the alphabet . . . Only known names in a known order, with direct entry under them as in alphabetical catalogues, or with references to another known order as in the classified catalogue, or to the codings of mechanical selection, will indicate information . . . Alphabetical order is the world's most important precision tool, because it is the most important device in indexing, and only familiarity has bred the stupid contempt with which it has been treated by so many supposed authorities on indexing.' (1)

No one can deny the validity of this argument. But retrieval is something more than the 'indication of information'. Let us look at another justificatory passage, this time from Metcalfe's *bete-noir*, S R Ranganathan: 'Classification means division into groups based on likeness, and arrangement of things in a more or less helpful sequence is an inherent habit of man. Such arrangement is a neural necessity. It is instinctive, almost biochemical in nature, and involuntary . . . The complexity of the universe of things and of ideas exceeds the capacity of involuntary classification. Deliberate classification becomes necessary . . . Sharpness in thinking, clarity in expression, expedition in response, and exactness in communication depend ultimately on the deliberate exercise of the innate power of classification.' (2)

A little reflection makes evident that classification, in one form or another, at one stage or another, is almost universal in information storage and retrieval. It can be avoided at the indexing stage: an index based on document titles, for example, simply uses the 'known names' assigned to documents by authors, and lists them in a known order. Retrieval from such an index can on occasion avoid classification, if the 'name' known to the searcher happens to match a title entry. But the moment that he looks for alternative 'names' to express the topic he seeks, he has classed these names alike. As soon as we depart from title indexing, and use a standard vocabulary of indexing terms, the indexer must of necessity class variant topic words as alike, all to be represented by a particular standard term, and the searcher must do the same. Nearly always in information storage and retrieval, at either the indexing stage, the search stage, or both, a classifying activity is implicit.

However, the theme of this paper is more specific: it is concerned with the *explicit* use of classification in alphabetical indexes and alphabetical index vocabularies. 'Classification' involves one or both of two operations: (a) grouping and division: putting together entities that are alike in some way, and keeping apart those that are unlike; (b) sequencing: arranging the entities of a group in a meaningful sequence.

Either the first or the second operation is essential—without one of them no classification has taken place. If either is used, the other is optional: entities may be sequenced without grouping, and grouped entities may be arranged in a sequence not related to meaning.

Modes of using classification
In a list of index terms such as the following, no classification has been introduced:

Art paper
Bevelled edges
Cartridge paper
Cloth binding
Flexible binding
Gold blocking
Guillotined edges
Hand binding
Paper boards

Rough edges
Silver blocking
Supercalendered paper
Wooden boards

By the use of *inverted headings,* classified groupings are at once introduced:

Binding,	cloth
	flexible
	hand
Blocking,	gold
	silver
Boards,	paper
	wooden
Edges,	bevelled
	guillotined
	rough
Paper,	art
	cartridge
	supercalendered

'Gold blocking' and 'silver blocking' are classed as types of blocking, and similarly with the other entries.

A second list of subject 'names' without classification is as follows:

Binding of books
Censorship of books
Illustration of books
Preservation of books
Printing of books
Publishing of books
Royalties for books
Selling of books
Transport of books.

Rotation to produce *subheadings* immediately forms a meaningful group:

Books,	binding
	censorship
	illustration
	preservation
	printing
	publishing
	royalties

selling

transport

Another form of rotation, exemplified by the KWIC index, groups together all titles (or index phrases) that include the same word:

SE-ORGAN)/	ANESTHESIA AND RECEPTIVE FIELDS(SEN
N)/ TEACHING OF GENERAL	ANESTHESIA FOR DENTAL SURGEONS(MEI
DE(CENTRAL DEPRESSANT)	ANESTHESIA IN CATS/ CARBON-DIOXI
ERLY AND AGED PATIENTS/	ANESTHESIA IN OPERATIONS FOR GASTRIC
NE(CENTRAL DEPRESSANT)	ANESTHESIA IN RESPIRATORY STUDIES/ C
EVALUATION IN PERIDUAL	ANESTHESIA OF LIDOCAINE, MEPIVACAINE
SURGICAL OPERATIONS OR	ANESTHESIA 1935-1939 AND 1956-1960-(
WITH DIFFERENT TYPES OF	ANESTHESIA/ PARAMETERS OF THE OXIDA
PPARATUS, SIDE-EFFECTS,	ANESTHESIA RESPIRATION/ ELECTRICAL
NEBULIZATION DURING	ANESTHESIA(APPARATUS,-MAN)/
AN ELECTRIC CURRENT IN	ANESTHESIA(DOG, RABBIT) USE OF
DUCTION OF HYPO THERMIC	ANESTHESIA(RAT, RABBIT, GUINEA-PIG
SPECIALTY (PHILOSOPHY)/	ANESTHESIOLOGIST'S VIEW OF HIMSELF A
AND THEIR IMPORTANCE IN	ANESTHESIOLOGY-(MAN)/ EFFECTS OF ION
HISTORY OF THE JOURNAL	ANESTHESIOLOGY/
DEPRESSANT)A NEW LOCAL	ANESTHETIC AGENT/ COMPARATIVE EVALU
OF INFLUENCE OF SEX ON	ANESTHETIC MORBIDITY AND MORTALITY
RABBIT, RAT)/ EFFECT OF	ANESTHETICS ON THE DURATION OF EMBO
AT,MONKEY/ EFFECTS ON	ANESTHETISED ANIMALS OF AN OXYTOCIC
S(HISTORY)/ LIFE AMONG	ANESTHETISIS: RECOLLECTIONS OF 40 YE
NE(CARDIO VASCULAR) IN	ANESTHETIZED PATIENTS/ CIRCULATORY I
RIPHERAL CIRCULATION OF	ANESTHETIZED PATIENTS/CRITICAL CLOS

In all these examples, classificatory grouping is used, but only alphabetical sequences. Meaningful sequences of subheadings may also on occasion be found, particularly in book indexes, as in the following example:

Sulphur,

        sources of supply

        use in gunpowder

           insulation

           matches

           vulcanization

        deleterious effects on blast-furnace iron

                    coal-dried melt

                    glass coloration

Sulphuric acid,
>> early methods of manufacture
>> lead-chamber process
>> contact process
>> use in preparing alum
>>> ether
>>> explosives
>>> paraffin
>>> soda
>> use for bleaching
>>> electric batteries
>>> petroleum refining

The final aspect of classification found in alphabetical indexes and vocabularies is that which is implied by *cross-references:*

Aeronautics *see also*   *Aerodynamics*
>> Airplanes
>> Civil aviation
>> Flight

refer from   Aviation

The implication is that all the terms so linked form a meaningful group or class, alike in some (unspecified) way.

The development of computer search of word indexes has led to a new form of classing—the grouping together of a set of words all of which include the same sequence of letters, by the technique known as *truncation.* A search for *CELL* (where the asterisks mean 'irrespective of what letters appear in the word at this point') collects together entries containing such words as:

>> Cell
>> Cells
>> Cellular
>> Cellulose
>> Cellophane
>> Celluloid
>> Cellar
>> Cello
>> Cellist
>> Micelle
>> Hermicellulose
>> Unicellular
>> Cancellation

123

The aim is to produce a meaningful group—and the art of truncation is to achieve this aim with minimum admixture of the irrelevant.

The three main ways in which classification is introduced into alphabetical indexes and vocabularies are thus inversion of headings, formation of sub-headings, and the use of cross-references. Classification can be—and often is— introduced casually, as practical experience in the development of an index suggests its utility. But attempts have been made to put forward principles to guide its use, or at least to establish consistent practice. Some of these ideas will now be examined.

Principles of classification use
The inversion of compound subject names, as we have seen, leads to the formation of classified groupings. However, inversion is not by intention a classificatory technique, whatever may be its effect. In considering a compound name such as AGRICULTURAL CHEMISTRY, C A Cutter (3) was concerned to enquire, under which word in the compound would the user expect to look if he sought this particular topic? The rules that he discussed were therefore concerned with specific entry, not with classing, and this has been the case with others who have put forward rules for inversion.

Cutter recognized three types of phrase that might be inverted: (a) the noun preceded by an adjective, such as AGRICULTURAL CHEMISTRY; (b) the noun preceded by an adjectival noun, such as DEATH PENALTY, and (c) the prepositional phrase, such as FERTILIZATION OF FLOWERS. He discussed three possible rules: (1) never invert, (2) invert only type (a), and (3) invert any type of compound name if doing so brings to the front what we consider to be the 'most significant' word of the phrase.

The first rule would introduce no grouping other than that provided by natural language, *eg:*

Agricultural	botany
	chemistry
	economics
	history
	implements
	land
	machinery
	rents

The second rule, as far as classification is concerned, implies that the noun is the preferred basis of grouping, *eg:*
124

System	economic
	educational
	financial
	social
	solar

The third rule, recognizing that both the others are too absolute, leaves inversion to the discretion of the indexer—in fact, it is no rule at all, and offers no classificatory guidance.

Eric Coates (4) intensively analysed adjectival phrases according to the semantic categories of their components, and applied his principles in the construction of the alphabetical *British technology index.* (5) He recognizes four semantic categories into which words may be classed:

Thing—*eg,* Beams, Inks, Buses, Engines

Material—*eg,* Aluminium, Steel, Wood

Action—*eg,* Moulding, Welding, Labelling, Collision

Property—*eg,* Velocity, Thickness, Hardness, Fertility

Other words in phrases may represent the type or purpose of a thing, material, action or property. Binary combinations of categories give rise to a dozen kinds of compound name, and a rule as to the inversion of each is put forward by Coates:

Example	*Categorical analysis*	*Invert?*
Aluminium beams	Material type of thing	Yes
Research satellites	Action type of thing	Yes
Illustrated books	Property type of thing	Yes
Anodised aluminium	Property type of material	Yes
Injection moulding	Action type of action	Yes
Elastic collisions	Property type of action	Yes
Printing inks	Action purpose of thing	No
Rocket engines	Thing, part thing	No
Rocket research	Thing, action	No
Lightning fires	Action type of action	Yes
Hardness ratio	Property of property	No

Thus as far as classification is concerned the main effect of Coates' rules is to group by purpose, if present, otherwise by the 'thing' word, if one is present. The analogy to preferred groupings in schemes of faceted classification is evident, and the primacy of 'things' corresponds to the primacy of 'concretes' in the earlier work of J Kaiser. (6)

When Coates does not invert, he introduces the colon as a separator between the words in the phrase:

125

Printing:	inks
Rockets:	engines
Rockets:	research
Hardness:	ratio

In form and in fact, the phrase becomes a heading and subheading. This opens the way to rules for compounds other than adjectival phrases, such as the following:

Example	Categorical analysis	Invert?
Welding by lasers	Action by thing	Yes
Thickness of beams	Property of thing	Yes
Labelling for packaging	Action for action	Yes

A further step is to develop rules for compounds of more than two words, *eg* 'Welding of foil by lasers' is analysed as 'action on thing by thing', and the heading formed is FOIL: WELDING: LASERS. To sum up, the grouping found in the *British technology index* is controlled by the classing of terms into categories and a pre-determined combination sequence of categories, in a way that is completely analogous to the principles used in faceted classification.

It is interesting to find that the technique has been rediscovered in the USA by H Skolnik (7)—who believes it to be 'a new concept'. For a chemical index, he categorizes terms as product, reactant, process, catalyst, use or property, and combines them in headings in that sequence.

Grouping in the alphabetical index may also be controlled, not by directly categorizing terms, but by inserting one of a small set of 'relational operators' between each pair of terms, accompanied by similar sequencing rules. A scheme of this kind was put forward by Jason Farradane (8), using relations named as concurrence, self-activity, association, equivalence, dimensional, appurtenance, distinctness, reaction and functional dependence. In this case, it is the word-pair relations that must be classed.

The principles of categorical analysis and relational operators have been combined and applied to alphabetical indexing by Derek Austin and Peter Butcher for the *British national bibliography*. (9) They start with a natural language phrase expressing a topic, for example:

(a) Plating the spokes of bicycle wheels
(b) Contamination of rivers by power station feedwater
(c) DDT for controlling aphid predation on roses

They first categorize each term as 'entity' or 'attribute'. An 'entity' is comparable to Coates' 'thing' or Kaiser's 'concrete': it is defined as 'a

126

thing, whether concrete object or mental construction'. Grouping is first of all by entity. Attributes are the properties of entities, their activities, or the properties of activities.

Next, among all the entities present in a phrase, it is necessary to decide which is the 'focal concept'—the idea in the subject which is to be regarded as its key, the direct concern of the author. Other concepts are regarded as non-focal 'differences'. So in examples (b) and (c) above, the entities RIVERS and ROSES may be considered to be focal concepts. In example (a), the focus of attention is 'the spokes of bicycle wheels'. This must be further analysed by means of the 'possessive' or 'thing-to-part' relation into:

system—bicycles
subsystem—wheels
subsubsystem—spokes

and its components assembled in that sequence. The remaining term in this example—PLATING—is an attribute, and the complete heading is:

BICYCLES. WHEELS. SPOKES. PLATING

In example (b) there is a second entity, 'power station feedwater', analysed by the possessive relation into POWER STATION. FEEDWATER. This is linked to RIVERS via the attribute term CONTAMINATION, which is an 'effect produced on' RIVERS by the FEEDWATER. So the complete heading is RIVERS. CONTAMINATION. POWER STATIONS. FEED-WATER. In example (c), there are two other entities, DDT and APHIDS, and two attribute terms. PREDATION links ROSES and APHIDS in an 'effect produced on . . . by . . .' relation; CONTROL links APHIDS and DDT in the same way. The full heading is thus:

ROSES. PREDATION. APHIDS. CONTROL. DDT

The net effect of this detailed categorical analysis is to form index headings grouped by the principal systems of focal entities, with sub-grouping determined by relational analysis—once again in a way comparable to facet analysis. In all these principles of alphabetical indexing developed by Coates, Farradane and Austin, limited classificatory effect is achieved by methods similar to—and in fact derived from—those used to obtain more extensive grouping in faceted classification. The limitation is that, within any grouping, the sequence is alphabetical. No hierarchical sequence of terms is introduced.

This last stage is brought into alphabetical indexes in the form of cross-references. These, too, are considered by the writers just discussed but they have come to their full flower in thesauri, which tend to replace the traditional subject heading lists. Whereas the latter presented meaningful

127

groupings simply as 'see also' references, the former use a more refined relational analysis. A cross-referenced term may be part of the same classificatory hierarchy as the term referring to it—either the genus to which it belongs (broader term, BT) or a species of it (narrower term, NT). On the other hand, the two terms may be collaterally (species in the same genus) or semantically linked in some non-hierarchical way, and both these types are referred to as 'related terms' (RT). A typical thesaurus extract is as below (10):

Chemical properties

BT	Chemistry
NT	Acidity
	Alkalinity
	Calorific value
	Chemical reactivity
	Heat of absorption
	Heat of combustion
	Heat of crystallization
	Heat of formation
	Heat of fusion
	Heat of hydration
	Heat of reaction
	Heat of solution
	Heat of vaporisation
	Latent heat
	Thermo chemical properties
	Valence
RT	Chemical bonds
	Molecular weight
	Optical activity
	Physicochemical properties
	Thermodynamic properties

The result of this relational analysis is that the terms referred to as BT and NT all fall within the same conceptual facet as the referring term, whereas the RT may be either collateral terms in the same facet or terms from another facet: in effect, facet structure has partly been introduced into the displayed grouping. In some thesauri, the 'concealed classification' lying behind the cross-reference structure is made explicit by a second sequence of terms which presents the hierarchy within each facet used, for example:

128

Chemical properties
        Acidity
        Alkalinity
        Chemical reactivity
        Thermochemical properties
          Heat of absorption
          Heat of crystallization
          Heat of reaction
            Calorific value
            Heat of combustion
            Heat of formation
              Heat of hydration
          Heat of solution
          Latent heat
            Heat of fusion
            Heat of vaporization
        Valence

The explicit display of structure is taken one step further in the Thesaurofacet described by Jean Aitchison. (11) The basic hierarchical relations of each index term are displayed in the schedules of a faceted classification. Thus the entry TELEVISION CAMERA TUBES, MCE, in the alphabetical thesaurus refers to class MCE in the classified schedule:

M	Electronic engineering (BT)
MA	Electron tubes (BT)
MBT	Electron beam deflection tubes (BT)
MBV	Indicator tubes
MBW	Trochotrons
MC	Cathode ray tubes (BT)
MC2	Image converter tubes (RT)
MC4	Image intensifiers (RT)
MC6	Storage tubes (RT)
MCE	Television camera tubes
MCI	Colour tubes (NT)
MCL	Television picture tubes (RT)
MCO	Colour tubes (RT)
MCQ	X-ray tubes

The terms marked BT, NT, RT might be so referred in a typical thesaurus. In the Thesaurofacet, references to these broader, narrower and collateral terms in the same facet are *not* made in the alphabetical sequence.

129

The latter is reserved for semantic relations to terms in *other* facets, thus:

Television camera tubes, MCE
    RT Photomultipliers
        Phototubes
        Television cameras
    BT (A) Television apparatus

The BT (A=auxiliary or additional) does not lie in the hierarchy to which TELEVISION CAMERA TUBES belongs, although these tubes are indeed a species of television apparatus. The net effect of the Thesaurofacet is to make the classificatory structure behind cross-references even more explicit.

The value of classification

Is all this introduction of classificatory techniques—inversion rules, categorial analysis, relational analysis, facet hierarchy—anything more than biochemical urge, a neural compulsion? Has it value in information retrieval? Is the complexity it introduces justified by results? Would we not be better served by known names in a known order, and nothing more?

The advocates and users of classificatory principles in alphabetical indexing would make answer on two counts. First, as soon as the 'name' of a topic is something more complex than a single word, problems of sequence arise which the alphabet cannot solve—there is no longer a universally known order. Second, there are few areas of knowledge in which terminology is so settled and so widely accepted that each topic has a single known name.

The first problem immediately neccessitates some principles of ordering, so as to achieve a consistency in indexing that will facilitate search. It is this that has given rise to inversion rules, categorial and relational analysis, and these in turn create classificatory groupings in the index. The second problem, contrariwise, necessitates some principles of variation and interrelation, so as to achieve a flexibility in the choice of search terms. It is this that has given rise to the whole cross-reference structure and its elaboration, with the creation of classificatory groupings in the index vocabulary.

Index entries constructed according to a consistent pattern are particularly important in retrieval systems that rely on visual search. An entry such as:

ROSES. PREDATION. APHIDS. CONTROL. DDT

130

is more readily comprehensive to the human searcher than one in which, perhaps, the index terms follow each other alphabetically:

APHIDS. CONTROL. DDT. PREDATION. ROSES

The latter system is used in the SLIC Index developed by J R Sharp (12) and also in *Excerpta medica* indexes, where it leads to entries such as:

Ammonia, ATP, brain cortex, cerebellum,
          Glucose, glutamate, glycogen,
          lactate, methionine, seizure, white
          matter

A sequence of ordered entries, however, produces an alphabetico-classed grouping in which a searcher may more readily browse to pin-point a topic to follow up.

A cross-reference structure aids search whether it is humanly or mechanically performed. Particularly in the computer searching of indexes based on text language (titles or abstracts), to capture all the variant word forms whereby a concept may be expressed it is necessary to search for a whole group of semantically related words and truncations. For example, a search for 'carbohydrates' in *Chemical titles* offers the following search terms:

CARBOHYD*	*URONIC
SUGAR	*SONIC AC*
*OSE	GLUC*
SACCHARID	GLYCER*
OSAMIN	XYLON*
ITOL	ARABIN*
QUINIC	GALACTO*
SEPTIC AC	*OSIDE*
SHIKI*	RIBON*
STREPTA*	*NNONIC*

The value of classificatory techniques in otherwise alphabetically based retrieval systems is established both by logic and by their use in practice. The alphabet is indeed a basic precision tool, but it is not the whole answer. As Peter Mark Roget wrote in 1852, 'words are the instruments of communication, though we often remain unconscious how much we owe to this potent auxiliary of the reasoning faculty . . . Yet frequently we seek in vain the words we need, and the appropriate terms—notwithstanding our utmost efforts cannot be conjured up at will. They come not when we call, and we are driven to the employment of a set of words and phrases either too general or too limited . . . ' Because of this defect—which holds for indexer and searcher as strongly as for

131

author—Roget set about the production of his classified thesaurus of words and phrases.

He outlined its benefits in the following way: 'The inquirer can readily select, out of the ample collection spread before his eyes, those expressions which are best suited to his purpose, and which might not have occurred to him without such assistance. In order to make this selection, he scarcely ever need engage in any elaborate or critical study of the subtle distinctions (upon which the classificatory analysis has been based)—an instinctive tact will rarely fail to lead him to the proper choice . . . Some felicitous turn of expression thus introduced will frequently open to the mind a whole vista of related ideas.'

This is the very crux of the matter. An index is more than an 'indication of information'. It is a tool to aid *search*. It needs to be a 'potent auxiliary' of the information-seeking faculty. Classificatory techniques are introduced to make it something more like the 'precision instrument' that we need.

REFERENCES
1 Metcalfe, J: *Information indexing and subject cataloguing.* Scarecrow Press, New York, 1957.
2 Ranganathan, S R: *Prolegomena to library classification.* 3rd edition, Asia Publishing House, London, 1967.
3 Cutter, C A: *Rules for a dictionary catalog.* 4th edition, US Bureau of Education, Washington, 1904.
4 Coates, E J: *Subject catalogues—headings and structure.* Library Association, London, 1960.
5 Coates, E J: 'Aims and methods of the British technology index'. *Indexer, 3,* 1966, p 146-152.
6 Kaiser, J O: *Systematic indexing.* Pitman, London, 1911.
7 Skolnik, H: 'The multiterm index'. *Journal of chemical documentation, 10,* 1970, p 81-84.
8 Farradane, J and others' *Report on research and information retrieval by relational indexing.* Part I, 1966.
9 Austin, D and Butcher, P: *PRECIS—a rotated subject index.* BNB MARC Documentation Service Publication No 3, London, 1969.
10 *Thesaurus of engineering and scientific terms.* Engineers Joint Council, New York, 1967.
11 Aitchison, J: 'The thesaurofacet'. *Journal of Documentation, 26,* 1970, p 187-202.
12 Sharp, J R: 'The SLIC index'. *American Documentation* 17, 1966, p 41-44.

Appendix: Comparison of a thesaurus with classifications
The degree to which classificatory hierarchies have penetrated thesauri may be illustrated by a sample comparison undertaken by Aslib in 1969. The thesaurus examined was TEST (10) and a sample from it
132

was compared with the Dewey (17th edition), Bliss, Colon and UDC classifications.

TEST, a thesaurus of engineering and scientific terms, was published in 1967, but is related to an earlier thesaurus of engineering terms published in 1964. A collective work and the joint product of the US Office of Naval Research and the Engineers' Joint Council, it includes over 17,000 index terms (and over 5,000 USE references) in science and technology. The main sequence is alphabetical—each term is listed independently. Italicized terms are USE references. Below each allowed term are cross-references: UF (used for) referring to a term not allowed in indexing; BT (broader term) to a term higher in a hierarchy; NT (narrower term) to a term lower in a hierarchy; and RT (related term) to a term having a close but non-hierarchical relation. A dash against any term in the NT or RT lists implies that it too has narrower terms associated with it.

A second sequence in the thesaurus lists twenty two major fields (such as Physics) and sub-fields within each (such as Acoustics), and lists terms that occur within them. A third sequence extracts all broad terms that have at least two levels of narrower terms associated with them, and presents each hierarchy. There is no explicit indication of facets, chains are clearly displayed in each hierarchy, all arrays are in alphabetical sequence and there is no coding. By linking the second and third parts of the thesaurus, longer chains can be derived, for example: Chemistry—Physical and General chemistry—Chemical reactions—Decomposition reactions—Solvolysis—Hydrolysis—Saponification.

From the third part of TEST, we extracted fifty four hierarchies in science rather than technology, and coded them by four general classifications. A single example is presented in Table 1. It will be seen that (a) of the forty nine terms in the hierarchy, we located only nineteen in Dewey, eleven in Bliss, eight in Colon, and twenty nine in UDC; (b) some of the locations were not specific, *eg* more than the topic Thermal expansion is covered by Dewey 536.41 or Bliss BHQ, and is indicated by the $<$ signs preceding these codes in the table; (c) the topics in a hierarchy may be scattered in a general classification, *eg* Thermodynamic properties as listed by TEST occur in Dewey classes 536.7, 536.4, 541.3, and 537.65.

In Table 2 a summary of the comparison is presented showing the hierarchies examined, the number of terms in each, the numbers located in each general scheme, and comments on specificity and scattering. In some cases, the highest term in the hierarchy (recorded on the left) could not be found, and this is signalled by an asterisk: for example, it appears not to be possible to pull together a hierarchy 'body fluids' from any of the four classifications. The overall result of examining fifty four hierarchies containing 1,893 terms is:

	Dewey	Bliss	Colon	UDC
Terms found in	493	402	256	961
Highest term not found	21	20	26	6
Comment 'not specific'	24	30	6	1
Comment 'scattered'	20	20	13	17

As far as term content is concerned, even in the best performed, UDC, only 961 (51 percent) were located, with Dewey (26 percent), Bliss (21 percent) and particularly Colon (14 percent) being even more inadequate. Scattering was a common occurrence in all four classifications, but UDC was rarely 'not specific' and usually contained the highest term of the hierarchy. The sample suggests, nevertheless, that none of the four classifications contain as many detailed terms as TEST, and that the hierarchies established by TEST differ considerably from those in the classifications.

TABLE 1: Sample comparison with TEST

	Dewey	UDC	Bliss	Colon
Thermodynamic properties	<536.7	<536.7	<BHB	<C4:7
Dissociation energy		—		
Enthalpy	536.73	—	BHE	
Entropy		536.75		
Free energy		536.77		
Gibbs free energy		<536.775		
Helmholtz free energy		<536.775		
Solidification points	<536.42	536.421.4	<BGV	
Thermal expansion	<536.41	536.41	<BHQ	
Thermochemical	<541.362		CDP	
Heat of ablation		—		
absorption		—		
activation		—		
adsorption		536.658		
crystallization		—		
mixing		—		
Heat of reaction	<541.362	536.66		
Calorific value		—		
Combustion	<541.362	536.662		
Dissociation		536.657		
Formation	<541.362	—		
Hydration		536.664		

TABLE 1 continued
Thermodynamic properties
Thermochemical (continued)

	Dewey	UDC	Bliss	Colon
Heat of solution	<541.362	536.653		
transformation		536.656		
Latent heat		536.65		
of fusion	<536.42	536.652		C4:514
of sublimation	536.445	536.654		
of vaporization	<536.443	536.655		C4:554
Thermophysical				
Boiling point	<536.443	536.423.1	<BGV	C4:552
Critical point	<536.443	536.44	<BGV	C4:582
pressure		—	<BGJ	
temperature		—	<BGV	
volume		—		
Emissivity			<BHW	
Melting point	<536.42	536.421.1	<BGV	C4:512
Peltier effect		537.322	BKW	
Pyroelectricity	537.65	537.227		
Seebeck effect		—		
Sensible heat		—		
Softening points		536.421.2		
Specific heat	536.63	536.63	BHJ	C4283

TABLE 1 continued

	Dewey	UDC	Bliss	Colon
Thermodynamic properties				
Thermophysical (continued)				
Sublimation pressure		536.422.15		
Surface energy		–		
Thermal conductivity	536.2012	536.2.022	BHU	<C424
Thermal diffusivity	536.2014	–		
Thermal stability		536.423.15		
Vapour pressure		536.423.16		
Volatility				

TABLE 2: Summary of comparisons with TEST

Hierarchy	Terms	Dewey	Bliss	Colon	UDC	Comments
Acid halides	6	1	1	1	6	B and C not specific
Acyclic alcohols	9	1	6	6	9	B not specific
Aerodynamic characteristics	14	10	1	0	11	B not specific
Aldehydes	10	5	1	6	10	B and D not specific; D scattered
Algebra	54	15	19	18	23	B, D, C not specific & scattered, U scattered
Alkaloids	26	1	1	1	24	B not specific; C scattered
Alkene compounds	32	2	3	9	32	
Aluminium alloys	16	1	1	1	16	
Aluminium inorganic compounds	13	3	1	13	13	Some B not specific; C scattered
Amides	43	6	1	4	35	B, D, C not specific, D scattered
Analysis (maths)	90	19*	42	40	42	B often not specific; B, C, D scattered
Aquatic animals	49	45	45	7*	16	D and U often not specific, B sometimes; B, C, D, U scattered; U has few vernacular names in schedule.

*Highest term not in schedules.

TABLE 2 continued

Hierarchy	Terms	Dewey	Bliss	Colon	UDC	Comments
Bacteria	180	24	38	1	48	D often not specific. B scattered
Beams (radiation)	12	2*	1*	1*	6	D and B not specific, U scattered
Body fluids	13	8*	10*	4*	8*	B, G, U scattered, B and D not specific
Bosons	9	4*	2*	1*	3*	B not specific, U scattered
Capacitors	12	1	1	0*	11	B not specific
Carbides	18	18	0*	18	18	B scattered
Carbohydrates	33	6	20	13	30	
Cardiovascular system	13	10	8*	8	12	B and D not specific
Celestial bodies	32	25	25	20	24	B and D scattered
Cements	26	3*	2	1	7	
Chemical properties	27	9*	3*	2*	12*	D not specific and scattered, U scattered
Chemical reactions	92	27*	4*	4*	32	B, C, D scattered and not specific
Chemical tests	30	21*	14*	11*	25	B and D not specific, B, C, D, U scattered
Circuits	48	2	1	0*	8	B not specific, U scattered
Computer systems, hardware	37	2	0*	1	13	C not specific

*Highest term not in schedules.

TABLE 2 continued

Hierarchy	Terms	Dewey	Bliss	Colon	UDC	Comments
Congenital abnormalities	37	1	10	0*	30*	D not specific, B, U scattered
Crystal defects	10	0*	0*	0*	1	
Crystals	13	1	2	1	6	
Diodes	12	2	0*	0*	6	
Dispersions	16	7*	3*	3*	6	B scattered, D not specific
Drugs	89	22*	20*	1	54	B and D not specific
Earth atmosphere	36	12	6	1	5	D scattered, B not specific
Electrical properties	32	10*	11*	1*	15*	B and D scattered and not specific, U scattered
Electric current	18	4*	4	3	12	B, U scattered
Electromagnetic interference	23	0*	1	0*	17	B not specific
Electromagnetic properties	23	15*	11	11*	14	B, C, D scattered, some not specific, U scattered
Electromagnetic radiation	63	12*	12	14	26	B, C, D, U scattered
Electron tubes	46	14*	5	0*	27	B and D not specific; D scattered
Enzymes	76	12	5	3	27	D scattered
Magnetic properties	22	12	7*	5	12	
Mechanical properties	118	20*	6*	0*	53	B and D scattered and not specific
Mechanical tests	37	12	0*	0*	19	D not specific

*Highest term not in schedules.

TABLE 2 continued

Hierarchy	Terms	Dewey	Bliss	Colon	UDC	Comments
Mechanical waves	22	6*	4*	2*	11	B, D, U scattered
Number theory	23	8*	9	4	14	B and D not specific, B, C and D scattered
Numerical analysis	25	4	7	4*	8	B and D not specific; B, C, D, U scattered
Operations research	22	2	0*	0*	1	B and D not specific
Particle accelerators	17	8	3	0*	12	B and D not specific, B scattered
Spectra	29	8	8	4	23	B and D not specific, B scattered
Statistical analysis	38	1	1	0*	6	
Stochastic processes	5	0*	0*	0*	0*	
Thermodynamic properties	49	19	11	8	29	B and D not specific; B, C, D scattered
Welding	48	10	5	0*	33	D not specific
Totals	1,893	493	402	256	961	
Asterisks	—	21	20	26	6	
Not specific	—	24	30	6	1	
Scattered	—	20	20	13	17	
Hierarchies	54	—	—	—	—	

*Highest term not in schedules.

Prospects for classification suggested by evaluation tests

E M KEEN
College of Librarianship,
Wales

EDITOR'S INTRODUCTION: In this paper, the performance and potential merits or faults of classificatory index languages are assessed in the light of results from testing. The author has had extensive experience in the latter sphere in relation to ISILT and Cranfield. He is currently directing project EPSILON (Evaluation of Printed Subject Indexes by Laboratory InvestigatiON) at College of Librarianship, Wales.

A variety of different activities have been described as evaluating index languages. Firstly there is the time-honoured technique of examining the vocabulary of a particular classification or other index language, in isolation from any documents, users or search requests, to assess such things as properties of the notation, up-to-dateness, flexibility, and so on. Secondly, there is the process of examining and comparing one or more index languages by indexing or classifying particular documents, again quite divorced from an actual index or the operation of searching. Such observations as a lack of suitable locations for specific topics and an assumed unhelpful shelf order are frequently made. These two activities, particularly prevalent in library school education, represent an approach of very limited value because the whole process of information retrieval in practice involves steps missing from these evaluative speculations, and because the opinions and arguments advanced are in the main quite untested. It is not denied that the factors uncovered by such exercises do enter into real working situations, but there is no way of distinguishing the unimportant and trivial from the vital. A third approach to evaluation therefore takes the form of testing a complete information retrieval system, whether in the controlled environment of a laboratory experiment or the real-world situation of an operating system. The testing of classification that has been done in the last fifteen years or so has been entirely within the information retrieval field. Although restricted to

142

retrieval problems as exhibited in certain subject areas and not free from weaknesses or from some valid querying of the methods employed, it does represent an attempt to taste the pudding itself rather than to make comments about the colour and texture of the uncooked ingredients. The *desiderata* of an index language in practice go beyond such things as a short notation or an assumed helpful order to the end product, namely the ability of the total indexing system to recover items relevant to the user's needs while excluding items irrelevant to the user's requirements. There are also matters such as the time required in practice by system operators and users in the operations of index language construction and maintenance, indexing, physical index contruction, and searching. Economic factors are obviously of vital concern too.

Before considering the findings of some of the evaluation tests that have been made of index languages, it must be decided what kinds of index language fall within the scope of the expression 'classificatory'. Such a consideration will also prepare the way for a later discussion about what constitutes the basic properties and differences between index languages. Classification for information retrieval in a general sense implies two things. Firstly, the establishment of classes of terms which, when used in the indexing of documents, identify classes of documents to which the terms have been assigned. Such things as the kind and scope of these term classes will be of importance. Secondly, there is the establishment of relations between these term classes to permit class adjustment at the time of search, either broadening to find more documents or narrowing if too much has been retrieved. Again, such things as the kind and amount of such provision may be of importance. In a rather stricter definition of the word classification, traditional library usage has implied systematic arrangement, of books on shelves or cards in a catalogue, and also the formal recognition in classification schedules of the relations among terms displayed hierarchically. For the purposes of this paper any index language exhibiting hierarchical linkage will be considered to be classificatory, whether or not systematic arrangement is also provided and thus a thesaurus distinguishing Broader and Narrower from Related terms will be included. Many would regard a faceted classification as the zenith here, and mention of this raises a further matter sometimes labelled classification. That is the provision of syntactical devices in an index language, devices that establish in varying degrees of accuracy the relationships between the elemental topics in a compound subject. A faceted classification applied in a pre-coordinate index provides a fair degree of accuracy in specifying these relationships. Much less accuracy is inherent in the post-coordinate approach if the

143

syntactical devices of links and roles are not used. The peak of accuracy is claimed for schemes of relational operators, such as those devised by J Farradane and by D W Austin. Since any kind of index language, classificatory or not, can use any of these ways of specifying relationships, even the use of a faceted classification in a post-coordinate index is a quite feasible combination.

A selective progress review of evaluation tests covered more than twenty major projects. (1) Most of these have shed light on index language performance, and either explicit classificatory languages or languages employing some degree of hierarchical linkage have figured in many tests. (Reference will be made to the findings of some eleven tests in this paper, but for details of these projects the reader is directed to the references that are supplied.) What are the findings of these tests?

The first general finding is that different types of classificatory index language do not substantially differ in performance merit. The first Cranfield project, which was a laboratory comparison test, investigated both UDC and a faceted classification in the field of aeronautics. (2) The measurements made included that of recall—the ability of the index languages to retrieve, for this test, the single relevant document on which each request was based. The difference in performance between UDC and facet was very small indeed: in the main results UDC scored 76 per cent recall and facet 74 per cent. But in most of the different tests conducted facet results were lower than the other languages, and although the differences were not statistically significant the personal observations of the searchers, reinforced by an analysis of individual search failures, showed that there was a considerable weakness due to the use of a fixed citation order and chain index. In a supplementary test a sample of the index was reconstructed by providing multiple entry in the classified file supported by a simple alphabetical index, and this arrangement gave an 8 per cent improvement in recall. But neither this nor the main comparisons can be regarded as showing any real difference between UDC and facet.

Moving from one of the first laboratory tests to the latest one, another faceted classification has been compared with a thesaurus in the field of library and information science (3) in a project here abbreviated to ISILT. The faceted classification, described as the Hierarchically Structured language in the test, was based on the Classification Research Group's draft scheme of library science. For the tests of this scheme in a post-coordinate manner the facet isolates were used without synthesis at the indexing stage, and thus without a fixed citation order: the
144

notation and hierarchical linkage were retained, and the optical coincidence file was thus arranged in schedule order. The thesaurus was known as the Compressed Term language since the basis of this was a minimum vocabulary list compiled by Aslib's research department. A structure of related terms was incorporated, and included a small number of broader and narrower term references. This was naturally again a post-coordinate system using optical coincidence cards. Although a laboratory test, most of the sixty three requests used represented real information requirements which were posed directly at the time of the test or had previously been submitted to Aslib or the Library Association. The entire collection of 800 documents was examined in order to trace every document that could be regarded as relevant to every request, and this was done by independent judges who were neither the requesters nor connected with the test in any other way. This meant that search results could be measured in terms of both recall (expressed as a ratio, relevant retrieved as a proportion of total relevant), and the number of non-relevant documents retrieved (in some tests expressed as the Precision ratio, relevant retrieved as a proportion of total retrieved). The searching was designed to simulate real-world conditions as closely as possible, so the search of each request in each system was arranged to cover four variants of recall target. For example, a minimum recall target of only one highly relevant document per request represented the needs of one type of 'High Precision' user, whereas a maximum recall target of all the partially and highly relevant documents in the file represented the hypothesized needs of one kind of 'High Recall' user. A means was supplied to the searchers of knowing when the recall target had been reached to enable the termination of the search at that point, unless a time limit had previously expired.

In the results, both Hierarchically Structured and Compressed Term easily attained the two variants of recall target set for the high precision needs, but in terms of non-relevant documents retrieved, Hierarchically Structured was best having 1.1 non-relevant retrieved on average compared with 2.8 in Compressed Term, in one of the tests. This small difference was not statistically significant, but turning to the high recall needs slightly larger differences were seen. In one test Hierarchically Structured retrieved 6.4 non-relevant on average, and Compressed Term 13.1, but in achieving this result Compressed Term had the edge on recall: 87 per cent as against 81 per cent in Hierarchically Structured. The worse performance of Compressed Term as far as non-relevant go was not unexpected since the minimum vocabulary approach needs careful modification in the light of use to achieve specific retrieval. But one cannot escape

145

the general conclusion that the performance differences were not large.

Further results from this test illustrate a second general finding, namely that non-classificatory index languages do not have a substantially different performance from classificatory ones. The results just presented included a third index language known as Uncontrolled, which consisted of natural language single words derived from the documents by the indexers, with no synonym control or any kind of related word structure provided beyond an alphabetical list. For the high precision needs again no difficulty was experienced in reaching the desired low recall targets, and in terms of non-relevant retrieved, Uncontrolled performed almost identically with Hierarchically Structured. For high recall it achieved 84 per cent in the test already mentioned, at a cost of 8.9 non-relevant documents retrieved on average, slightly worse than Hierarchically Structured but better than Compressed Term. If this result comes as a surprise to some then it should not be so: this kind of result has the support of many previous tests. In the first Cranfield project, for example, a uniterm post-coordinate system was tested in which no more than synonym recognition was provided, but it still reached the same recall level as the others. The alphabetical subject headings also tested contained no 'see also' reference structure, but again proved just as good. In the second Cranfield project a series of twenty nine artificial index languages, each isolating just one of the many control devices that go to make up a complete language, showed the lack of need for classificatory languages. (4) The series of languages most similar to a faceted classification (known as the simple concept languages) performed as a group slightly worse than the thesaural languages, a series of controlled terms based on the Engineers Joint Council Thesaurus, and in turn these languages were eclipsed by the performance of the uncontrolled, single term languages. Among the latter group, the confounding of variant word forms gave the best results, whereas the inclusion of loosely related terms or even hierarchical groupings of terms worsened the result. It should be noted that these comparisons were all based on measurements of both recall and precision, also combined for convenience into a single number measure of merit known as normalized recall.

In another recent laboratory test designed to enable correct choice of index language for an envisaged operational system, there is an interesting correspondence between the classificatory thesaural language tested and the free language non-classificatory one. (5) The thesaurus had been

146

developed for a parallel investigation into SDI, and the free language terms were just the indexers' concept indexing record in uncontrolled language before being translated into the thesaural terms. The search results did show a small advantage in performance for the thesaurus, but the free language was chosen as the one recommended for use. What this project and the evaluators' recommendation suggest is that it may not be necessary to use a controlled classificatory language at the indexing stage because if some control is needed it can be supplied at the search stage in the form of a thesaurus or classification of natural language words to be used optionally by the searchers.

What is now needed to advance the understanding of index languages and how they perform is a means of identifying the really important properties or characteristics that determine performance. Both B C Vickery and C W Cleverdon have provided a most valuable analysis in terms of index language devices, and Vickery's set of fourteen questions (6) again supply a useful operational picture. But these methods are too detailed for the purpose in hand since there are too many factors and too many combinations. Grosser measures are needed, and in many ways the traditional ideas of class definition and relations between classes already mentioned provide the kind of characterization required. Class definition regulates the specificity, or hospitality for specificity, of an index language, the degree of specificity being definable as 'the preciseness of subject description allowed at the time of searching an index language'. It is, of course, the amalgam of index language devices in use that control this preciseness. As was suggested in the second Cranfield project there is an optimum level of specificity for a particular situation. If the language is under-specific the precision performance will suffer, and if over-specific there may be difficulty in attaining good recall which may in turn also lead to a poor precision. Specificity is in some circumstances directly related to vocabulary size, but with post-coordination the true specificity of the term combinations cannot be measured this way. So in the ISILT work the best measure of specificity was obtained by observing the number of documents retrieved in a series of specially regulated searches in which the search formulation for each request was kept quite identical in each language. In one of these results Uncontrolled retrieved 0.7 documents on average, Hierarchically Structured 2.8 and Compressed Term 20.5. Since a language of high specificity is defined to be one that will retrieve only a small number of documents until the search is broadened, Uncontrolled is seen to the the most specific, just a little more so than Hierarchically Structured, with the very much lower specificity of Compressed Term a clear explanation for its poorer performance in suppressing non-relevant documents. There is no evidence so far that the class definition that gives the best performance must be explicitly classificatory in origin: what matters is whether the optimum level for given circumstances is approached or not, by whatever means employed. In the second Cranfield project the Simple Concept language terms with their fairly high level of pre-coordination were over-specific and caused a broadening of the searches to obtain recall that, as a result, decreased precision seriously; the hierarchies that were then used improved the position because by lowering the specificity they moved towards the optimum. On the other hand the hierarchies used with the Single Term languages led to a worsened performance because they were lowering specificity beyond the optimum point.

The broadening of searches to improve recall raises a second characteristic of index languages, that of relationships among terms. Formal linkage may be defined as 'the provision of substitute index language terms (indicated by cross-references or hierarchies) for optional use in the broadening of searches to retrieve additional items'. Searchers will naturally utilize their knowledge in the form of informal linkage but formal provision has long been assumed to be a vital task of a controlled index language, and one particularly well performed by an hierarchically structured language of the faceted classificatory type. Measurement of formal linkage was attempted in ISILT by adapting a measure used for thesaural languages by M Kochen and R Tagliacozzo. (7) This enabled the amount of cross-reference structure or linkage formally provided in the schedules of each language to be compared. Both Compressed Term and Hierarchically Structured had around 4½ 'cross-references' per term, while Uncontrolled had less than one derived only from the accidentally helpful collocation of terms in the alphabetical list. If formal linkage were vital to the obtaining of high recall then a language like Uncontrolled in ISILT would be expected to fail: not only did it not do so, but the language with facet-based hierarchies did not perform as well. Assuming that the human variables, inescapable in search tests of this kind, were adequately controlled, which it is believed they were, this result points either to the use of adequate informal linkage by the searchers of Uncontrolled or to the fact that dropping terms off the search request is a perfectly good way of gaining recall.

All this leads to the third general finding, that formal hierarchical linkage has not been found to be essential to high recall. This can already be deduced from what has been described of the Cranfield-1 results. In Cranfield-2 it was most clearly observed on the recall versus precision

148

plots that to drop a term off the search combination was better than to keep all the terms and add substitutes from a thesaurus or hierarchy: for example, using an intelligent selection of three basic controlled terms in one test achieved on average 31 percent recall at 40 percent precision; dropping to combinations of two terms improved recall to 58 percent at 21 percent precision; and keeping the three terms but adding suitable related terms from the thesaurus gave 53 percent recall at 14 percent precision. In the ISILT result it seems that the complexity of the Hierarchically Structured language may have led either to the searchers failing to recognize potentially useful substitute terms or to termination of some of the searches due to the excessive time required to use a language of this kind. Further analysis of this matter is in progress.

It may be argued that hierarchical linkage is useful just to enable the indexer and searcher quickly to find the correct subject area particularly when the information need is not yet clear. The value of this use of linkage is not denied, but evaluation testing has rightly covered only the use of linkage once the search request has been finally formulated. It may also be pointed out that it is the finding of both experience and one test (8) that use of hierarchically specific terms is of considerable value: it seems that in a complex controlled vocabulary there is greater need for such linkage, but it does not gainsay the finding that an uncontrolled language with virtually no formal linkage performs just as well.

A fourth general finding is that syntactical devices as precision improvers have a small and a minority value. Apart from the normally provided precision device of coordination (the ability to search and match term combinations), a very frequently met extension is the use of pre-coordinate entries in which the index terms are combined in particular sets and particular orders. Just combining particular index terms without considering their order is the device of partitioning: it is probably an effective way of dealing with a multi-topic document so that incorrect combinations of terms are prevented at the search stage. Many post-coordinate systems do not even contain partitioning, so some tests have examined this device alone. The first result came in the Cranfield test of a special facet catalogue as part of the Western Reserve University experiment (2, 9), where post-coordination gave 76 percent recall at 30 percent precision, and the device of partitioning improved precision by 4 percent for a 6 percent loss in recall. A similar comparison from ISILT showed only a 1 percent drop in recall for partitioning, but the precision gain was small in that non-relevant retrieved dropped only from 4.0 to 3.9, and these differences averaged over sixty requests were confined to 10 percent of the requests. This particular device certainly has only a small and minority value.

More powerful precision devices are claimed to be schemes of role indicators and of relational operators. Tests of role indicators have been reviewed by F W Lancaster (10) and he explains why they have rarely proved to be worthwhile. The best known scheme of relations is that of J Farradane. In a laboratory test of the scheme, in the subject of sugar technology, in isolating the direct benefit of the operators themselves he found that they altered the performance of some 23 percent of the requests and resulted in an average gain of 6 percent in precision for a 10 percent loss in recall. (11) The ISILT work also conducted a similar but not identical experiment in which the operators provided an improvement to 10 percent of the requests, non-relevant retrieved dropping to 3.65 from 3.87 while worsening 3 percent of the requests in dropping 2 percent in average recall. Now it is not difficult to find individual cases where relational indexing is beneficial: for example, one particular document was indexed in ISILT as follows:
Information retrieval/; Systems/; Using/; Users/; Requirements/-Investigating
This makes it clear that the investigation is of the user requirements, not of the IR system, and the benefit from cases of logical structure like this was the suppression of several non-relevant documents. The distinction between past and present processes by the /; and /- operators, respectively, also had a beneficial effect. In another example, an apparently clear subject 'the use of UDC for retrieval of reports' when indexed by relational had to include parts of the subject not stated explicitly, in this case the fact that retrieval is not by UDC directly but by means of a catalogue constructed according to the rules of UDC, as follows:
UDC/=General Classification schemes
/;Classified catalogues
Reports/-Information retrieval
In this case, though, the result was the suppression of a relevant document, so the important questions about this language are: how often are these valid distinctions useful in retrieval performance? Do they in practice suppress many non-relevant documents? Do they lead to any unwanted suppression of relevant documents? Is their increase in cost, as seen in indexing time, file size and complexity, and search time, justified? Relational schemes have yet to be tested operationally, unlike role indicators, but both laboratory tests of the former and field tests of the latter
150

suggest that their use is only justified in rare circumstances, and only with difficulty in these cases.

The mention of syntactical devices in connection with pre-coordinate systems raises a problem of definition. What is the essential difference between a pre- and a post-coordinate system? After all, by means of partitioning and role indicators a post-coordinate system can be made to perform in a quite identical manner to a pre-coordinate one as far as the matching of the search terms against the index is concerned. The really essential point, which is rarely mentioned, was covered in a very early definition: 'pre-coordinate implies that the coordination of separate concepts is done at the time of indexing and the entries in the subject index will show this coordination'. (9) The latter clause is the vital part because the provision of the entries constitutes a 'preserved context', to borrow the very apt name for PRECIS.

It is this context, which is not always provided in full in every entry in some systems, that enables the searcher of a pre-coordinate file to select and reject entries on the basis of index terms provided in the entry that were not originally part of his search strategy. Of course this selection and rejection can go on in post-coordinate systems as well but not in the search file of an optical coincidence system: this would have to be carried out on the documents themselves, or using a file of document titles or abstracts. Again, avoiding testing the value of this purely to clarify ill-formed requests, one experiment in ISILT supplied to the searchers the equivalent of a rotated chain index so that the full context of the pre-coordinate entry (derived from the Hierarchically Structured language) could be used to select and reject entries. When compared against the obligatory selection of all the entries that contained the chosen search terms, this strategy gave a useful improvement in non-relevant retrieved, dropping from 5.3 to 2.9 on average, for a 14 per cent loss in recall. Some 63 percent of the requests were affected by this strategy, 56 percent improved on non-relevant and 33 percent worsened in recall. This result does not at the moment refute the fourth general finding since it is more the provision of context terms rather than that of syntax that is involved here. However, further tests are needed to see whether simple lists of terms with no syntax at all—as are sometimes provided in the accession ordered file of a post-coordinate system—provide as good a result.

A fifth and final general conclusion from evaluation tests is that the index language, as one of several sub-systems in a complete IR system,

151

is of minor importance. This can be seen from the various 'failure analyses' that have been conducted in which particular cases of retrieval failure are investigated to trace the cause, such as incorrect indexing, an error in searching, a weakness in the index language, misunderstanding with the user in question negotiation. or misjudged relevance of a document. In the cases of UDC and facet in Cranfield-1, for example, only 6 percent of the failures to retrieve relevant documents were due to the index languages, whereas 70 percent (UDC) and 54 percent (Facet) were due to indexing faults, 11 percent (UDC) and 24 percent (Facet) were due to search errors, and the remainders due to questions. In the test of the Western Reserve University index itself, which contained extensive classificatory devices and role indicators, 13 percent of the recall failures and 30 percent of the precision failures (that is, unwanted retrieval of non-relevant documents) were due to the index language. But among the chief causes of the fairly large numbers of precision failures there were problems with role indicators and interfixing, devices that would probably have led to recall failures if used, so corrections here would have led to other weaknesses. The most important and extensive test of an operating retrieval system so far supplies similar data. (12) This covered the retrospective demand search mode of the Medlars machine searched system The subject headings list, which is used in a post-coordinate manner, contained some explicit classification in the form of tree structure displays. The average performance of Medlars at this time was found to be 58 percent recall at 50 percent precision, and in the failure analysis exercise some 797 and 3,038 individual cases of recall and precision failure, respectively, were examined. The major causes of recall failure were again indexing and searching, 37 percent and 35 percent respectively. Another 25 percent of recall failures were due to request negotiation problems, and some 10 percent were attributed to lack of specific terms in the index language. However these latter cases were recall failures only because the appropriate 'see' references in the lead-in vocabulary had been omitted, surely a failure due to lack of index language maintenance rather than a weakness in the index language itself; provision of specific terms might not have been warranted. One point at which the linkage provided may not have been adequate was among the 21 percent of failures in which searchers did not cover all reasonable approaches to retrieval. But all supporting examples showed that appropriate linkage was available and the searchers just failed to make use of it. In the precision failure analysis the largest single cause was indeed the index language at 36 percent, with indexing 13 percent, searching 32 percent and request negotiation 17 percent. Of the index language failures half were caused by
152

lack of specific terms in the vocabulary, which again reflects on poor vocabulary maintenance rather than any deep seated fault in the language itself. The other half were false coordinations and incorrect term relationships, and although they are naturally unwelcome, some of these problems are inevitable with a role-free post-coordinate system, and they are probably best lived-with in return for an easier recall and reduced effort. So, in justifying the viewpoint that an index language is of minor import, it has been assumed that updating will be carried out in the form of adding new terms when clearly required, and providing an adequate lead-in vocabulary, essentially the task of the indexing subsystem since the need for these operational modifications cannot be foreseen at the index language construction stage. Such maintenance just reflects changes in subject matter over time, and if carried out strictly in accordance with rules of the original language it is merely an updating task: specificity and linkage are not radically altered, and the basic strengths and weaknesses of the language will remain. Another indication of the minor role of an index language is seen in the laboratory test results of the kind already mentioned, where languages have not been found to differ greatly from each other, and statistically significant differences are rare.

One reaction to these five suggested general findings may be that all the factors involved in the use of classification for information retrieval have not been covered. This is undoubtedly correct since it has been those situations requiring exhaustive indexing of journal and report literature in limited subject areas within the sciences that have figured in these tests. The systematic arrangement of compound and complex topics either in the form of a helpful sequence of documents on shelves, or cards in a catalogue has not been tested since its use is more rare for this kind of literature and information need. But the conclusions about the effectiveness of linkage, in say the Hierarchically Structured scheme in ISILT, are probably fairly indicative of the usefulness of systematic arrangement for specific searching (not browsing): systematic arrangement just cannot collocate all related material at the compound topic level, but even the vastly richer collocation provided by a post-coordinate use of the faceted classification schedules did not lead to as good recall as Uncontrolled terms. Book level summarization indexing has not really been tested, and some of the factors that are unique to the use of published printed subject indexes have not yet been evaluated. There are also some untouched matters concerning sheer user convenience, as well as factors affecting economics. For example, it is obvious that for manually indexed and searched systems a controlled vocabulary, even one with a limited number

153

of terms, is likely to be very convenient for indexing, searching and file size; whereas an entirely uncontrolled natural language system might pose impossible practical problems of implementation in such a manual environment.

Another reaction to test findings is to query the test techniques employed. Some of this caution is justified: for example, the small scale of some tests in terms of size of document collection and request set makes extrapolation to the larger sizes in operational use very difficult, although in one test of UDC the experiment simulated this by sampling from a collection of 196,000 (13) and of course the operational Medlars test was of the complete file of more than half a million documents and over 300 search requests. Comments are sometimes heard about the controversy over statistical interpretations of the actual test figures obtained. If by this is meant that the use of alternatives to recall and precision as performance measures is urged by some, then it should be realized that several tests have used different measures with near identical results. This was done in the case of Cranfield-2 with the normalized recall measure, although Vickery does correctly note two points of disagreement with the full recall versus precision plots. (6) Then in the INSPEC index languages investigation all the major results were calculated by five different methods, yet there was very strong agreement in the resulting comparisons. If attention is being drawn to the matter of statistical significance then one can only say that little work has yet been done in this area, and that in practice some fairly *ad hoc* decisions have to be taken about what constitutes a worthwhile difference.

Another quite different matter is the impact of mechanization on information retrieval systems. It may be asked if any tests have suggested whether it is likely that classificatory methods will have any part to play in the machine indexed and searched systems of the future. The very extensive test programme conducted on the SMART automatic system provides some answers to this question. (14) Based on unedited natural language input and using document abstracts for most of the present experiments, this computerized system has tested a wide range of manually and automatically constructed index languages in several subject fields. The manually constructed thesauri tested, when constructed according to certain rules such as allowing for the frequency of occurrence of terms in the document collection, does provide some increase in performance over the simplest machine-compiled word stem languages. One hierarchically arranged thesaurus was tried, but the standard thesaurus used alone was found to be superior. It should be realized

154

that any operational version of SMART would be unlikely to provide a wide variety of kinds of index language as options because it has not been possible so far to achieve useful performance improvements by mixing different languages in some way. Thus it seems unlikely that it will employ any manual classification techniques beyond that of a simple thesaural grouping of related terms.

Turning to the subject of machine generation of index languages, a quite large amount of work has been done, some of it described as automatic classification. Very few of the schemes tried have been tested, but three results can be mentioned. A series of automatically obtained keyword classifications have been tested using the documents and requests of the Cranfield-2 experiment. (15) By choosing just the right kind of classification clustering, based in the first stages on term co-occurrence characteristics that are computed on the particular indexed collection supplied, some improvement over the use of keywords alone can be achieved. Some queries remain about the individual nature of the parameters used, and the effects of changes in collection size and topic, but this result does suggest that automatically produced clusters of overlapping related terms may achieve something not possible with manual methods and with less effort. Another large-scale test using word associations and clusters found that although they produced useful results in that it was easier to adjust the searches to produce the required number of documents, the results of word stems without associative methods had virtually as good a performance. (16) In the SMART system also the associative retrieval procedures tested did not prove to be a reliable substitute for the manually constructed thesauri. (17) Also, work on automatic thesaurus construction has again not produced as good results as manual versions, but recent developments in automatic common word recognition and automatic refinement of the manually produced thesaurus classes are showing some promise. (18) So it may be concluded that no explicit classificatory methods are yet in sight in the mechanized field, though machine construction may have something to offer.

This paper has questioned the benefits of classificatory index languages, so it may be asked where the logical foundation usually advanced for such methods may be at fault? One answer may be that the theory is sound enough, but no way has yet been found to realize the benefits in practice because the gains are outweighed by losses. In providing controlled languages their artificiality and complexity introduce new opportunities for misunderstanding and error. But another answer may be that the logical foundation presupposes a false view of the objectives of document

155

retrieval systems. Users rarely require to see every single fully and marginally relevant document in a particular file, and they do not always expect that every non-relevant document in the file can be withheld. The varieties of user requirement facing a system mean that the objectives in terms of recall and precision will alter: for the user who needs only low recall, extensive linkage in an index language will rarely be required, for example. So, the logical basis for the use of index languages of particular kinds has yet to be clearly established.

The next decade will see the usual mixture of kinds of IR system, some manual, some mechanized, and some new ones approaching automation. It will also see the protagonists of particular kinds of index language sticking to their guns in spite of the evidence. This paper has suggested that on considerations of retrieval performance there is ample evidence that, in the kind of situations covered by tests so far, relatively uncontrolled languages used at the indexing stage cannot be improved on by controlled languages, and that in many cases even the use of controlled language aids at the search stage will not be necessary. Those who use classificatory languages for IR without first establishing by evaluation test methods whether such techniques are necessary, in the particular circumstances applicable, are in danger of wasting huge amounts of effort. A report of Ranganathan's group some years ago stated that their estimate of the time required to establish depth schedules for subjects in the applied sciences was 5,000 man-years. (19) How fortunate that such effort is unnecessary!

REFERENCES
1 Cleverdon, C W: 'Evaluation tests of information retrieval systems' (Progress in documentation series), *Journal of Documentation, 26,* 1970, p 55-67.
2 Lancaster, F W and Mills, J: 'Testing indexes and index language devices: the Aslib Cranfield Project'. *American Documentation, 15,* 1964, p 4-13.
3 Keen, E M and Digger, J A: *Report of an information science index languages test,* College of Librarianship, Wales. 2 vols, 1972.
4 Cleverdon, C W: 'The Cranfield tests on index language devices'. *Aslib proceedings, 19,* 1967, p 173-194.
5 Aitchison, T M and others: *Comparative evaluation of index languages.* INSPEC Reports R70/1, 2, The Institution of Electrical Engineers, 1969-1970.
6 Vickery, B C: *Techniques of information retrieval.* London, Butterworth; Hamden, Conn, Archon Books, 1970.
7 Kochen, M and Tagliacozzo, R: 'A study of cross-referencing'. *Journal of Documentation, 24,* 1968, p 173-191.
8 Freeman, R R: *Evaluation of the retrieval of metallurgical document references using the Universal Decimal Classification in a computer-based system.* Report AIP/UDC-6, American Institute of Physics, 1968.
9 Aitchison, J and Cleverdon, C W: *A report on a test of the index of metallurgical literature of the Western Reserve University.* Cranfield College of Aeronautics, 1963.

10 Lancaster, F W: 'On the need for role indicators in postcoordinate retrieval systems'. *American Documentation, 19,* 1968, p 42-46.

11 Farradane, J: *Report on research on information retrieval by relational indexing.* The City University, part 1 1968.

12 Lancaster, F W: 'MEDLARS: report on the evaluation of its operating efficiency'. *American Documentation, 20,* 1969, p 119-142.

13 Atherton, P, King, D W and Freeman, R R: *Evaluation of the retrieval of nuclear science document references using the Universal Decimal Classification in a computer-based system.* Report AIP/UDC-8, American Institute of Physics, 1968.

14 Salton, G and Lesk, M E: 'Computer evaluation of indexing and text processing'. *Journal of the Association for Computing Machinery, 15,* 1968, p 8-36.

15 Sparck-Jones, K and Jackson, D M: 'The use of automatically-obtained keyword classifications for information retrieval'. *Information storage and retrieval, 5,* 1970, p 175-201.

16 Vaswani, P K T, and Cameron, J B: *The National Physical Laboratory experiments in statistical word associations and their use in document indexing and retrieval.* Computer Science Report 42, National Physical Laboratory, 1970.

17 Lesk, M E: 'Word-word associations in document retrieval systems'. *American Documentation, 20,* 1969, p 27-38.

18 Salton, G: *Experiments in automatic thesaurus construction for information retrieval.* Section VII of Report ISR-18, Department of Computer Science, Cornell University, USA, 1970.

19 Current Research and Development in Scientific Documentation, Number 24. National Science Foundation, 1966. (See section 5.52)

The CRG research
into a freely faceted scheme

DEREK AUSTIN
Head, Subject Systems Office,
The British Library, London

EDITOR'S INTRODUCTION: In this far-ranging and now updated paper on the CRG/BNB research programme, it is stressed that a preferred citation order is needed for concept linkage within computer systems, but that it should be based on linguistic analysis rather than on an attempted order of 'decreasing concreteness' or diminishing significance. PRECIS and its history are described. It will be seen that the author has expressed the view that he now holds, namely that 'a highly articulated, language-independent coding system' eliminates the need for a sophisticated general classification on faceted lines both for shelf arrangement and within the context of machine searching.

Introduction
In classification and indexing, as in other fields, advances often begin as changes made on the bench to an existing system. In these cases the immediate intention is not to produce a new kind of system, but to improve the performance or usability of a particular scheme, and the scheme itself is expected to survive the modification. Changes of this kind, especially any which are adopted later outside the system for which they were intended, are sometimes seen in retrospect to demonstrate the emergence of a new principle, even though it might have been difficult at the time to set down the reasoning which prompted a change made simply on grounds of expediency.

The first task of basic classification research, on the other hand, is to seek for the general principle outside the context of any individual scheme. The research may be goal-oriented, in that broad objectives may have been laid down as guidelines at the start of the work, but until basic principles have been established no attempt should be made to devise procedures or mechanisms which will transform these principles into a working system. For example, no attempt was made to devise notation during the early stages of the classification described in this paper; this

158

should be seen in contrast to the development of the Decimal Classification, which started with a scheme of notation, then tailored its principles to fit the rule of ten. Ideally, the researcher should be free to relate means to ends, structure to function, in whichever ways seem appropriate for the purpose in view, and he should further be able to modify any of these factors as necessary during the course of the research.

Work of this kind is demanding in terms of both time and effort, and depends upon the creation of special opportunities and a favourable environment. Despite the obvious needs for controlled access to the sense content of increasing amounts of literature, and the role which classification can play in this, very few centres in the world which could have provided the right conditions have seen fit to channel their resources into fundamental classification research. Apart from the work described in this paper, the only other projects which come readily to mind are, first, the development of the Broad System of Ordering (BSO), and secondly the research being conducted at the Documentation Research and Training Centre (DRTC) in Bangalore, though in the latter case the emphasis appears to be more on developing the Colon Classification than on fundamental research as defined above.

In this paper I shall try to set down the postulates and findings of a particular research project: that which was initiated by the Classification Research Group in London (CRG), was sponsored by the NATO Science Foundation, and was accommodated by the British National Bibliography (at that time an independent entity, but now absorbed into the British Library). Such a host organisation possesses one special characteristic essential to work of this kind, in that any hypothesis which appears to be feasible on purely theoretical grounds can be tested immediately against the stream of documents on all subjects which continually passes through the organisation.

In a paper on innovation in information science, Fairthorne (1) said that: "Given genuine privacy, possessing some particular skill, and taking the opportunity to extend and alter one's viewpoint, anyone can do research about anything. Judgements on the research must be based on the results, not on the topic". On the grounds that no tangible results (such as printed schedules or a manual of instruction) arose from the work described here, it might be hard to justify a place for this account in a collection of essays on the well-established classification schemes. It is true that the verbal index system, PRECIS, did evolve directly out of this research (and in the account which follows a close relationship between classification and subject indexing is taken for granted), but this

159

index system should perhaps be seen as an interesting by-product of a search for a general classification scheme which did not achieve its intended goal, and is also, I believe, unlikely to do so, for reasons considered later.

The project described here is sometimes referred to as the CRG approach to classification. I should add, however, that not all the members of this heterogeneous collection of individualists would accept as their own the aims and viewpoints presented here, many of which have evolved, and are still evolving, out of research into the uses of PRECIS now being conducted within the British Library and elsewhere.

Aims of the classification research
The CRG's plan for research into a new general classification was formally launched at a Conference held in London in 1963. (2) At the end of this conference certain guidelines for the project were laid down, and these can be summarised under four main heads:

(a) The new classification should be for manual retrieval of books on shelves and entries in indexes, but it should aim to reach the maximum possible compatibility with machine retrieval systems.

(b) The first task to be undertaken should be a systematic arrangement of "organised fields of knowledge". These were described as subject areas having professional societies, schools of studies, journals etc.

(c) It was recognised that it would be necessary to work out a system of categorisation of terms, and in addition at least a minimum set of relations.

(d) It was recognised that complex terms need analysis or dissection up to a certain point, but this point has to be determined.

On the face of it, the approach indicated by these points would have led to the construction of a fairly conventional faceted scheme, with the Colon Classification serving as the obvious model. Like CC, the scheme was seen primarily as a means for the physical ordering of documents and the arrangement of index entries, while the organisation of machine-held files of subject data was regarded as a desirable but secondary target. It was also intended that the scheme should be founded, again like the Colon Classification, upon a system of main classes or disciplines; how else should we interpret "systematic arrangement of organised fields of knowledge"? Within these basic classes, concepts would have been organised into facets or categories, but the idea of developing completely general categories of concepts was not then seriously considered.

160

It is doubtful whether many members of CRG would now subscribe to these aims as they stand, and the priorities which are implicit in the first three of these points had generally been reversed by the end of the project. The intention was then no longer to establish mutually-exclusive classes of the universe of knowledge, each divided into facets, but instead to assign concepts on a once-and-for-all basis to general categories from which they could be selected as needed in the building of any compound subject. The aim of producing a new faceted scheme for the ordering of documents as physical objects had therefore been abandoned in favour of a system intended specifically for machine storage and retrieval. Consequently, although the proposed scheme would still make use of analytico-synthetic techniques, the Colon Classification could no longer be regarded as its prototype. This change of direction had been noticed by A C Foskett (3), who pointed out that: "Starting with the theories of analytico-synthetic classification developed by Ranganathan, the Group has moved forward in a rather different direction from Ranganathan himself; for a variety of reasons, it seems probable that future developments are likely to be along the lines indicated by the CRG rather than those used in CC".

No deliberate decision to alter the course of the research was ever taken, but hindsight suggests that a steady modification of views occurred within the Group, and that this should be related to a general change in the climate of information work throughout the 1960s.

Without doubt the introduction of the third generation of digital computers must count as one of the major factors in this shift of attitude. Not only did these machines offer much faster processing than was possible with any of their predecessors, but their increased storage capacity meant that the rapid handling of large volumes of subject data became feasible for the first time. Ways of organising files of concepts which, however desirable, had previously seemed impracticable, were no longer shrugged off by data processing personnel as impossibly difficult or expensive.

Coupled with these developments, BNB's involvement in the MARC Project had shown not only that bibliographical information could be transmitted successfully between national centres through the medium of magnetic tapes, but that cataloguing data could be tagged or coded in such a way that any specific datum could be identified in a machine-readable file and individually retrieved. Nothing approaching this facility existed at that time for subject data in the form of class numbers. The MARC format does make provision for certain class marks, such as DC and LC

161

to appear on every record, and it is unlikely that these schemes will be superseded by any machine-oriented system for the purpose of organising libraries as collections of physical objects. But no one could seriously claim that these shelf order schemes also represent the last word in retrieving subject data by computer. R E Coward (4), then Head of the UK MARC Project, emphatically made the point that: " . . . there is one thing that can be said with certainty about Dewey and the Library of Congress classifications. They are totally unsuitable for machine systems. This might turn out to be a good thing. The field is open for a general classification designed for use in computer systems. If one were developed now there is a good chance that it could become established".

It seemed, therefore, that there was an urgent need at that time for a classification system designed specifically for the creation and exploitation of machine-held files, and designed from the outset to perform a variety of tasks which lay beyond the capabilities of existing shelf order schemes. The main function of such a system would be the rapid identification of document citations in response to enquiries made through subscribers' terminals, which might be located at a distant agency. In addition, such a system should be capable of providing a general format for the exchange of subject data between different information centres. Over and above these documentation functions, the system might further serve as a research tool in its own right. The potential functions of such a system could be summarised in the following six points:

1 It should be capable of direct interrogation by the user under any term, and should permit the rapid identification of all documents in which a particular *concept* has occurred.

2 The user should be able to discover, under any entry term, a full account of all the *combinations of concepts* in which a particular term has appeared.

3 It should allow the user to establish which of these combinations is relevant to his enquiry by distinguishing between the different subjects which can be constructed out of the same elements, indicating how one concept is related to others.

4 It should permit the user to broaden or narrow his search at the individual concept level by offering on demand any collateral or higher or narrower terms appropriate to the subject of his enquiry.

5 It should also permit a search to be varied at the whole subject level, the system being capable of indicating subjects in which the same concepts have occurred in different kinds of relationship, or between subjects which are structurally similar, but which contain a greater or lesser number of concepts.

162

6 Finally, since both storage and retrieval, at least within the system, would be conducted in the medium of codes or notation, the system should be neutral with respect to any one natural language, and should be capable of interrogation regardless of the language of the questioner.

The creation of a single system capable of meeting these requirements has to be reckoned a considerable undertaking by any standards; one which would go beyond all reasonable ambitions if it meant designing the system from scratch. The point is, of course, that the CRG were not starting from scratch. If these points are considered one at a time, it will be found that each had independently been the subject of enquiry by information workers concerned with the computerisation of various different kinds of local system. It was therefore felt that the major task would consist more in examining these separate lines of enquiry from the viewpoint of a general unifying theory, rather than in initiating a major original project.

In the search for these unifying principles various fields of work which were then regarded as outside the scope of library science were considered from the special viewpoint of documentary classification. It was found, for example, that the approach of the general systems theorist could contribute to a better understanding of a compound subject as a set of discrete but identifiable elements linked by their interrelationships. The connection between citation order and grammatical structure was also carefully considered, and it seems possible, in indexing research, that developments in the field of modern linguistics may have a bearing on the concept of a general model for determining the order in which the parts of a compound subject should be set down. These and other studies have undoubtedly thrown new light on some of the basic problems of a general system for concept organisation, machine-oriented or otherwise, and in some respects they caused the CRG to modify its approach to the representation of compound subjects. But it was felt that they also tended to confirm, rather than undermine, the soundness of those general principles of subject analysis and synthesis which are already the foundations of modern faceted classification.

Structure related to function in a general classification
Put in its simplest terms, the basic teaching of analytico-synthetic classification is that any compound subject, however complex, can be broken down into its separate components, or facets, and that these can be re-organised consistently into a standard pattern by reference to a general decision-making model. This approach to concept organization rests on two assumptions which appear to be reasonable at the theoretical

level, though they have not so far been adopted as working principles in the construction of any faceted general classification. These are:

(a) that any compound subject is made up of separate elements which exist as entities in their own right, so that, for example, the meaning of a basic concept such as 'Iron' is not considered to change in any fundamental way when it appears in different contexts such as geology, metallurgy and plumbing. Consequently, it should be possible to represent this concept by a single symbol which would identify it once-and-for-all for retrieval purposes regardless of the various subjects in which it has appeared.

(b) that a general citation order can be established which holds good across the entire spectrum of knowledge, so that, for example, a formula which controls the order of terms in physics applies equally well in music and politics.

Although analytico-synthetic techniques are employed in faceted schemes such as UDC and CC, their approach to the organisation of knowledge has not been generalised to anything like this extent. The notation which represents a particular concept can vary greatly from one main class to another, and the order in which facets are cited also tends to be regulated by their main classes, a feature which these schemes share with enumerative classifications. In fact, no attempt has been made in these schemes to establish completely general categories of concepts and a universal citation order, nor is it possible to see how such general principles could be imposed upon them without introducing such radical changes in their structures that they would cease to be fully effective for the purpose for which they are principally intended, which is the organisation of libraries as collections of physical objects.

While it may be easy to question on theoretical grounds the extent to which knowledge can be broken down into watertight compartments, from the practical viewpoint of library organisation main classes confer such obvious advantages that if they had not evolved already we should have to invent them. Classification by fields of common interest does more than bring documents on a given theme together at some reasonably obvious place on the shelves. It also, and more importantly, allows complex subjects to be represented by the relatively short and uncomplicated symbols which are necessary for shelf organisation, and which clearly show how one subject should be filed with respect to another. It further ensures that citation order can, in faceted classifications, be varied according to the different needs of each subject field.

The achievement of a brief notation for library organisation purposes can be traced back to the ways in which classes are formed during the

164

first stage in the design of these schemes. This can be visualised as a direct approach to the universe of knowledge, which is broken down in successive steps by the application of various principles of division, first into those 'organised fields of knowledge' which figured in the original CRG proposals, then into subclasses, and so on down to the point at which the individual concept is identified and notated within the context of a particular class. Although faceted classifications incorporate a measure of categorisation within classes, it is rare for a concept to be represented by the same notation when it belongs with equal right in more than one major division of knowledge, except in the usual cases of form, place and time concepts. For example, the notation which represents the concept 'Iron' is represented by at least the following different symbols in UDC:

546.72	iron as a chemical element
553.3	iron ores
622.341	mining of iron
661.872	iron as an industrial material
669.1	production of iron
672	iron wares

But although the division of knowledge into classes leads to an obvious order on the shelves and a definite gain in notational brevity, it also gives rise to a certain rigidity of structure which makes these schemes unwieldy for the purpose of citation retrieval, and we have to accept, as part of the price of economy in notation, a concomitant loss of expressiveness. It must count as a considerable achievement that an entire 'packet' of subject information, such as 'Iron ores considered as geological species of economic importance', can be represented by a code of only five characters including the decimal point. But we can hardly then expect this code to identify separately the different parts of this complex subject in such a way that each can be used as a retrieval label anywhere in an information store, while from the viewpoint of machine retrieval it would clearly be cheaper and more efficient if the concept 'Iron' could be represented throughout the store by a single code.

A main class structure and its parallel system of hierarchical notation also have to be considered as contributory factors in the familiar problems of currency and hospitality. When designing a classification based on main classes it must be difficult, to say the least, to make sufficient and accurate allowance for the insertion of new and unforeseen topics into an existing hierarchy, nor can users of the scheme anticipate exactly how its editors are going to notate these advances in knowledge when they do occur. A lack of currency and hospitality are often regarded as failings in schemes which are used for library organisation, but they are far more serious

165

from the viewpoint of a machine-based citation retrieval system, since they directly affect its performance at the very point where it should be especially sensitive; that is, in the identification of recent material. It was felt, however, that both of these problems could be overcome at one and the same time if subjects were to be constructed freely out of their separate elements as and when they were encountered. Given access to a sufficiently comprehensive source of concepts, it seemed reasonable to assume that most new subjects could be accommodated as they arose. It is generally recognised that knowledge advances more through the juxta-posing of already familiar concepts, perhaps in unexpected ways, rather than in the evolution of entirely original ideas.

The main classes which are a feature of existing schemes also regulate citation order to a considerable extent, even in classifications which claim to be freely faceted. Although Ranganathan's PMEST formula is often regarded as a general decision-making model, the classifier cannot in practice decide which concept should be assigned to the fundamental category Personality, and therefore cited as the first element in a subject statement, until the subject as a whole has already been assigned in his mind to some appropriate class. This means that an element of intuitive perception has been left in the system which makes it difficult to lay down hard and fast rules for recognising Personality. (5) But it also ensures that the citation order which is most appropriate for, say, chemistry, is not imposed arbitrarily upon completely different fields such as music and criminology. It is doubtful whether a completely general order can be established which will prove equally satisfactory in each of the various classes into which libraries are organised.

But though the use of a class-sensitive citation order model ensures that at least a proportion of the documents on a given topic are brought together on the shelves, it leads at the same time to an inevitable scatter of concepts which are regarded, for shelving purposes, as subordinate to the primary facet or shelving factor. This scatter is dealt with to a certain extent in the subject index, which is organised on an alphabetic as opposed to a classificatory basis, and so acts as a supplementary route to subject information. However, even this alternative can incur some kind of loss; most methods of subject indexing in use at the time of the CRG enquiries, such as keywords, subject headings and chain procedure, made little if any attempt at expressing the *whole* of a compound subject under *each* of its separate elements. Even in the chain index, which is often regarded as fully pre-coordinated, a subject is not expressed in its entirety until the final element has been added to the chain.

166

This situation, however, need not exist in machine-held files, since a computer can be programmed to restructure a string of subject components to form an inverted file which brings each element in turn to the lead position. We should still need to establish some preferred order for building concepts into strings in order to ensure: (a) that the contents of the file are organised consistently to the same pattern for collocation purposes; (b) that we can distinguish between the different subjects which can be made out of the same ideas. However, the need to identify some single 'most significant' concept on a basis which varies from one discipline to another no longer then applies.

It follows that a scheme which is intended for library organisation has to concern itself principally with subjects as entities in their own right, and can identify separate concepts only secondarily and with difficulty. A citation retrieval system, on the other hand, which sets out to identify documents by matching enquiries term by term against a machine-held file, also has to operate at the level of individual terms or concepts.

A system of main classes which suits the purposes of library organisation should not therefore be expected to serve as a starting point in the design of a mechanised citation retrieval system. Insofar as machine-retrieval systems operate at the level of the individual concept, their approach to the organisation of knowledge is bound to be entirely different. Their first requirement can be seen as a thesaurus organised in such a way that specific concepts can be located readily for use in the building of any subject as and when it is encountered. As noted above, it is desirable that some preferred order for subject building should be established, and since concepts can be related together in different ways to convey different subjects, this order should also take account of the relationship which exists between citation order and meaning. But the need to identify one of the elements in a compound subject as 'most significant' from a shelving point of view does not apply when we are dealing with machine-held files. The goal of a general subject building formula which, because it is related to linguistic structure, can be applied across the entire subject spectrum, then becomes feasible.

The role of relationships in concept organisation
Two kinds of control can be introduced to improve the chances of a match between the terms of an enquiry and the subject file. In the first place vocabulary can be controlled to ensure that the same idea is represented as consistently as possible by the same term or terms. Secondly, the order of terms in a subject statement can be regulated to convey some

particular meaning. The use of codes or notation rather than words to represent specific concepts introduces a third kind of control with special functions which will be considered later.

The need for two different kinds of control, one operating at the level of the concept, and the other concerned with the combination of concept can be explained in terms of two fundamentally different kinds of relationship. The first concerns those familial and other categorial relationships which link a particular concept to the class or classes of ideas of which it is a member, in the way, for example, that the entity 'Dog' is a member of such categories as 'Canines', 'Carnivores' and 'Mammals'. The second concerns those syntactic links between the separate elements of a compound subject which endow a subject statement with meaning, in the way, for example, that the terms 'Dogs', 'Sheep' and 'Herding' can be linked together in a particular way to express the subject 'Herding of sheep by dogs'. As A C Foskett (3) has pointed out, the first of these are present by implication and can be distinguished as *a priori* relationships, while the second cannot be known until after they have been made explicit, and so are *a posteriori* relationships. They can be recognised respectively as Gardin's paradigmatic and syntagmatic relationships, and will be distinguished here as: (a) semantic or categorial relationships; (b) syntactic relationships.

These distinctions are of little account in a classification which is based upon main classes, and schedules frequently display both semantic relationships (e.g. genus-species) and syntactic relationships (e.g. an action and its agent) in the same hierarchy. For example, a schedule such as:

```
621.3      Electrical engineering
621.31     Generation
621.312    Generating plant
621.31213  Central stations
```

displays in a single sequence both (a) a class of actions and a specific action, and (b) a class and a subclass of agents.

During the CRG research it was considered that these differences would be of fundamental importance in the design of a totally synthetic classification, and that each of them would need to be handled by an entirely different mechanism. Semantic relationships offer a ready-made basis for constructing a general thesaurus, each concept being assigned to its appropriate category on a once-and-for-all basis ready for use in building any subject. Syntactic relationships, on the other hand, would be indicated by a separate system of coded relators or operators expressing
168

those inter-concept roles which are common and basic to all subjects. These operators, when built into the subject string, would not only serve to indicate the role played in the subject by the concept which follows the operator; they could also determine, through their relative filing values, the order in which the concepts should be cited in the act of subject building.

With certain exceptions which will be considered later, this means that the higher of two adjacent terms which are semantically related should normally be excluded from a subject string. Higher generic terms are, of course, already excluded as a general rule from pre-coordinated index statements; indeed, it is hard to see how these terms could be incorporated into a subject statement without allowing the phrase to sink under its own weight. This is a characteristic which indexing shares with natural language; we would not, for example, include terms such as 'Canine' and 'Mammal' whenever we write or speak of 'Dogs'. It was felt that we could, however, overcome this loss of semantically related ideas from a concept string by devising a system of machine-readable codes or notation which would not only identify each concept individually, but also specify the category of which the concept is a member, so that both factors could be 'read' from the notation itself. It was felt that this would effectively add a second dimension to any subject statement, permitting a machine display of the higher, lower and coordinate terms which relate to any one concept.

Assuming that a suitable thesaurus and a system of codes or operators to indicate syntactic relationships could be created, input to the information file would then have consisted in a four stage process:
(a) a document would be analysed, and the classifier would establish those terms which he considers are essential to a summary statement of its subject content.
(b) terms would be located in the thesaurus, and translated into notation.
(c) the role of each term in the subject would then be determined and indicated by the choice of an appropriate code or operator.
(d) these notated elements, plus the relational codes, would finally be organised into a string ready for keyboarding and input to the computer. With the exception of the two points in this sequence at which notation is applied (first to concepts, and then to the coding of syntactic relationships) these stages are already common practice in many human-based indexing systems.

During the course of research various relational systems, such as citation order formulae and schemes of relational operators, were examined with a view to identifying which particular relationships should be regarded as essential for the special purposes of a completely synthetic general classification. A number of these were established, the most important being the genus-species relationship which links a concept to its taxonomic type or group, the possessive relationship which links a specific concept to its properties or attributes, and the interactive or patient-action-agent relationship. These were then considered further from the special viewpoints of both thesaurus construction and subject building.

Thesaurus construction: the deductive approach
The word 'thesaurus' is used here in its original (or Roget) sense to indicate terms which have been organised systematically into categories according to their basic meanings, the systematic section being supplemented by an alphabetical index. It does *not* refer to a simple alphabetical list of words, with a few inter-term relationships possibly indicated by supplementary devices. It is recognised that different terms may belong to the same category when they share a common meaning; at the same time, a given term may also and logically belong to more than one category.

The point was made earlier that the first stage in constructing a traditional classification can be visualised as a direct approach to the universe of knowledge, which is broken down by the successive application of various principles of division to the point at which a specific concept is identified and notated within the context of its class. This procedure is entirely analytical, and by its very nature cannot lead to the creation of general categories of concepts. In contrast, the making of a general thesaurus must involve a direct approach to the universe of concepts, the intention being to organise the basic ideas out of which all subjects are constructed.

Two approaches can be adopted in the construction of a general thesaurus, one analytical and deductive, the other synthetic and inductive. Using the list approach, we might confront the universe of concepts directly, breaking this down on an *ad hoc* basis into more manageable proportions by applying various kinds of difference. It could, for example, be postulated that 'action' concepts differ in some fundamental way from 'thing' concepts, and should therefore be assigned to a different part of the thesaurus. This analytical procedure is clearly similar to the way in which the universe of knowledge is fragmented into classes in the making of a traditional classification, and would lead to the establishment
170

of fairly broad categories which could later serve as a basis for organising concepts when these are considered individually, a particular term being assigned to this or that part of the thesaurus according to the basic kind of idea which it represents. Ultimately, however, concepts have to be considered one at a time as they are encountered during indexing or in the examination of existing classifications, categories being created synthetically as homologous or near-homologous meanings are recognised.

The first of these techniques had already been expounded to the CRG by Farradane (6) when describing his research into relational indexing. He had established four broad groupings of concepts which he had labelled 'Entities', 'Abstracts', 'Activities' and 'Properties'. These had then been divided further into various sub-groups, such as 'Pre-concept properties' and 'Physical abstract activities', which Farradane considered should be capable of accommodating concepts of every kind. He was, however, concerned with developing a non-printed verbal index system rather than a classification, and was working more at the level of the word than the idea. For example, he assigned terms such as 'Circular' and 'Beautiful' to the category 'Abstract pre-concept properties', but treated 'Circularity' and 'Beauty' as quite different notions which he labelled as 'Abstract measurable properties', despite the obvious paradigmatic links which exist between 'Beautiful' and 'Beauty', 'Circular' and 'Circularity'.

A different principle was adopted during the research carried out under the NATO Grant, and attention was paid particularly to the basic meanings of terms, leading to what was called the 'root concept' principle. According to this principle, the term 'Beautiful', despite the fact that it consists of a single word, would be recognised as a compound conception; that is, the substantive element 'Beauty' plus a grammatical qualification meaning 'Used in its adjectival sense'. The terms 'Circularity' and 'Circular' would be differentiated on grammatical grounds in the same way. Since a relational code had been devised which indicated that 'The concept following this code has been used in its adjectival sense', there could then be no point in creating special categories for adjectival terms such as 'Beautiful' and 'Circular'. This left the designer free to concentrate on substantives in category building, while ensuring at the same time that paradigms would share a common notational base for retrieval purposes.

Just as the main classes found in one discipline-oriented scheme are seen to recur in another, even though the schemes themselves may differ radically in their inner structures, so the main divisions of the universe of concepts which were established during the NATO Research bore an obvious resemblence to those established by Farradane, even though the

171

inner structure of each of these categorial systems was also entirely different. This would suggest that there are certain basic kinds of idea, such as 'Things', 'Properties' and 'Actions' which are so fundamental to a subject-building system that they cannot be overlooked, just as there are certain divisions of the universe of knowledge—for example, 'Physics' and 'Languages'—which have to be recognised in all discipline-based classifications.

The evolution of these main groupings of concepts, and the similarity between this analytical approach and the creation of main classes, can be demonstrated by considering briefly the ways in which categories were established during the CRG research, various differences being applied to the universe of concepts to break it down into smaller and more manageable proportions.

To begin with, concepts were divided into two basic kinds, 'Things' being distinguished from all other types of concept. This apparently fundamental division has, as A C Foskett (3) points out, a respectable ancestry going back at least to Aristotle. Besides featuring in earlier classifications, such as those of Kaiser and Brown, it had also been observed by members of CRG as an appropriate starting point in the construction of various specialist schemes.

Things were themselves divided into two basic kinds, 'Naturally occurring entities' being distinguished from 'Artificial entities', and the latter were then divided into two further groupings, 'Concrete objects' or artefacts (such as chairs and aircraft) being distinguished from 'Abstract constructs' or mentefacts, a category which had been postulated by Kyle to accommodate concepts such as systems of belief and products of the imagination.

'Non-thing' concepts were also seen to fall into two main kinds, roughly distinguishable as the 'Attributes of things' and 'Activities of things'. Two subdivisions of Attributes were then established:
(a) Properties, such as weight, colour and size, which are perceived through our senses, or are amenable to measurement, so that we can reasonably assert that they belong intrinsically to an object; (b) those characteristics which, though generally attributed to entities, tend in fact to reveal some kind of subjective reaction on the part of the observer rather than an intrinsic characteristic of the thing observed. In contrast to Farradane, it was not considered that 'Beauty' could be categorised as an intrinsic or *measurable* property of any object, and conceptions of this kind were assigned to a special category of 'Evaluative' concepts. A property such as 'Colour', on the other hand,

172

was considered to be a perceived and intrinsic characteristic, on the grounds that it can be related directly to a precisely measurable factor, the frequency of light. This still acknowledges the validity of the argument set out in Newton's 'Opticks': "If at any time I speak of Light and Rays as coloured, I would be understood to speak not philosophically and properly, but grossly and according to such conceptions as vulgar People in seeing all the experiments would be apt to frame. For the Rays to speak properly are not coloured. In them there is nothing else than a certain Power and Disposition to stir up a sensation of this or that Colour".

Conceptions of action turned out to be especially difficult to categorise, mainly because they are frequently amenable to division by more than one principle at a time. We should need, for example, to distinguish between purposive and non-purposive activities, and also between transitive and intransitive actions. During the research period there was time to establish only an outline sequence of categories for these ideas, attention being paid mostly to non-purposive physical actions on the grounds that these are the easiest to define and organise. This still left a great deal undone at the end of the project, mostly related to the organisation of human purposive activities, including informational concepts such as 'Measuring', 'Analysing' and even 'Categorising'.

It is hardly possible to embark upon the systematic establishment of categories in this way without also giving some thought to the ways in which the categories should be related one to another within the thesaurus. Should we, for example, have tried to set down activity concepts earlier or later than thing concepts, and should artificial entities follow or precede naturally-occurring entities? These are the kinds of matter which were discussed at some length during meetings of the Classification Research Group, mainly with a view to establishing a linear sequence of concepts which would serve as a basis for ordering documents classed by the scheme. By that time the use of the scheme as a shelf-order system no longer appeared to be entirely feasible, but there still seemed to be good reasons for considering this matter of linear order. A systematic order can not only further the task of thesaurus construction, insofar as an obvious gap in an otherwise logical sequence would suggest that a certain area of knowledge called for further investigation, but it could also play a part in category construction, in that a sequence of homologous concepts would tend of its own accord to suggest some higher generic grouping which could then be made exploitable in a machine-searching system.

173

Various principles, such as simple-to-complex, time-dependency, etc., were considered as bases for achieving an apparently logical sequence of categories, but none proved to be entirely satisfactory. The most attractive proposal, in that it suggests a connection between concepts of quite different kinds, was found in an idea put forward by D J Foskett (7), who suggested that Integrative Level Theory might provide a logical basis for linear order. This theory postulates that a sequence of entities can be established according to their different levels of organisation, a new level being recognised as the point at which entities from lower levels come together, acquire a new identity, and are characterised by properties which are not found in the entities at lower levels. Molecules, for example, possess properties and structural characteristics which are not found at the level of their constituent atoms, while unicellular living organisms possess attributes over and above those of their molecular components. This suggests that it should be possible to establish parallel and corresponding sequences of entities and also of their various attributes.

As it stands, the Theory of Integrative Levels contains some elements of very doubtful logic, and it certainly led to difficulties when an attempt was made to establish a linear sequence of categories according to its precepts. It leads, for example, to a number of branching structures, not to a linear order, and it takes no account of the products of disintegration, nor of the fundamental differences which distinguish things produced by integration, such as molecules and compounds, from non-coherent and non-stoichiometric wholes which are the products of aggregation, such as alloys, families, and even research groups and committees. It must be emphasised, however, that we were looking at that time for a basis on which to build a working classification, not for a system of philosophy. This meant that we could justifiably select just as much as we found useful from any hypothesis such as Integrative Level Theory, then go on, perhaps with greater confidence, to further experiments. As Dr Alex Comfort said in a television interview: "The thing about theories isn't that they have to be right, but that they get you working".

Working along these lines, a sequence of fairly detailed categories was established by the Group, the outline of which has been re-published by the Library Association. (2) However, neither the order in which these categories are set down, nor the contents of the categories themselves, could ever be regarded as more than speculative; there were obvious gaps in the sequence, not all of which could be attributed to the fact that the NATO Grant ran out just as a suitable methodology and an experimental scheme of relational codes or operators had been devised.

174

However good the methodology, there must come a point beyond which categories can no longer be formulated on an entirely deductive basis, with different principles of division being applied in turn to the universe of concepts, each being taken to its limit before a new one is sought and applied.

Thesaurus construction: the inductive approach

Ultimately, as noted earlier, we reach the stage at which concepts have to be considered one at a time as they are encountered in the day-to-day business of classing and indexing. The research moved on to this inductive phase during the OSTI-supported development of PRECIS conducted at BNB. In this machine-produced verbal index system the terms which comprise a summary subject statement are ordered into a linear sequence or 'concept string' according to rules for filing which are invested in a schema of relational marks called 'Role operators'. Any term which serves only to establish the wider category to which the next term belongs is generally excluded from the string (the exceptions are considered later). For example, if 'Rodents' and 'Rats' appeared as consecutive words in a string, 'Rodents' would be deleted on the grounds that it is already present by implication. Category-establishing terms of this kind are handled instead through a complementary system of machine-generated references, '*See also*' references being made between related terms, or from higher to lower terms, and '*See*' references from unused synonyms to their preferred alternatives.

As this system is applied to books passing through the British Library, strings are examined term by term with a view to establishing, from dictionaries, classification schemes and existing thesauri, any semantically related term or terms which might occur to the user as alternative access words. The terms above and below a reference, together with the specific kind of relationship which links them, are then separately coded and keyboarded ready for input to a machine-held file. Once this step has been taken, each higher term is itself considered in exactly the same way, so that a further level of references is established, and this procedure is repeated until a network of semantically related terms has been established, and assigned to the computer. Any term in this network can then be extracted at any time simply by quoting, as part of the PRECIS input, a random-access number which identifies the address of that term in the machine-held file. It is then the computer, not the indexer, which traces its way through the network, extracting all relevant terms, and generating appropriate printed references. Since these semantic networks are created in the first place in response to the separate and individual terms in a string, but are not necessarily related to the subjects in which these terms occurred, the same coded reference can be used whenever a particular concept is encountered during the building of any number of different compound subjects.

It can be seen that a general categorial system is, in this fashion, being established heuristically and, as it were, from the bottom up, in contrast to the downward or analytical procedure considered during the classification research. Ultimately it is intended that the contents of this file should be printed out and critically examined with a view to producing a systematic thesaurus. It will then be interesting, to say the least, to see how closely the categories created in this way correspond to those which were postulated during the original classification research from which PRECIS evolved.

This work on PRECIS led to some rethinking of the basis on which we recognise one term as being 'higher' than another. It was generally assumed during the classification research that categories should be founded consistently upon the genus-species relationship; that is, the relationship which links a specific concept to the type of kind of which it is a member. This relationship is, of course, the familiar basis on which taxonomic groupings are constructed in the natural sciences. It establishes the fact, for example that 'Robins' are regarded, by common consensus, as members of the category 'Passerine birds', that 'Birds' are 'Vertebrates', and so on. This particular relationship is amenable to a relatively simple test, in that we can apply the logical 'Some' when reading down a hierarchy (e.g. 'Some birds are robins') and the logical 'All' when reading up a hierarchy (e.g. 'All robins are birds'). By applying this test, it is possible to establish taxonomic groupings of many kinds of concept besides the entities which are the common concern of, say, chemists and biologists. We can, for example, determine that 'Red' is a kind of 'Colour', that 'Rotation' is a kind of 'Motion', and 'Screws' are kinds of 'Fastening devices'.

This was regarded as the principal (almost the only) relationship which could serve as a satisfactory basis for thesaurus construction during the classification research; it was generally assumed that other kinds of relationship, such as whole-to-part and patient-action-agent, would be dealt with at the stage of subject building, these different kinds of concept being linked together into strings of notated elements, and their interrelationships then indicated by the choice of an appropriate operator.

While it remains true that classes, in the strict or taxonomic sense of the work, may be founded only upon the genus-species relationship, work
176

on PRECIS has established that higher generic terms are not the only kind of concept which can usefully be assigned to a thesaurus and excluded from index strings. It was suggested earlier that pre-coordinate indexing shares with natural language the characteristic of generally shedding those 'higher' terms which relate directly to the individual elements in a subject statement. There is obviously no need, whenever we speak of 'Rats', to spell out the fact that we regard these creatures as belonging to various categories such as 'Rodents' etc. Indeed, to do so would amount to explicating commonly accepted frames of reference to the point where a smooth flow of communication is seriously disrupted. Since the 'higher' terms are, in all these cases, present in a subject statement by implication, and frequently constitute part of the definition of the lower term, they can safely be handled through a system of references, without loss of meaning in an index entry.

This situation also occurs, however, in certain cases where the higher term is the greater whole of which a specific concept is the part, not the family of which it is a member. When we use the term 'Veins', for example, we naturally recognise its coordinate relationship with the concept 'Arteries', together with the fact that both terms imply the wider concept 'Cardiovascular system', which in turn is subordinate to 'Circulatory system'; yet none of these terms is linked by the genus-species relationship, and the logical 'All' and 'Some' test clearly does not apply.

It is not suggested that the whole-part relationship should therefore be accepted as a basis for thesaurus construction in any circumstances; it is, in fact, generally not suitable for this purpose. Speaking in a different context, Fairthorne (1) rightly pointed out that "We have to avoid taking one man as a small crowd, or the leg as being a small man". But it is worth noting that some categories can logically be based upon these whole-part relationships, and allowance for this has been made in a recent International Standard (8) (IS 2788), upon which the whole of the semantic component of PRECIS is now firmly based.

The concept of 'neutral' categories

It was suggested earlier that the principle of the 'root concept' could be used to ensure that common paradigms in a general classification would share common notational roots. This principle was also considered, during the CRG research, as a means for bringing different terms together within a general or 'Neutral' category when they are seen to convey the same basic idea, regardless of whether or not they share a common linguistic stem. This is, of course, no more than a rediscovery

177

of those principles which were first made public by Peter Roget over a century ago.

Although some terms appear to be limited in their use to a particular discipline, so that to a certain extent they identify the viewpoint of the user, they nevertheless share an element of common meaning with terms which are appropriate in entirely different contexts. For example, the engineer's use of the term 'Fuel' overlaps to some extent the physiologist's use of the term 'Food' and the farmer's use of 'Feedingstuffs'. It was therefore regarded as conceivable that all three of these terms could be assigned to places within a general category which collocates terms expressing the idea of 'Sources of chemical energy', and they could even share some common element of notation.

This does not mean that we intended to impose affinities upon concepts where non validly exists, and notational distinctions would have been made between terms which have similar but not identical meanings. Since, however, terms of this kind are not likely to be confused in practice ('Food', for example, is not used in the context of 'Cars'), there would be no point in assigning them to entirely different and unrelated categories. We would even have anticipated certain gains, in terms of increased recall, if their membership of the same general category was acknowledged by using the same notational root to identify all three concepts. In this way the physiologist who is studying the use of a particular technique for measuring the rates of combustion of food would have been able to detect, through a relatively simple change of notation, any relevant documents which describe the use of this same technique in the study of fuel combustion rates.

It was felt that if these homologous meanings were to be exploited effectively, terms should be assigned to categories which are, as far as possible, neutral with respect to the various contexts in which a specific idea can occur. This idea of neutral or context-independent categories does, indeed, emerge as an important factor in the design of a totally synthetic and freely-faceted general classification. In effect, we would need to consider each term as a basic unit of meaning, and assign it on this basis to the category, or categories, which appear most likely to remain valid in each of the different contexts in which it might occur. Exactly the same thing can be seen in Roget. This means, for example, that concepts of action such as 'Flow', 'Migrate', 'Transfer' and 'Conduct' should all be assigned to places within a category which brings together terms expressing the general idea of 'Transfer from A to B', and neither the labelling of the category, nor the notation which indicates

178

categorial membership, should predicate that one of these terms is generally used in the context of fluids, another is usually applied to living things, and so on. Whichever context is correct for the topic being classed could then be established during the act of subject building, the general notion of 'Transfer' being related to an appropriate system (i.e. 'thing transferred') by the fact that both thing and action concepts occur together in a string, and are linked by the correct and appropriate operator indicating, say, the 'patient-action' relationship. This should be seen in contrast to the various UDC numbers which represent the concept 'Iron', where each different symbol is limited to a particular aspect or context, none of which might be entirely appropriate for the document to hand.

Syntactic relationships and citation order

If a general system of categories, as represented by terms and their notational symbols arranged systematically into a thesaurus, can be visualised as the vocabulary of an information system, we should next consider the 'grammar' of the scheme; that is, we would need to establish a set of rules or a decision-making model which tells us how to organise concepts into strings according to their syntactic relationships.

Certain requirements of a subject building system have already been briefly considered, the most important being:

(a) that is should enable us to construct subjects freely as they are encountered

(b) that we should be able to re-format strings in such a way that the whole of a compound subject can be located under each of its significant components.

It has also been postulated that a predetermined citation order is necessary, not only to ensure the consistent organisation of strings in a machine-held store, but also to convey the meaning of a particular combination of concepts.

These different points are not necessarily interrelated. Although the chances of a successful search are probably lower in a large pan-disciplinary data base, it is conceivable that a machine-retrieval system could be designed which allows both unrestricted subject building and access to a compound subject under any of its component terms without imposing the extra burden of organising terms into pre-determined sequences. An unorganised set of keywords representing a total subject packet could still be filed under each of its significant elements in turn, and it would not strictly be necessary to organise these terms into any particular pattern to allow the machine to identify citations in which certain terms or sets of terms have co-occurred. Such a system would possess certain definite advantages over manual post-coordinate or key-word indexes; computers are much better than human beings at remembering terms, and much faster at matching them; they are also (so far as we know) not prone to the minor irritations and mis-rememberings which sometimes accompany the manual searching of coordinate indexes.

But while it might be a relatively simple matter to set up and run such a system, it is doubtful whether its performance would be rated as entirely satisfactory beyond a certain limited range of subject fields. These are those areas of knowledge, often referred to as the hard sciences, in which authors and their readers usually tend to share common and well-established frames of reference, and use the same term or terms when referring to the same objects or phenomena. In the harder disciplines terms also usually suggest, of their own accord, the grammatical roles they are most likely to adopt in the majority of subjects being indexed. In these circumstances it would be hard to justify the extra effort of achieving a fully structured subject statement. Given that certain terms, such as 'Flow', 'Wings', 'Boundary layer' and 'Swept back', together constitute the subject of a document, we should reasonably expect a user familiar with the frames of reference which hold within the field of aeronautics to be able to relate one term correctly to another, and so deduce the whole subject correctly from its parts. It would be hard, for example, to construe 'Flow' as a kind or part of 'Wings', or to regard 'Swept back' as an attribute of 'Boundary layer'.

We cannot assume, however, that these favourable circumstances hold in every indexing situation. We cannot, for example, presume the existence of a single frame of reference if we are classing or indexing across the entire subject spectrum. Nor can we dispense with structure, except at the risk of ambiguity, when we are dealing with subjects at the 'soft' end of the subject spectrum, in which the meanings of terms tend to vary according to the different contexts in which they are used.

This applies particularly to studies relating to man and his social activities. In the physical sciences we can generally infer the relationships between different entities from the presence of terms which indicate either their interactions or the effect which one thing has produced upon another. But at the soft end of the subject spectrum, especially in fields such as politics and sociology, we not only find that concepts of action are more complex, but that the object-subject relationship also tends to be interchangeable, so that we cannot deduce from a simple co-

180

occurrence of terms who has done what to whom. Concepts such as 'The individual', 'Expectations', 'Role' and 'The State', for example, can be related together in various ways to produce quite different but equally valid subjects. These are also the fields in which the exact meaning of a term often cannot be known until after it has been placed within the context of some other term or terms, and the relationship between them has been made explicit.

We therefore have to take account of the relationship between meaning and structure in a subject statement when we are: (a) classing or indexing across a range of different disciplines; (b) dealing with media at the soft end of the subject spectrum. Both of these circumstances have to be taken into account in the design of a general system.

Models for regulating citation order
Since structure in a subject statement concerns (a) kinds of concept, and (b) relationships between concepts, rules for ordering the parts of a compound subject into a linear sequence could theoretically be based upon either of these factors. We could, for example, focus attention upon conceptual types (such as Matter and Energy), and order terms into a sequence according to the different kinds of idea they represent. Alternatively, we could concentrate on the relationships *per se*, so that terms are arranged entirely according to the basic kinds of relational links which occur between them, such as possession or causality.

It is doubtful whether an order based solely upon kinds of concept could ever be a practical proposition. To a certain extent the PMEST formula of Ranganathan is based upon conceptual types, insofar as it postulates that terms which refer to Matter should precede those which convey the notion of Energy, and so on. This serves well enough as long as we are dealing with simple propositional statements, but relational factors (in the form of 'rounds' and 'levels') have to be introduced as soon as we go beyond a certain level of complexity.

Farradane (6), in his study of relational indexing, explored an alternative route, and tried to develop a system based entirely upon abstract relationships. His basic relationships, however, such as Equivalence, Appurtenance and Distinctness, proved difficult to teach or to understand, and the system he developed does not strictly amount to a precedence formula, nor does it seem capable in all cases of producing linear strings of concepts suitable for machine storage.

It appeared, therefore, that a satisfactory precedence formula should take account of both conceptual types and inter-concept relationships.

181

Consequently, the whole question of these relationships was closely examined during the NATO Research, and certain basic kinds were established, either empirically or from a study of existing citation order formulae such as Vickery's 'Standard order'. The most important of the relationships determined from these studies appeared to be as follows:

(a) the generic relationship (genus-species)
(b) the possessive relationship (whole-part)
(c) the attributive relationship (thing-property or action-property)
(d) the interactive relationship (thing-action-thing)

Each of these relationships was then considered separately, and rules of precedence were established which determined the order in which concepts should be cited when linked by one or the other. It was postulated, for example, that a thing should be set down before its properties, a whole before its parts, a patient before an action, and an action before the agent.

As stated earlier, a system of coded prefixes or operators was then established which identified which of these various roles, such as action, property or part, was being assumed in the subject to hand by the concept which followed the operator. For example, we should need to write one operator in front of an activity concept, but a different operator as a prefix to the agent of the action if this should also be present in the subject. These operators consisted of numbers, and carried a prescribed filing value which determined the order in which concepts should be cited when writing a string of codes and notated elements to represent a compound subject.

In designing such a coding system we were, in effect, trying to establish a comprehensive decision-making model to ensure that the subjects held in an information system would be organised into meaningful sequences in accordance with a set of generalised rules. Two problems had to be faced if these rules were to be applied effectively by different people, or by the same person at different times. Firstly, the codes would have to be sufficiently comprehensive in scope to deal with any role which could occur in any compound subject, regardless of its complexity; secondly, the filing order prescribed by these codes would need to be logically obvious, or at the very least logically inoffensive. That is to say, the system should lead to the production of strings which represent subjects unambiguously and even predictably.

Various attempts were made to establish a unified scheme of codes which could satisfy these requirements, but difficulties were encountered in applying the codes to really complex subjects. The rules considered above, and based on fairly simple inter-concept relationships, led to a
182

coding system which allowed the construction of short phrases consisting of two or three concepts, such as patient-action-agent, but this did not amount to a really comprehensive model capable of determining the order in which complex sets of phrases so constructed should be cited, nor did the model indicate a correct procedure when the same relationship occurs more than once within a given compound subject.

The subject considered as a system

In the search for this comprehensive model, we found that we had to consider the compound subject as a *gestalt* or system in its own right, regarding it as a set of data conveying different kinds of information, any element of which may itself consist of more than one concept. This is, of course, exactly the way in which the systems analyst considers the objects or phenomena he is studying, regarding them as wholes which are composed of various subsystems, any of which may be considered as a further system made up of lesser constituents. There are clear implications in this approach for the analysis of compound subjects, and since the techniques of systems analysis have been applied successfully in a variety of subject fields, ranging from the hard to the soft end of the subject spectrum, the procedure appeared to have an obvious bearing on the design of a general classification.

A compound subject was therefore reconsidered as a set of information units, and insofar as information in documents pertains to objects or phenomena, whether real world or abstract, which are theoretically amenable to systematic analysis, an attempt was made to relate a generalised conception of the subject to the analyst's conception of a system. All the essential features of a system may be found in the following definition by Macmillan and Gonzalez (9): "A system is a set of objects (subsystems) together with relationships between them and their attributes. Since a system never occurs without an environment, a characterisation on this basis is incomplete without reference to the total system, i.e. the system plus its environment. All systems have thus to be identified by means of constraints which delineate their true position and that of their subsystems vis-a-vis the environment. The only exception is the universe, which has no environment and thus constitutes the only true total system".

The conceptual elements which are highlighted in this definition, such as the attributes and parts of a system, simply confirmed rather than added to those which had been deduced already from a study of inter-concept relationships. The important point to note here is the special

183

emphasis given to the role of the environment, which is seen as a concept whose principal function is to establish the context in which a system is being considered. No reference is made to any interaction between the system and its environment beyond that of constraint; and direct interaction would entail the incorporation of the environment as part of the system, which in its turn would then call for the naming of a new environment. The significance of this from the viewpoint of citation order will be considered later.

If we now relate these factors to the subject elements which had been established earlier from a study of inter-concept relationships, we can go on to establish the following provisional list of roles which concepts can potentially assume in any compound subject:

(a) the environment of a system

(b) the system itself, whether concrete or abstract, considered in terms of:

      (i)   its attributes

      (ii)   its subsystems

      (iii) interactions between the subsystems, perhaps involving both active and passive components

      (iv) the attributes (whether parts or properties) of the subsystems

This is clearly the beginning of a model which offers a completely generalised approach to subject analysis and building. Owing to the iterative nature of systems analysis it can also be used to extend an analysis to any depth required by the subject in hand. Any component of a system can serve as the starting point for a new level of analysis, the subsystem at one level becoming the system under review to another, when it is reconsidered in terms of *its* parts and *their* interactions. For example, the motor car may be regarded as a subsystem for the purposes of a traffic survey, and will then be seen in terms of its interactions with other kinds of vehicle, yet on another level the car can be viewed as an entity in its own right, and is then considered in terms of various parts, such as its engine and bodywork, which would not have been especially relevant in a road traffic survey.

The development of a general citation order
Any analysis which proceeds like this from one level to another in systematic steps suggests that it should be possible to organise the parts of a compound subject in the same way. The filing order prescribed by the coded roles should then have ensured, for example, that the environment
184

is stated before the system, the system before its parts, the passive component before any action which links it to the active component, and so on, the concept named at one step helping to explain the role of whichever factor is introduced at the next. This is, in fact, the order which is currently used in preparing strings for PRECIS, though an entirely different route was followed in developing this input order of terms for the index system.

This citation order is not only predictable, it is also sufficiently generalised to be neutral with respect to subject field, and could therefore be used to regulate the ordering of concepts across the whole of the subject spectrum. It was not, however, seriously considered when general systems theory was examined during the CRG research, mainly on the grounds that it would be unsuitable for a dual-purpose classification intended for both library organisation and also machine storage and retrieval. It is clear that collocation under environment, which would usually be the name of a country or a geographical region, would not provide a satisfactory basis for organising the stock of a library. Consequently, this factor was de-emphasised in the model developed at that time, and an order was established which ensured that concepts expressing location (except when place is the main theme of a document) would appear at the end of a string during the act of subject building, just as it is when using the PMEST formula. In many respects the citation order model which was developed at that time bore a close resemblance to Ranganathan's, with concepts generally ordered according to some prior conception of their relative significance as shelving factors. However, allowance had been made for the inclusion of factors such as 'Parts' and 'Properties', which were missing from the earlier schema, and the proposed model also included codes which would handle problems noted in the early stages of the research. For example, one code was introduced to identify concepts having an adjectival function, i.e. it would indicate a logical 'difference' which defines a subclass, in the way that the activity 'To weld', for example, can act substantively in subjects such as 'Welding of steel', but can also assume an adjectival role and define a special class of material such as 'Welded steel'. Another code established the quasi-generic group to which a concept might belong from the restricted viewpoint of the particular document in hand, in the sense that the concept 'Rats', for example, which belongs intrinsically to the class 'Rodents', might also be viewed as a member of *a posteriori* groupings such as 'Pets' and 'Laboratory animals'.

The research had reached this stage, with the establishment of an outline system of categories and a provisional citation order model, when the

185

funds from the NATO Science Foundation ran out. The next stage of
the research was first supported by BNB, and later OSTI, and was concerned with the production of a subject index from a single string of
descriptors taken from the MARC magnetic tapes. These experiments
with a pre-coordinated subject index might seem a far cry from research
into a notated meta-language, but, in terms of basic methodology, it is
considered that the principles underlying these two approaches to citation order are essentially similar.

The development of PRECIS

It is not the intention to devote much space to an account of this verbal
indexing system. Its historical development, including its evolution from
the CRG research, has been described elsewhere (10), and the operation
of the system has been set down in a 'Manual' (11) which is now regarded
as definitive, at least as far as indexing in English is concerned. During
the initial stages of the *BNB* research, the intention was to automate the
production of the chain index to a DC organised file which had been a
familiar feature of the national bibliography for some twenty years.
However, this venture proved to be abortive, and later researches have
increasingly tended to take a different direction—one which owes more
to modern linguistic theories than classificatory principles.

Expressed in completely general terms, the original intention was to
explore a new approach to subject index production, using the computer
to manipulate a single input string of terms in such a way that:
(a) any significant term in the string could be pre-selected by the
indexer, and would then appear in the lead position in the entry, serving
as the user's access point.
(b) a full summary statement of the subject would be presented in a
meaningful form to the user under each of these pre-selected terms.
This second point should be seen in contrast to a set of keywords or subject headings assigned to a document, none of which may be fully coextensive, and also to the chain index, which achieves a full subject
statement only when the final concept has been added to the chain.

Early experiments with various entry formats led to the establishment
of a layout of terms on the page in which the lead term is followed by
others which set the lead into its wider context, while this part of the
entry may also be further extended by terms which are themselves
context-dependent on the lead, and are indented below on a second line.
This gives a potential for the three part entry structure which is now
186

typical of the PRECIS index as it appears in *BNB* and various other catalogues and bibliographies:

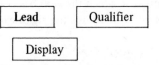

Once this basic format had been established, it was a relatively simple matter to program a computer so that it shunted terms in input strings through these various positions to generate a full set of entries. The most commonly-used routine in the entry generation program simply calls for terms to be shunted sequentially out of the display position, into the lead, then across into the qualifier, as seen in the first of two sample sets of entries below. In most cases it was found that the entries generated in this way during the early researches could be readily comprehended, regardless of which term was in the lead position. In some cases, however, entries were decidedly ambiguous, while in a few instances the meaning of the subject had been lost altogether. It was deduced heuristically that the cause of this loss of meaning could be attributed to only one factor, i.e. the order in which terms were organised in input strings. At that time, this was in accordance with the system of roles developed during the CRG research, and which had, of course, been intended to reflect some prior conception of relative significance judged from the viewpoint of shelf arrangement.

Following further experiments, it became clear that the idea of organising terms according to their relative value as shelving factors was not only responsible for the loss of meaning in some of the index entries; it is also entirely irrelevant in an index such as PRECIS, where any term pre-selected by the indexer can be marked as a lead, and will then dominate the entry and appear to assume the role of 'most significant' concept. In these circumstances, it is obviously more important to organize terms in such a way that the meaning of the subject can be conveyed with a minimum of ambiguity, regardless of their relative importance as indicators of shelf position.

A clue to this matter of meaningfulness came from a study of those entries which had failed to meet the criterion of ready interpretation. This indicated that the correct meaning of a set of index entries could be preserved throughout a series of manipulations provided that: (1) each term in the original string was directly related to the next term or set of

187

terms, rather as the words in a sentence frequently form a one-to-one related sequence; (2) terms are set down in such an order that each establishes the wider context in which the next has been considered by the author, without regard for their 'relative significance'. This can be represented by a diagram:

$$A > B > C > D$$

indicating that the author has studied the concept D in the context of C, C in the context of B, and B in the context of A. The order finally established, which generally corresponds to the order of terms in the passive declarative sentence in English and other languages, is obtained at the stage of concept analysis by assigning codes representing grammatical roles or cases to each of the terms in a summary subject statement. These terms are then set down as an input string according to the filing value attached to each of the principal codes. This schema of codes, called 'role operators', is shown as Table 1.

The use of these codes can be demonstrated by applying them to a straightforward subject such as 'The migration of birds in Canada'. This would first be analysed into its three substantive elements, 'Birds', 'Migration' and 'Canada', each of which is then checked in turn against the schema to determine how its role in the subject should be coded. A rule of the system requires that every string must include at least one concept which is coded '1', representing a 'Thing', and/or a concept coded '2', representing an action or its effect. The action term, if present, is usually regarded as more important, since it tends to determine how the rest of the string should be coded, much as the verb tends to dominate the sentence in traditional grammar. In this example we can recognize 'Migration' as an action which should therefore be coded '2', e.g.

(2) migration

After using this code, the indexer would then tend to check the subject for the presence of a thing associated with this action; in the present example, this is the term 'Birds', which functions as the agent of an intransitive action, and should therefore be coded '1'. Since the main line operators have ordinal filing values, the string produced so far would read:

(1) birds
(2) migration

This still leaves the locality 'Canada' to be considered, which calls for the use of the operator '0', indicating a location or environment. This gives the final sequence of operators and terms:

188

(0) Canada

(1) birds

(2) migration

—forming a context-dependent string ready for the addition of machine instructions, then input to the computer. Assuming that the indexer wishes to provide access under each of these terms, the machine would respond to his coded decision and produce the following set of entries:

Canada

Birds. Migration

Birds. Canada

Migration

Migration. Birds. Canada

These entries demonstrate the standard shunting algorithm described above, with terms shifted successively from the display into the lead and then into the qualifier. Two other formats are also available, and the formatting of entries is regulated entirely by the computer in response to the role operators.

Experience has shown that this method of coding terms according to their syntactical roles is easy to teach, and is capable of handling subjects at any level of complexity. In certain circumstances, iteration is allowed, meaning that some of the operators can occur more than once in a string; consequently, the system is able to deal with whatever depth of subject analysis is required by the document to hand.

Besides this use of operators to deal with syntactical relationships, PRECIS includes a supplementary system for generating, from a machine-held thesaurus, references between semantically related terms, e.g.

Aves *See* **Birds**

Vertebrates

See also

Birds

Ornithology

See also

Birds   etc.

These references are produced automatically whenever the numbered address of an indexing term is quoted in the appropriate field in a subject data record. It should, perhaps, be emphasised that these numbers represent addresses in a random-access file, and do not resemble notation in the usual sense: that is to say, the number associated with any given term does not indicate its hierarchical or other kind of relationships. Links

TABLE 1: *Role operators used in PRECIS*

Main line operators

Environment of observed system

0	Location

Observed system (Core operators)

1	Key system: *object of transitive action; agent of intransitive action*
2	Action/Effect
3	Agent of transitive action; Aspects; Factors

A

Data relating to observer

4	Viewpoint-as-form

Selected instance

5	Sample population/Study region

Presentation of data

6	Target/Form

Interposed operators

Dependent elements

p	Part/Property
q	Member of quasi-generic group
r	Aggregate

Concept interlinks

s	Role definer
t	Author attributed association

Coordinate concepts

g	Coordinate concept

Differencing operators
(prefixed by $)

h   Non-lead direct difference
i   Lead direct difference
j   Salient difference
k   Non-lead indirect difference
m   Lead indirect difference
n   Non-lead parenthetical difference
o   Lead parenthetical difference
d   Date as a difference

Connectives
(Components of linking phrases; prefixed by $)

C

v   Downward reading component
w   Upward reading component

Theme interlinks

x   First element in coordinate theme
y   Subsequent element in coordinate theme
z   Element of common theme

between the contents of these addresses are indicated by a separate system of machine-readable codes which identify the basic thesaural relationships specified in IS 2788. One special advantage accrues from this use of random access addresses: the system has infinite hospitality, since new terms can be introduced into the thesaurus at any time without fear of disturbing a system of expressive notation.

The prospects for a freely-faceted classification
It was stated earlier that the organisation of terms in PRECIS strings is based on linguistic rather than classificatory principles. Consequently, these strings are theoretically neutral with respect to subject field, and it should be possible to assign a subject expressed in this way to some 'most obviously correct' place in each of several shelf order classifications, no matter which factor was emphasised in any particular scheme. For example, the subject expressed in a set of PRECIS entries such as:

Shipbuilding industries
    Inventory control. Applications of computer systems
Inventory control. Shipbuilding industries
    Applications of computer systems
Computer systems. Shipbuilding industries
    Applications in inventory control

—might be classed with documents on special industries in one scheme, at inventory control in another, and with computer applications in a third. Each of these factors is emphasised in one entry or another, yet the initial analysis would remain the same in all cases. The point therefore arises: Could this initial analysis function as the basis for a new freely-faceted classification scheme?

The answer is 'Almost certainly no', for a number of reasons which have been explored elsewhere. (12) Nevertheless, it could function as a medium for exchanging subject data in a coded and language-independent form, leaving local classification schemes undisturbed. This concept of a meta-language which is language-independent, while remaining neutral with respect to shelf order systems, is likely to become increasingly important as the exchange of subject data across national and linguistic frontiers spreads with the growth of MARC or MARC-type systems. This is the area in which research is most needed at present, special attention being paid to what Neelameghan (13) has called the concept of an 'absolute syntax': that is, a set of principles for organising concepts into sequences which convey basically the same meaning in several, if not all, human languages.

192

Some work along these lines is now being undertaken as part of the PRECIS project. Current research is directed towards the addition of a switching component to the system, so allowing an indexer to write his strings in, say, English, and have these converted, via a machine-held intermediate concept file, into codes which will lead to meaningful and correctly formed index entries in a range of different target languages. At present the research is limited to English, French and German, and a number of interesting problems have already been highlighted. New codes are needed, for example, to deal with compound terms and inflections in the Germanic group of languages. Thanks to the cooperation of indexers in a number of European countries, specifications for these new codes have already been prepared, and now await programming and testing. More importantly, however, experiments conducted in a number of different languages appear to show that PRECIS is based on logico-linguistic principles which do, indeed, hold good in all the languages tested so far. There appears to be a direct relationship between the syntactical roles used in PRECIS and the 'deep cases' (14, 15) recognised in modern linguistics.

Inevitably, this conclusion leads to a further question: If it is possible to devise a highly articulated, language-independent coding system which could be used not only for data exchange and the searching of machine-held files, but also for the production of co-extensive and pre-coordinated index entries in terms drawn from a range of different natural languages, do we also need to devise highly-articulated compound class numbers to organise documents on library shelves? An attempt at a personal answer to this question was presented at the FID/CR Conference on Classification Research held in India in 1975 (12): "When the third generation of computers was evolving in the early 1960s, a sense of disquiet could be detected in writings on the future of enumerative classifications. It was vaguely suspected that this new range of machines, with their increased capacities for storing and manipulating quantities of data, might mean the beginning of the end of schemes such as DC. The balance appeared to be tipped in favour of faceted classifications, such as CC and UDC, which already tended to treat subjects as strings of discrete data elements. But the evidence now available, backed by more experience in dealing with computers, suggests that these fears were unfounded ... It would appear that the enumerative classification can, indeed, co-exist with the machine-based system, provided that its editors are not tempted into offering more than just mark-and-park facilities by introducing features which belong more rightly within the computer. At the risk of seeming to be icono-

193

clastic, it could be argued that it is the future of faceted schemes which is now in doubt. In trying to meet two conflicting sets of requirements, i.e. shelf order and concept specification, they might be judged as satisfying neither".

REFERENCES
1 Fairthorne, R A: 'Innovation resulting from research and development in the information field: a researcher's view'. *Aslib proceedings,* 22(11), 1970. p 550-558.
2 Classification Research Group: Classification and information control: papers representing the work of the Classification Research Group during 1960-1968. Library Association, 1969.
3 Foskett, A C: The subject approach to information. 2nd ed. London, Bingley; Hamden, Conn, Linnet Books, 1971.
4 Coward, R E: 'BNB and computers'. *Library Association Record,* 70(8), 1968. p 198-202.
5 Roberts, N: 'An examination of the Personality concept and its relevance to the Colon Classification scheme'. *J. Lib.* 1(3), 1969. p 131-148.
6 Farradane, J E L: Report on information retrieval by relational indexing: Part 1, Methodology. City University (London), 1966.
7 Foskett, D J: Classification for a general index language: a review of recent research by the CRG. Library Association, 1970.
8 International Standards Organisation: Guidelines for the establishment and development of monolingual thesauri (IS 2788). I.S.O. 1975.
9 Macmillan, C & Gonzalez, R F: Systems analysis: a computer approach to decision models. Irwin, 1968.
10 Austin, Derek: 'The development of PRECIS: a theoretical and technical history'. *J. Doc.* 30(1), March 1974, p 47-102.
11 Austin, Derek: PRECIS: a manual of concept analysis and subject indexing. Bibliographic Services Division, The British Library, 1974.
12 Austin, Derek: Differences between library classifications and machine-based subject retrieval systems: some inferences drawn from research in Britain, 1963-1973. *In* Proceedings of the Third International Study Conference on Classification Research, Bombay, January 1975. FID/CR (in press).
13 Neelameghan, A: Absolute syntax and structure of an indexing and switching language. *In* Proceedings of the Third International Conference on Classification Research, Bombay, January 1975. FID/CR (in press).
14 Fillmore, C J: The case for case. *In* Universals of linguistic theory, *ed.* by E Bach & R T Harms. Holt, Rinehart and Winston, 1968.
15 Sørensen, Jutta and Austin, Derek: PRECIS in a multilingual context: Part 2: a linguistic and logical explanation of the syntax. *Libri,* Summer 1976. (in press).

194

Classification in computer-based information systems of the 1970s

ROBERT R FREEMAN
Environmental Science Information Center, National Oceanic and Atmospheric Administration, US Department of Commerce, Washington

EDITOR'S INTRODUCTION: The author was closely associated with mechanized classification throughout the 1960s, especially in the context of the American Institute of Physics AUDACIOUS project. His 'state of the art' overview is produced here in substantially the same form as in the first edition for—while he points out to me that he is no longer directly connected with this kind of work—the following account remains a most useful broad picture of research and exploration in this sphere.

Preface

It seemed fitting that the UNISIST World Science Information System feasibility study (1) crossed my desk as I first began to transform the outline of this paper into its final form. The 1970s, it is clear, are the decade of the consolidation of the technical advances of the 1960s into large-scale, multi-organizational, multi-national information systems. While we have not yet seen all the requisite degree of cooperation and standardization that are needed to carry out the development of such systems, the need is clearly perceived and the institutional mechanisms are functioning with greater strength than ever before.

The purpose of this review is to examine the role of classification as a part of the information process in the light of discernible broad trends. These trends will result in fundamental changes in the ways in which we organize to make recorded knowledge available for present and future use. Although quite clearly related to technology and methods, the trends are most importantly institutional.

The reasons for these institutional changes are largely reflections of the economics and organizational patterns of modern industrial societies. As a basis for recommendations for a National Advisory Commission on Libraries, Cuadra (2) and his associates identified these factors as (i) a rising volume of documents, (ii) rising educational level, (iii) rising salaries and manpower shortages, (iv) competition for funds with other urgent

195

political and social priorities, (v) emergence of new fields of study by coalescing or dividing of older fields, and (vi) new ways of looking at old problems. Except for the problem of manpower shortages, which has already proved to be non-permanent and related to shifting social priorities, the list is still valid. The identifiable results of this economic pressure are trends towards centralization of the cataloguing of books and reports and towards information networks.

Institutional Components of Networks
To remain within the scope of this paper, only secondary processors of published information will be considered as components of networks. Secondary processors are those organizations which store and disseminate documents and/or provide means of access to their collection or to some definable body of published information. Several distinct types of secondary processors have emerged in recent years as components of what are gradually coming to be networks. The process of institutional change is by no means one which follows a clear, rational plan, however.

One component is the *document depot* or warehouse. These organizations provide for relatively long-term access to large, general collections of documents, supplying copies for sale or, in some cases, for loan to users.

The *information supplier* is a second component. Information suppliers traditionally have been abstracting and indexing services which published periodical journals of abstracts, as well as some centralized bibliographic cataloguing services, notably the various national bibliographies and the US Library of Congress. Three developments have begun to change this picture considerably.

Firstly, the larger organizations performing this function have diversified, making available for sale or lease large varieties of new products and services, sometimes incorporating the same information into new categories, sometimes into different media (such as magnetic tape or microfilm), and sometimes developing products which are entirely novel.

Secondly, the information suppliers, traditionally single organizations, are becoming the focal points of decentralized, often international input networks. Thus, a sharing of the work of identifying, obtaining, cataloguing, abstracting, and indexing is evolving. In each case, the objective is the continuous updating of a data base from which the variety of services and products are produced.

Finally, the diversification of the larger producers, the increased flexibility of their products, and the high cost of information services
196

are combining gradually to reduce the likelihood of survival of highly specialized information suppliers of this type. It seems likely that there will be fewer and larger information data bases in the future, especially those which are publications only. This does not mean that there will not be specialized information services. To the contrary, the emerging institutional forms described below provide more specialized, personalized services than heretofore.

A third institutional component of the information networks of the 1970s is the *information dissemination centre* or 'information middleman'*. These centres, which exist in numerous sites in both North America and Europe, concentrate their efforts on providing information retrieval services using data bases which have been purchased or leased from the suppliers. Most centres do not create data bases as a result of their own work, relying entirely upon outside sources. However, some information suppliers also function as information dissemination centres for their own data base.

The usefulness of the institution of information dissemination centres stems from complexity. The management of several complex bibliographic data bases requires a degree of sophistication in both information systems and the various scientific and engineering disciplines which most organizations have not yet developed at present. Despite promising trends toward standards there are so many technical variations in the characteristics of data bases from the many suppliers that only centres with a sufficiently broad base can afford to provide staffs with sufficient knowledge of each data base to manage it economically.

The fourth component institutional form consists of the *information and data analysis centres*. In contrast to the previous types, these centres emphasize a very thorough knowledge of a tightly-defined field, usually of fairly limited scope, and close continuing contact with a user community. These centres often produce critical reviews of data and literature within their scope and seek to reinforce relationships with users of their services by involving them in the reviewing and analysing process.

A final institutional role is one which might be termed *'authority supplier'*, by which is meant the maintenance and promulgation of classifications, thesauri, subject heading lists, and other authoritative guides to accessing information files. This role is often played by the information suppliers, but it is distinctive enough to be given separate recognition.

Having identified these major components of information networks, I should like to review relatively recent work which may give some

* A term emphasized by Dr Burton Adkinson in several lectures.

197

indication of the role of classification in information retrieval systems.

Of all of the institutions described above, the information dissemination centre is uniquely a phenomenon of the 1970s. It serves user requirements on the basis of bibliographic data bases in whatever form and with whatever content they are available from producers. These centres face not only more serious problems of input and total storage volume than the processor of a single data base, but also the formidable problem of methods of file and record organization and classification and indexing which differ from one data base to the next.

There are two important aspects of the problem. One is how to process any one file efficiently. The second is how to process efficiently several files which are organized differently and which vary in content and description of content.

1 Extremely large files already are being generated and sold (or leased) to user organizations. While the capability to store and process large files has increased dramatically and costs per unit have fallen, the question of whether classifying, partitioning or otherwise reorganizing the file will aid in achieving maximum search effectiveness continues to require careful examination. Thus the problem is to maximize effectiveness, by whatever measure is chosen, while minimizing the sum of file organization (including classification) and maintenance costs, storage costs, and search and display costs. The problem is made more difficult by the inverse (or even more subtle) relationship between organization, maintenance, and storage costs on one hand and search and display costs on the other.

2 The technical and costs problems of providing direct access to extremely large data bases, described by Cuadra (3), may not be a uniformly large problem for all organizations, if classification techniques are used. Many technical information centres serve a clientele whose interests are well-defined and more limited than the scope of a single given data base. Consequently, data bases can be either: (1) reclassified at the input stage in order to maximize the likelihood of rapid access to segments (classes) which are most probably relevant; or (2) subjected to a selection process, whereby only that portion of the file deemed most relevant is retained. For example, if the magnetic tapes of *Nuclear science abstracts* were to be used as a data base to serve scientists in the oceanic, atmospheric, and geophysical sciences, certain sections of the file, amounting to probably no more than 5 per cent of the total, could be selected to enter the system. Regardless of

198

which technique is applied, there is a significant role for classification in this process. Potential solutions to this problem can be seen in three areas, namely (1) automatic classification techniques, (2) concordance on 'switching language' techniques, and (3) use of manually pre-selected classification codes.

Most bibliographic data bases include some form of pre-selected classification as a data element in each record. For example, element 0067-01 in the *Chemical abstracts condensates* file in the CAS revised Standard Distribution Format represents the class (from a total of eighty) to which each item has been assigned.

If an information centre serves a well-defined information-seeking clientele, it can reasonably hope to take any incoming file which is classified in some manner and select that portion which is likely to be of use to that clientele. However, if tue centre repeats this process with other files, it is still left with a collection of heterogeneous files, the indexing and classification of which was done in consideration of the original file contents and a different or more general set of users. There are a number of approaches to solving this problem.

Wall (4), for example, devised a method of 'vocabulary filtering', based on the assumption that the receiving organization has a well-developed thesaurus which represents the interests of its users. The filtering algorithm would convert the vocabulary of the incoming files into that of the receiver.

In contrast, most practising information dissemination centres keep each data base separate and train search analysts to become expert in the vocabulary and other characteristics of each data base. Separate software packages also have to be maintained unless the incoming files are converted to the receiver's standard. Most centres make the conversion to a single format.

According to another possible approach, recipient organizations could select and/or reorganize input records by using existing input class designators and then establishing concordances between these classes and other class designations chosen for relevance to the processor's interest.

A much more sophisticated technique would apply automatic classification methods to what might be termed 'automatic reclassification'. The interests of the recipient centre's clientele would be represented and related to the vocabulary of the incoming file by whatever technique is suitable for the chosen automatic method (clumping, factor analysis, etc). Incoming records would be assigned to new categories (or rejected) according to the computer degree of relevance to those categories and

199

the resulting file organized so as to take advantage of these segments. Thus, reclassified, reorganized, and distilled, the remaining input records could then be added to a single established data base maintained by the centre.

Although this last technique still seems 'far out' to the information system operator of today, there continues to be a spectrum of research and development which perhaps will lead to such applications. Recent work focusses on three areas. These categories are (1) the sources of classifications, (2) the use of classification in the storage, retrieval, and dissemination of documents, and (3) the use of classification in the storage, retrieval, and dissemination of document surrogates.

The sources of classifications

In a practical, as opposed to philosophical sense classifications have as their sources derivation by human analysis alone, computer-aided classification-making, and fully-automatic classification-making programmes. Computer techniques have a limited, but extremely important use in the first of these: through the use of computer-output-to-microfilm (COM) and photocomposition devices, large computer-stored classification schedules and their entry vocabularies can be prepared, updated, and disseminated readily.

There is a gradual convergence taking place between the practices for organizing and displaying classifications and thesauri, with more specificity emphasized in classifications and more hierarchy in thesauri. As summarized by Surace (5), modern thesauri contain alphabetical, hierarchical, permuted, and categorial displays, the second and last closely resembling classifications. However, this convergence may have taken place just as formalized, highly structured and controlled vocabularies for indexing and retrieval purposes are becoming obsolete, as Klingbiel has concluded recently after a review of current computer capabilities for natural language text analysis. (6)

Considerable work continues to be done on the analysis of natural language text for the purposes of generating indexing languages and classifications and assigning terms to document surrogates and surrogates to classes. Batty has provided a review of this field. (7) The terms 'classification', 'indexing', and 'thesaurus' tend to be freely interchanged in recent writing, although Sparck Jones has made the effort to explain that automatically-derived classifications differ fundamentally from those derived by humans. (8)

200

Larger amounts of text, derived from larger document collections is a goal which is being reached gradually. Lowe and Roberts, for example, describe an automatic document clustering system applicable to a collection of 40,000 documents and 100 million characters. (9)

In a similar vein, the full text of 25,000 United States patents will serve as the basis for research on computer-aided classification of patents. (10) This project, being carried out by a team from the US Patent Office and the National Bureau of Standards, investigates the creation of new classification structures based on computer analysis of the texts, rather than the assignment of patents to the existing Patent Office classification. But the need for larger amounts of text is only one of several technical, economic, and administrative problems which dampen the enthusiasm of operational information systems for automatically-derived and -applied classifications.

Especially in the case of libraries, Cuadra's conclusions of several years ago will probably continue to apply for most of the next decade: ' . . . use of computer-generated classification schemes is not yet appropriate for most libraries or even for most semiautomated retrieval systems. In addition to the fact that the relative merits of automated classification are yet to be demonstrated, there is the fact that all libraries presently use one or more existing conventional classification systems, and their personnel and patrons would require extensive training to reorient themselves toward computer-generated, adaptive classification systems. The cost of data generation and programming is also, for the moment, a prohibitive factor. For the present exploratory use of computer-derived classification categories is desirable primarily where documents are already deeply indexed, and where either the existing schedule is not considered satisfactory or there is no classification schedule at all . . .' (11)

Computer-aided systems for document dissemination
Relatively few published papers deal with computer-aided systems for document dissemination, by comparison with those concerned with reference retrieval and dissemination. Nevertheless, the increasing popularity of microfiche as an economical medium for storage of technical reports promises to stimulate the development of this application of classification in computer-aided information systems.

For example, the (US) National Technical Information Service initiated a selective dissemination of microfiche (SDM) system. While presently only semi-mechanized, this system permits large-scale microfiche users to receive automatically all new reports which belong to specified sub-ject classes. The classes may be selected from the COSATI Classification, the NTIS, CAST amd FAST categories, the Atomic Energy Commission's *Nuclear science abstracts* categories, or the NASA Scientific and Tech-nical Aerospace Reports categories.

The (US) Defense Documentation Center also has reported recently on experiments with an Automatic Document Distribution service. (12) The system is based on the DDC user studies, which showed that users of defence-related technical information (i) generally turn first (and often only) to local sources, not to national information centres and (ii) need fast service. According to the chosen scheme, microfiche copies of reports are selected according to organizational interest profiles and sent to the user organizations' libraries along with magnetic tapes containing bibliographic data, abstracts, and subject terms, which are used to generate individual user notices. The 188 categories of the modified COSATI classification are used for microfiche dissemination.

In contrast to these systems operated by large documentation centres, an advanced one-company system has been in operation at the Bell Laboratories since 1966. As described by Brown and Traub (13), the MERCURY system uses an internally devised hierarchical classification. Authors may specify subject classification codes as well as individuals and organizational units when arranging for distribution of their reports. The computer system matches these codes against stored user profiles and generates mailing labels accordingly.

Classification, storage and retrieval of document references
In reviewing the literature dealing with the use of classification in com-puter-based information systems, one is confronted with a variety of terms which overlap extensively in usage. In this section, I shall regard as a user of classification any system which (i) employs a set of relatively broad subject categories which may be used to select a portion of a file, or (ii) employs a controlled subject vocabulary or code which is primarily structured and used in a hierarchical form.

Many examples of the use of classification in information storage and retrieval systems have been reported in the last few years. The few reviewed below, along with many others, indicate that the 1970s will continue to see both the general classifications, including at least Dewey, Library of Congress, UDC and Colon, as well as a variety of special classifications used. If anything, this trend is likely to be promoted by the experience of the information dissemination centres, which collectively show great ingenuity in making use of any form of subject indicators introduced into a data base by the supplier.

General classifications
The use of the general classifications in computer-based systems will continue to spread rapidly as a direct impact of the MARC distribution system of the Library of Congress and the *British National Bibliography*. An example, reported by Bierman (14) and by Bierman and Blue (15), is the MARC-based selective dissemination service operated by the Oklahoma Department of Libraries. Interest profiles are encoded as Dewey and/or Library of Congress classification numbers. Notices are printed and sent to users in various university, state agency, and public libraries to aid in current awareness and selection of books to be ordered.

MARC-distributed files also are being modified to encompass classification codes which are not included in the MARC records. For example, the UK Atomic Energy Authority's Aldermaston library extracts records from the weekly MARC files by means of stored profiles consisting of about seventy Dewey classification numbers. Following this, UDC numbers are added to the selected records for local cataloguing purposes. (16)

In France, the Groupe informatiste de bibliothèques universitaires et specialistes (GIBUS), a consortium of eight organizations, has demonstrated a system that it is developing which will make use of data from the BNB MARC tapes with locally-added UDC numbers. (17) One member of the consortium, the Bibliothèque des Halles, opened in Paris about 1974 with an on-line, UDC-classed catalogue of the library's holdings of about one million volumes. (18)

Use of the Universal Decimal Classification in computer-based information systems has spread rapidly within recent years. Rigby has summarized reported work with UDC-oriented systems in eleven countries. (19) In addition to the MARC-oriented systems mentioned above, an operational SDI system for a metallurgical company has been described by McCash and Carmichael. (20)

At least one information retrieval system based on the use of the Colon Classification has been reported. The paper by Gupta (21) describes a set of fifteen programmes which provide for storing and updating a reference catalogue, a classification schedule, an alphabetical index to the schedule, and a catalogue of user profiles. Interactive retrospective searching and selective dissemination are the output options.

Special classifications

Most, if not all, of the computer-processable bibliographic data bases now available include a data element which indicates a broad class or classes to which each record belongs. Generally, the classification is especially developed for the data base or for the equivalent printed abstracting and indexing service. These codes provide a ready-made basis for selecting portions of a file for more detailed searching, while bypassing clearly non-relevant portions. Beyond this simple use of classification other measures are employed in order to permit detailed hierarchical searching.

For example, an on-line, interactive *Abridged index medicus* search system known as AIM-TWX is operated by the National Library of Medicine. It includes an 'explode' command which provides for hierarchical display of sections of medical subject headings desired by the user. As there is alphabetical access also, the hierarchy may be entered at any level.

A hierarchically-organized indexing language is used for indexing and retrieval of current research project descriptions at the Science Information Exchange of the Smithsonian Institute. The SIE system is discussed in a two-part paper by Hersey *et al,* who report evaluation studies showing both precision and recall to be well over 90 percent. (22)

In the field of architecture, a special classification was developed for use in a remote job entry system. (23) It is a manually-developed classification specifically intended for a computerized system of data storage and retrieval.

Schneider has developed an SDI system for biomedical information which is based on an enumerative, hierarchical decimal classification. (24) In a more recent paper he has advocated the wider use of enumerative hierarchical classifications in indexing large bibliographic data bases, arguing that the benefit would be 'to improve the precision and quality of matching scientists with useful documents'. (25) Schneider has compiled a preliminary annotated bibliography on classification-based automated information systems which is available on request from the National Cancer Institute, Bethesda, Maryland 20014.

Comparative studies

Comparative studies of the performance of indexing languages and classifications in the context of computer-based systems have continued to be produced. To an increasing extent, these studies are becoming concerned with problems of concordance or automatic switching between files which are differently indexed or classified. The work of Wall, cited above, is an example.

Troller conducted a study of the relative performance of a controlled keyword system versus that of a highly specialized analytico-synthetic, post-coordinate, hierarchical, faceted thesaurus. (26) As described in her paper, the Naval Reactor Information Center receives the magnetic tape data base equivalent to *Nuclear science abstracts,* containing USAEC keywords. Only a limited portion of the file is relevant to the interests of the Center, so a selection is made. The question investigated was whether a significant benefit would result from re-indexing the selected file items according to the specialized interests of the Center. The re-indexing would be done automatically by establishing a machine-stored concordance of the two indexing languages. The study concluded that (i) the precision ratio of the results obtained would be approximately the same with either language, but that the time of search formulation would be significantly less, with consequent large savings in manpower and costs if the specialized hierarchical vocabulary is used, and (ii) that the construction of the hierarchical vocabulary, including its arrangement and notation, plays a major role in the retrieval process, especially owing to the ability to retrieve ranges or classes of information which are not specified by a single term.

Another comparative study involving classification in mechanized systems is currently in progress at the Department of Computing Science, University of Alberta. This study is 'part of a major project concerned with the development of an on-line thesaurus-based information storage and retrieval system for water resources management. [. . .] As a preliminary choice, it was decided to investigate and compare the appropriateness of the UDC, the LC [classification] , and the United States Water Resources Thesaurus as indexing languages for the control of water resources planning literature.' (27) The MARC tapes, the machine-readable UDC schedules produced by the American Institute of Physics in 1965-68, the Water Resources Thesaurus supplemented by terms relevant to Canada, geological and water resources data bases are being used in the study.

Summary
The matter of switching among existing classifications and indexing languages used in machine-readable data bases will continue to be the subject of considerable effort throughout the remainder of the 1970s. A variety of classifications continue to thrive in the context of computer-

205

based systems, both as file-partitioning and as detailed subject searching devices. Large-scale use of automatic classification techniques is probably still at least a decade away.

Finding the balance of computer versus human analysis
The increasing likelihood of computer capabilities for classifying and indexing information and for deriving automatically the very basis for classifying poses a question for which we should have some answers prepared by 1980. We are already seeing how rapidly-growing technology and its side effects can cause sudden and unexpected stresses on our institutions and upon public policy, resulting in major dislocations and reorientation of goals and programmes. It has been well proven in the 1960s that advanced, industrialized nations can produce surpluses of highly educated and skilled people. The degree of permanence of this situation may well be low, but the possibilities of recurring episodes seem to exist.

There is a paradox which may become apparent by the decade's end. We have long accepted the premise that automation should relieve man of mindless, repetitive manual labour, freeing him to use his intellectual capability. But perhaps we are on the way to demonstrating in a few years that we can not only educate more people that we presently can employ productively, but that we also can teach computers to take over a portion of the intellectual analysis and classification of our recorded knowledge, thus even further reducing the need for the analytical skills.

I do not mean to conclude this paper by sounding like a Luddite; but there is a public policy question involved if technology helps to produce unemployment. Perhaps automatic text analysis and classification techniques will be used to stimulate even more thoughtful and creative review and critical analysis of recorded knowledge by revealing relationships not otherwise to be perceived. Perhaps also by the 1980s we may see the way more clearly to attaining the ideal of a user's 'virtual classification of a large information file. That is, by analogy to the 'virtual memory' of the computer time-sharing, the appearance to each user that the file is classified according to relevance to his interests of the moment. The point to advocate is that information science research in the late 1970s should be broadly conceived to take into account possible implications of the expected outcome.

206

REFERENCES

1 UNESCO and ICSU: *UNISIST: synopsis of the feasibility study of a world science information system.* Paris, 1971.

2 Cuadra, C *et al*: 'Technology and libraries', Section C, p 282-341 of Chapter VII in Knight, D M and Nourse, E S *(eds), Libraries at large: tradition, innovation and the national interest.* New York and London, R R Bowker Co, 1969.

3 Cuadra, C: 'On-line systems: Promises and pitfalls', *J ASIS* 22 (2), 1971, p 107-114.

4 Wall, E and Barnes, J: *Intersystem compatibility and convertibility of subject vocabularies.* Aaerbach Corp, Philadelphia, Technical Report 1582-100-TR-5, 1969.

5 Surace, C: *The displays of a thesaurus.* Rand Corp, Santa Monica, Calif. Report P-4331. March 1970.

6 Klingbiel, P H: *The future of indexing and retrieval vocabularies.* Defense Documentation Center Report DDC-TR-70-4, Alexandria, Va, November 1970. (AD 716 200).

7 Batty, C D: 'The automatic generation of index languages'. *Journal of Documentation,* 25(2), June 1969, p 142-151.

8 Sparck Jones, K: 'Automatic thesaurus construction and the relation of a thesaurus to indexing terms'. *Aslib proceedings, 22* (5), May 1970, p 226-228.

9 Lowe, T C and Roberts, D C: *On-line retrieval.* Informatics Inc, Bethesda, Md, Report RADC-TR-70-44. April 1970.

10 US Patent Office, Washington, DC, Office of Research and Development: *Computer-aided classification: report of the planning committee.* August 1 1970, p 137. Report No COM-71-00181.

11 Cuadra, C *et al*: p 615 *in* Knight and Nourse, *op cit.*

12 George, R L: *Automatic selective documentation services.* Defense Documentation Center, Alexandria, Va, Report DDC-TR-71-4. March 1971. AD722 425. Especially pages 8, 15, 27-28, 46.

13 Brown, W S and Traub, J F: 'MERCURY: a system for computer-aided distribution of technical reports'. *J assoc computing machinery, 16* (1), Jan 1969, p 13-25.

14 Bierman, K J: 'An operating MARC-based SDI system: some preliminary services and user reactions'. *Proc Am Soc information Sci, 7,* 1970, p 87-89.

15 Bierman, K J and Blue, B J: 'A MARC-based SDI service'. *J library automation, 3* (4), Dec 1970, p 304-319.

16 Eyre, J J: 'Structure and handling of MARC files for the AMCOS update programs'. *Program: news of computers in libraries, 4* (1), Jan 1970, p 30-41.

17 *GIBUS.* Brochure distributed by l'Association française des documentalistes et des bibliothecaires spécialisés. Oct 1970.

18 Beyssac, R: 'Utilisation de la CDU en recherche documentaire à la Bibliothèque des Halles à Paris'. *Proceedings of the 2nd seminar on UDC and mechanized information systems, Frankfurt (Main), June 1-5 1970.* Published as an FID/CR Report by the Danish Centre for Documentation in 1971.

19 Rigby, M: 'Computers and the UDC: a decade of progress, 1960-1970'. Presented at the International Federation for Documentation, 35th Congress, Buenos Aires, September 14-24 1970. Revised June 1971 for publication by FID in 1971.

20 McCash, W H and Carmichael, J J: 'UDC user profiles as developed for a computer-based SDI service for the iron and steel industry'. *Journal of Documentation,* 26(4), Dec 1970, p 295-312.

21 Gupta, B S S: 'Program package for a system for document finding'. *Library science (India), 7* (2), June 1970, p 179-191.
22 Hersey, D F *et al:* 'Conceptual indexing and retrieval of current research records: an analysis of problems and progress in a large scale information system'. *Methods of information in medicine, 7* (3), July 1968, p 172-187.
23 Brown, T B and Sinkey, L O: *ISR-1: information storage and retrieval system: an architectural information classification system and computerized data storage and retrieval system.* Computer-Aided Design Laboratory, Dept of Architectural Engineering, Pennsylvania State University, University Park, Report 69-3, April 1 1969. PB 192 830.
24 Schneider, J H: 'Experimental trial of selective dissemination of biomedical information in an automated system based on a linear hierarchical decimal classification'. *Proc Am soc information sci, 5,* 1968, p 243-245.
25 Schneider, J H: 'Selective dissemination and indexing of scientific information'. *Science, 173*(3994), July 23, 1971, p 300-308.
26 Troller, C E: *Comparative performance of two indexing languages for an operating information system: measurement of differences in content and construction.* Knolls Atomic Power Laboratory, Schenectady, New York, Report No KAPL-M-7056. June 1969, 100 pages.
27 Mercier, M, Heaps, D S and Cooke, G A: *The study of UDC and other indexing languages through computer manipulation of machine-readable data bases.* Preprint of a paper presented at the International Symposium on UDC in Relation to Other Indexing Languages, Herceg Novi, Yugoslavia, June 28-July 1, 1971.

Automatic classification

KAREN SPARCK JONES
Computer Laboratory,
Cambridge University, England

EDITOR'S INTRODUCTION: I welcome the one entirely new contri-
bution to this edition as the literature on automatic classification, or
'classification without classifiers' as I once heard it described, has grown
greatly and much of it is highly technical, whereas the present paper
assumes that the reader is not already very familiar with the subject.
Dr Sparck Jones, herself an active researcher and writer in this area, now
reviews some applications and experiments, keeping on-line situations in
mind. She proves to be relatively pessimistic concerning the more
immediate prospects of the classification that is statistically derived.

In 1976, the status of automatic information classification is unclear.
The suggestion that automatic, statistically-based techniques should be
used for classifying information entities (index terms, documents, journals, etc) was first made in the late nineteen fifties, and a good deal of
work has been done in this area since. Automatic classification has not,
however, been adopted in operational information systems. The choice
and application of automatic methods for classification are still problems for research, and their value for different library purposes, and particularly document retrieval, is still unknown. The character and direction of classification research have also changed since 1960, partly because
computational classification itself presented more problems than was
first recognised, and partly because general classification theory did not
provide appropriate tools; but mainly because the detailed properties and
requirements of retrieval systems were found to be ill-understood, so the
specifications to be met by classifications as parts of such systems could
not be provided.

This chapter reviews the main lines of work on automatic information
classification to date, and the prospects for automatic classification, particularly in the large, on-line retrieval systems of the future. I shall first consider briefly classification procedures in themselves, secondly their

application in the context of information systems, and thirdly the results of experiments in automatic information classification, and their implications. To anchor the discussion I shall start with two examples of hypothetical automatic information classifications and their use. These illustrate particular choices of classification data, grouping procedure, application, and evaluation. The rest of the paper is essentially concerned with the range of possibilities under each of these heads, and the extent to which they have been explored.

Example A: an automatic thesaurus
We take all the non-function words in the abstracts of a set of documents and select from them all those occurring more than once per abstract. We then compute coefficients of resemblance between these keywords, indicating their tendency to co-occur in abstracts: this is presumably correlated with a stable semantic relationship. We define resemblance as the ratio between the co-occurrences and total occurrences of the words. We then form classes of keywords by taking all sets of words in which each member has a resemblance greater than .5 to some other member. The resulting classes of strongly related words form index descriptors, which are used in searching to promote recall by allowing matches between one word member in a request and another in a document.

Example B: a journal selection system
We take a sample of journal issues from our present library input. For each paper in these we list the journals cited. We then obtain cited journal pair resemblance coefficients using, say, simple co-citation frequency; and we rank, for each journal, the other journals linked to it by descending order of resemblance. We apply a cutoff to the lists, perhaps after the top 5, and examine the resulting groupings to see how well our current journal intake reflects the actual status of journals in the subject fields concerned. Thus if we fail to take the most cited journal in a group, we should perhaps start to subscribe to it.

Classification procedures
There is by now a large literature on classification theory and processes, of a fairly technical character. My treatment here will be deliberately informal as it is intended merely to provide sufficient background to clarify the subsequent account of information applications and experiments. (1)

210

Statistical classification techniques, or more broadly, association techniques, are concerned solely with the distributional behaviour of the items to be grouped, for example the occurrence and co-occurrence of symptoms in patients, or of citations in documents. The characterisation of these procedures is couched quite generally in terms of objects and properties, ie. things having associations or forming groups on the basis of their property descriptions. Objects may, in fact, be genuine individuals, or logical individuals representing samples or collections. Properties may be qualitative, ie. yes/no, or quantitative, eg. x percent, y percent. Clearly, over the whole range of application of general classification methods, there are many questions to consider concerning the status and independence of both objects and properties. Fortunately, in information classification the situation is usually fairly simple, with qualitative properties all of one kind.

Though classes may be formed directly from the initial property descriptions of the objects, most classification techniques depend on an initial computation of resemblance or similarity co-efficients defining the relation between each pair of objects, which are then exploited to identify groups of mutually similar objects. In this case the statistical associations between objects are first defined at a simple level, and then at a more complex one; these levels provide dispersed and concentrated information respectively about the set of objects being classified, as the first refers to separate pairs of objects, and the second to groups taken together. (The expression "statistical associations" sometimes refers to both similarity and class relations, sometimes to the former only; "statistical classification" clearly implies the latter.)

We may characterise classification techniques from three points of view, as follows:

a) how properties and classes are related:

is the possession of one or more specific properties necessary to class membership, or is it sufficient that each member shares some properties with some other members?

b) how objects and classes are related:

is membership of classes exclusive, ie. is an object restricted to one class, or can objects appear in several classes?

c) how classes are related:

is there an ordering relation between classes, or are classes treated as wholly independent of one another?

In principle, the possibilities under each of these heads can be freely combined with those under the others, to define what may be called a type of classification. Thus for example, we may have classes with each member sharing properties with some but not necessarily all of the other members, which are not exclusive, and which are not related by any kind of ordering.

This typology characterises classifications only in a very general way. Each type can cover a whole range of formal definitions of object pair similarity and of class. The many definitions of similarity to be found in the literature include, for instance, Dice's co-efficient and cosine correlation, either of which would be appropriate to the measurement of similarity for classes of the type just mentioned. There is also a large choice of specific ways of defining a class: for example, classes may be defined as "cliques", or maximally connected subgraphs of the similarity graph, or as "clumps", ie. relatively well connected subgraphs. Again, either of these definitions would lead to classes of the kind described in the previous paragraph. For a comprehensive survey of approaches to classification, see Sneath and Sokal. (2)

At a lower level, different algorithms may be developed for finding classes according to a given definition. A number of procedures for finding cliques have been proposed, for instance. Translating a class definition into a class-finding program is not always a trivial matter, and good algorithms are needed for the complete classification of large numbers of objects.

Automatic classification

In the last fifteen years a great deal of work has been done on classification: computers have made classification on a large scale possible, and have stimulated theoretical and experimental research; but they have emphasised the need for fully adequate definitions which can be applied without any tacit reliance on the knowledge or intuition of the human classifier. Theoretical progress has been made, and substantial experience obtained, but it is not the case that a well-organised theory of classification and battery of definitions with supporting grouping programs exist, from which anyone attempting classification in a particular area like information retrieval can readily draw the techniques that he needs.

Of course, formal statistically-based classification methods do not in themselves require computers. But they can be very naturally applied automatically. Equally, computers have encouraged statistical rather than 'conceptual' approaches to classification. Thus in areas where
212

automatic classification is attempted, including information retrieval, this may be associated with changes in the view of classification itself: classification is seen as an *a posteriori* processing of a large amount of elementary data, where the power of the computer allows very complex procedures for building up a classification from many bits of information about individual objects. Even where the process is in fact quite simple, there is a real or felt difference between automatic and manual classification in that the computer can be more exhaustive and comprehensive than the human classifier. The penalty in mechanisation is that the classification can only be derived from the explicitly stated properties of the objects: so the intended purport of the classification must be consonant with the initial property data. This is not always easily achieved: for example, since word meanings are not directly accessible to computers, some assumption is required to the effect that property descriptions of words in other terms, eg. their textual behaviour, are related to their meanings and hence can be used to generate a meaning classification. Clearly, property descriptions become simpler or more obvious, there may be more difficulty in showing that they are an appropriate or adequate means of access to the underlying structure of the data. Thus, coincidence of words in whole texts may be only weakly correlated with their semantic relationships.

More generally, while all the essential points about classification apply in principle to manual and automatic classification alike, automatic classification differs from manual in practice because the computer is a mindless, strictly consistent black box. This means that all the information required for classification must be explicitly supplied, and that all the operations to be applied to it must be fully specified. The grouping procedures will be rigorously carried through, using exactly the given data: for good or ill, ad hoc responses and intuitive inferences are excluded. Again word classification illustrates the point: a human being classifying words can be expected to exploit his extensive linguistic knowledge, on the one hand avoiding procedurally forced mistakes, but on the other supplementing his initial information and adapting his class criteria to produce a sensible result. The application of purely mechanical procedures increases the separation between the input and output of the classification process, between the supplied data and choice of grouping technique on the one hand, and the resulting classification on the other. While this separation of input and output is in principle also a problem for manual classification, it is perhaps underestimated there because the classing process itself is observed. The computer tends to sharpen the question: have you got what you wanted?

Applying classification techniques to information management
For information management, as in other practical applications of general classification methods, it is necessary to make a choice of objects and, more importantly, of properties appropriate to the specific purpose for which classification is required; and equally, to select a type of classification and particular class definition suited to this purpose. It is important to recognise that a practical objective like document retrieval imposes an additional constraint on classification, and hence on automatic classification. We require not only that the object-property data we use should be appropriate to the general character desired of the classification, but that this character itself should match the purpose for which classification is required. Thus if our object is to promote recall, we may argue that a classification of keywords to form synonym groups is required, and that these in turn can be obtained from document context incidence information about the words. Clearly, the further the ultimate purpose is from the initial data, the more chance there is of a faulty argument, and the more difficulty there is in locating the source of failure. This has, for example, been the experience of those attempting automatic retrieval thesaurus construction.

A truly comprehensive classification theory would incorporate some specification of the links between the formal requirements of concrete purposes and classification procedures; but such a theory does not exist. In any case, the difficulties of translating rather broadly or informally couched statements of purpose needs (for example that a term classification should promote the retrieval of relevant documents) into formal ones are considerable. Research workers in information retrieval have increasingly found that this, rather than the choice of one class definition as opposed to another, is their main problem in attempting automatic classification. It is, of course, one which is encountered by anyone trying to understand or improve document organisation and retrieval systems, but it is compounded by the limited information sources readily available for classification, and restricted range of well-founded grouping procedures, which increase the difficulty of evaluating any classification which is constructed. Further, since the only proper method of evaluating classifications for such purposes as document retrieval is by testing them in use, and this presents substantial problems in the control of system variables and measurement of system performance, it will be
214

evident that determining the effectiveness of such classifications is a major crux. Research on automatic classification for information management and retrieval is necessarily related to work on information system characterisation and evaluation over the past fifteen years. There has been some progress in system understanding and the design of retrieval experiments, but in the one case not enough to determine the prerequisites for classification, and in the other not enough to support unequivocal statements about classification test results.

Retrieval system environments for classification
The work which has been done on automatic information classification must also be considered in the context of the great changes in operational information systems in the last fifteen years. While a great many libraries have continued, and will naturally continue, because of their small scale and limited resources, to run on traditional manual lines, there have been striking developments in the use of computers for library purposes. (I refer here to their use for indexing and searching rather than purely clerical operations.) Some very large computer-based systems are now operational. Automatic classification would appear to be a natural component of a large scale mechanised system, both because it requires substantial computing resources, and because it fits neatly into a system in which human beings are replaced by machines. But the situation is more complicated because an important use of computers is for on-line searching, ie. computer systems are exploited to remove drudgery from the human user, rather than to act as a substitute. These systems are either restricted to the simplest information, or incorporate, eg. manually constructed index languages. Automatic classifications could nevertheless in principle form parts of such systems, particularly since much of the data needed to construct them is easily obtained in a mechanised system.

Approaches to automatic information classification
Against this background, we can now consider different approaches to automatic information classification and their implications.

Automatic classification techniques may be applied to any of the obvious information entities: index terms (natural or controlled language), documents, citations, journals, authors; and indeed experiments have been carried out with most of these. Properties readily available for characterising them, and suited to automatic manipulation, come from the same list: terms, documents, citations, journals, and authors may equally figure as properties on which classification can be based. For example,

215

terms may be grouped by documents and by authors, citations by documents, by journals, and by authors, documents by terms, citations, journals and authors. Further refinement is possible: thus we may distinguish document sentences and classification may be extended to, eg. users, and libraries. But most experiments have been carried out with the more obvious entities and properties like indexing terms or documents, the latter via surrogates like titles or abstracts.

Clearly, the choice of object and property for classification is determined by the purpose for which the classification is needed. In some cases the choice is obvious: for example if a keyword thesaurus is to be created automatically, the initial information will consist of text words characterised by their occurrences in some document unit like a title or abstract. However, for some purposes which may be rather broadly specified, like document classification to reduce false drops, the best choice of property from the range available may not be obvious: for instance both terms and citations have been proposed as suitable properties for bringing co-relevant documents together. The specific set of objects and properties chosen may in any case be a subset of those available of the kind: for instance, a classification of words by their distribution in document titles might not include all the words, typically excluding stop words, but also other very common or rare content words; similarly, the subset of title words may be used as a property set for grouping the documents represented.

The purposes for which automatic information classification has been attempted have varied. Thus keyword classification has been undertaken to provide a search thesaurus, and to provide supporting information for organising a manual controlled indexing language. In the first case, too, the detailed objective may have been to provide recall-oriented higher level descriptors, or to lead to precision-oriented term combinations. Document clustering has been proposed primarily to focus searching, or to reduce file scanning.

The underlying motives for automatic classification have also differed, as some of the examples just mentioned suggest. From this point of view, experiments in automatic classification may be grouped under three heads: automatic classification may be aimed primarily at improving system, and especially retrieval, effectiveness; at increasing economic efficiency; and at obtaining sociological information. Thus an automatic keyword classification may be proposed as a device for achieving greater retrieval effectiveness by exploiting information about the actual behaviour of document words which is not readily identified and easily
216

managed by the maker of a manual thesaurus. Classification as an economic enterprise is best seen in document clustering: as exhaustive, and particularly iterated, scanning of very large files is expensive, searches should be confined to likely subfiles. Technological advances may make this a less important reason for clustering, but searching subfiles is cheaper than searching full ones. (The general point applies whether the basic file is serial or inverted.) What I have called sociological classification is intended to provide information about libraries or literature, their sources and uses. For example it has been argued that citation clusters can throw light on the development and structure of knowledge. Of course system data gathered under the third head may subsequently be exploited to improve system effectiveness or efficiency. Equally, material and practical considerations may coincide: for instance document clustering may be advocated on the grounds that it contributes to both effectiveness and efficiency.

It will be evident that an automatic classification may or may not be part of an automatic information system. In some cases automatic classification provides a data representation which is itself exploited automatically: an example is a keyword classification intended for use in automatic request or document characterisation and matching. In other cases an automatically generated classification may be designed for manual use, for instance a classification exhibiting term relations as a reference tool for indexers. Automatic classification may indeed have a very limited role in the guise of automatically sustained manual classification: for example, if a manual categorisation of some documents is available, statistical correlations between text words and manual category labels may be established which can be exploited to assign the labels to new documents.

When this variety of data, purposes, motivations, and environments is taken together with that of statistical association structures, ranging from sets of simple lists, or semi-classifications, to full classes, it is evident that automatic information classification has many options. Indeed experiments in this area have been very heterogeneous and are difficult to evaluate and compare. There have been very few tests sufficiently similar in objectives and execution to support firm conclusions about the value of automatic classification in particular contexts; and more generally work has been spread so thinly over the whole ground that an overall view of the actual or potential utility of automatic classification can hardly be attempted. In the next section, major or illustrative experiments are briefly described, and an attempt is made to summarise their implications.

217

But it must be borne in mind throughout that the conclusions to be drawn even about particular approaches to classification must be tentative: in the few cases where the same procedure has been applied to different data bases (collections of documents, requests and relevant judgements) it may perform differently, for non-obvious reasons; so the results of any individual experiments must be treated with caution.

Automatic classification experiments

Early work on automatic classification, primarily of index keywords, is recorded in Stevens. (3, 4) This research was derived essentially from Luhn's idea that statistical keyword distribution patterns, which can be identified computationally, reflect semantic relationships and hence can be validly exploited to group terms or documents. The work was mostly on an extremely small scale and lacked proper evaluation of the automatic classifications produced, particularly for retrieval effectiveness. It merely demonstrated the feasibility of automatic classification and the visual plausibility, or comparability with manual grouping, of its output. Many of the experiments were aimed at term grouping, and the classes were therefore deemed satisfactory if, for example, they consisted of synonymically or generically related words.

By the later sixties it became evident that some of the apparently obvious ideas on which automatic classification was based were not well-founded: for example that a recall oriented classification should consist of synonyms; and that some of the techniques investigated, like factor analysis, were computationally exigent. Further, it was recognised that automatic classifications designed for specific purposes, like retrieval, must be properly tested for effectiveness. Classification experiments were therefore implicated in the wider evaluation of retrieval systems in general exemplified by the Cranfield project. Work in the second half of the sixties was thus directed at clarifying the role of automatic classifications, in developing practical classification algorithms, and in studying the behaviour of classifications as components of retrieval systems. (5)

a Term classification

The main experiments in this period were carried out by Dennis (6), Jones and Curtice (7, 8), Salton and Lesk (9, 10), Vaswani (11), Minker (12), and Sparck Jones (13, 14). Some of the tests were quite large. For example, Dennis worked with 7000 keywords and 5000 documents, and Vaswani with 1000 keyword stems and 12000 document

218

abstracts. Salton and Lesk, Minker, and Sparck Jones carried out tests on more than one collection, and Sparck Jones investigated a large number of classificatory procedures. Some tests like Jones and Curtice's involved controlled language terms rather than keywords. In these tests taken together a whole range of questions were investigated: for example, whether first-order (direct) or second-order (indirect) associations between terms are most informative, whether full as opposed to semiclassification pays its rent, what sort of class, whether tight or loose, is needed, whether statistical classifications are more useful as recall or as precision devices, and so on.

In those experiments involving adequate retrieval performance measurement there was considerable variation in the value of the classifications studied. Taking the best option for each individual project, performance for classified terms, typically measured by recall and precision, ranged from no improvement to a modest one of about 10%. The best approaches seemed to limit classification to less frequent terms, in order to limit false drops through substitution, and to restrict groups to terms with high mutual similarity, to ensure a genuine text-based relationship. Simple request expansion strategies, allowing extra words to function as substitutes or coordinate specifiers, worked as well as any. It is of interest that, compared with manual classifications, most statistical association techniques generate semantically less obvious, (but on inspection well-grounded), rather mixed classes or words, which seem to be as effective as the more homogeneous manual ones. It also appeared that different class definitions were not necessarily correlated with performance differences.

In general, these results seemed very disappointing. Earlier doubts about the practicability of automatic classification on a large scale for operational systems were replaced by doubts as to its real value. In fact this may be due to uncertainty as to the exact function of a term classification. Manual thesauri are naturally multi-purpose, but it is not clear how an automatic classification based on distributional information can or should mimic a manual classification. It is also not clear exactly how the character and effectiveness of a classification is determined by the various distributional characteristics of a collection, including the frequency distribution of terms, and their incidence in requests as well as documents. Thus in those cases in particular where a classification is intended to have a specific character and effect it is difficult to ensure that it has. But more generally, these experiments cannot be taken as clear evidence for or against the retrieval value of automatic term

219

classifications because the test findings simply reproduce many others obtained in this period. The many retrieval tests carried out from 1960 onwards have shown that large changes in retrieval systems may have surprisingly little effect, and in particular that great variation in the index language used may have little impact on retrieval performance. Those workers interested in automatic classification have, therefore, been driven to the same depressing conclusion as other information retrieval research workers, namely that the behaviour of retrieval systems is very poorly understood.

The experiments described were aimed mainly at forming automatic term classifications intended to form parts of fully-automated retrieval systems. Work on grouping index terms has also been undertaken to provide human indexing aids, whether in the form of providing information for improving vocabulary control, or for assisting indexing. Thus Gotlieb and Kumar investigated LC heading associations for the purposes of vocabulary control. (15) Associative information may also be supplied as a reference aid to the on-line searcher, as in Jones and Curtice's system.

Rather little work on automatic term classification is currently in progress: the emphasis has been shifted on the one hand to methods of manipulating the index term vocabulary by, for example, statistical weighting, which appears to be quite effective, and on the other to classifying documents automatically.

b Document classification

Research on automatic document classification or clustering, as it is frequently called, got under way in the mid sixties. The initial motive was economic, namely to restrict searching to subfiles of a whole large collection. However, document clustering may also be justified intellectually as a means of concentrating like documents and hence improving the chances of retrieving only relevant documents.

Documents may of course be clustered by terms, but experiments have also been carried out using citations as descriptive properties. In document clustering the type of classification required is rather different from that of term grouping: overlapping classes, which are a natural response to different term meanings or uses, are at a discount. The main difference encountered in experimental work is between a simple one-level partitioning of the document set, and a hierarchy. Document classification presents evaluation problems not met with term classification: if only subsets of the whole document set are searched, and

220

performance measurements are based on these, it is not obvious how measurements derived from different size subsets are to be compared. Document clustering also involves an additional step, in that when classes have been formed they must be provided with some characterising tag, for use in searching.

The SMART project workers under Salton have conducted a wide variety of term-based document clustering experiments, mainly with rather crude partitioning techniques in which documents are grouped round 'cores'. (16) In general retrieval performance compared with full file searches has been poor, but it is claimed that the reduced search effort is adequate compensation. Experiments with hierarchies have been carried out by Litofsky (17) and by van Rijsbergen. (18, 19) Litofsky's tests were on a very large scale involving nearly 50000 documents; but unfortunately, though the classification was intended for browsing during searching, it was only evaluated by comparison with a manual classification on a range of structural properties, with apparently satisfactory results. Van Rijsbergen's single-link classifications have been designed for automatic searching, and performance compared with full search for a number of collections has been quite competitive. Experiments with citations as properties have been carried out by Schiminovich (20), to obtain a partitioning: the results were judged good by comparison with a manual subject classification.

Document clustering is currently an active field of research and has not reached the impasse of term classification. In particular, work is in progress on large collections. It seems to be the case that document clustering can be superimposed on a system in a way that is not possible with a term classification; experiments do not therefore require that understanding of the relationship between different system components that has been found necessary for term classification. With computer developments, on the other hand, document classification is less obviously an economic necessity, and is more attractive as a device for cutting down output from very large files.

As mentioned earlier, document classification, particularly using citations, has been investigated for other reasons than retrieval system organisation: Small and others, in particular, (21, 22) have conducted substantial experiments designed to throw light on the structure of the literature of a science. Such studies have a natural history character, and are thus rather difficult to evaluate.

Some experiments have also been carried out in grouping other information entities, like journals; but these have generally been of a limited

221

character, and are therefore mentioned only to show that classification work has not been confined to terms and documents.

Dynamic classification

So far, I have tacitly treated classification as a once-off operation. But this is clearly unrealistic. Both a natural language keyword classification, and much more obviously a document clustering, would have to be updated as a document collection grows. The problem indeed applies to any classification which is required to reflect fairly accurately, because it is in continual use, a continuously changing data base of distributional information. Clearly, complete reclassification is not generally feasible for every new keyword or document, but the extent to which classifications can be modified in a non-arbitrary or non-effortful way is limited, some types being more hospitable than others. Some experiments in updating document clusterings by relatively crude methods have been carried out, for example by Murray (23), which showed that classifications may not be very sensitive to ad hoc alterations; but there have been no real studies of appropriate strategies for updating classifications not amenable to gradual but consistent change.

The phrase "dynamic classification" has, however, another interpretation, as reclassification of a given data set in response to further information obtained from its use. For example, information about the occurrence of terms in queries, or about the relevance and non-relevance of documents with respect to queries, may be exploited. Experimental work showing that such strategies can improve classification performance has been carried out by the SMART project. (24) Classification modification could clearly be of value in interactive search systems. Another form of dynamic classification suited to on-line searching might be the construction of 'personal' classifications of items selected from a neutral data file or structure, to reflect the particular interests of an individual system user. For example, given a term classification reflecting the behaviour of index terms in the filed documents, some may be selected, and their association increased, by their co-occurrence in a request.

Present situation and future prospects

As noted, there is little current research in automatic classification; there is most interest in automatic document clustering, but this is not a widespread topic of research. This modest level of effort is perhaps surprising, given that the use of computers for information systems is now common, so the practical problems which concerned early workers

222

are now unimportant. One reason for the lack of effort may be that research workers have been discouraged by the dearth of solid findings; indeed research workers have to face the problem of constantly rising experimental expectations: as fast as they conduct experiments, the requirements for methodological soundness and operational relevance become more exigent; the latter in particular means that as operational systems grow, the scale of experiments must increase, and this is extremely costly.

But there is, perhaps a more fundamental reason for the lack of research. In the nineteen sixties it was believed that the use of computers would in some way allow novel approaches to retrieval systems, and in particular to the treatment of standard system components like index languages. Interest in statistically-based automatic classification was one manifestation of this. Since 1970, advanced information technology has developed primarily in one direction, towards the searching of very large files on-line. In one way, this is simply mechanising old-fashioned library use, though the sheer speed of scanning available does allow the user options which are closed to manual systems. Concentration on the interface with the user, on the other hand, has meant that other system components have either simply been taken over from manual systems, or more usually, have been progressively simplified. Thus in some cases manual thesauri continue to be used, while in others the searcher is provided in a straightforward way with titles and word lists, etc, supported by frequency counts, truncation options, and the like. It is assumed that any defects in these sources of information about the filed documents, particularly in the second case, are offset by the range of search keys, and the speed with which batteries of them can be assembled, or journeys through the system can be made.

These systems have in one sense overtaken research, partly for the scale reason mentioned, but also because proper methods for carrying out experiments involving on-line searching have yet to be developed. But in my view such large files call for more sophisticated, ie. classificatory, forms of control than are currently supplied with them. More generally, we still lack an adequate understanding of retrieval systems. When this has been achieved we may be in a better position to address ourselves to automatic, statistical classification: for this appears to offer some distinctive advantages, in that it can take account of the kind of information about the actual behaviour of information entities like terms or documents in a system which is not readily grasped by the human indexer or searcher, and can characterise the data in a direct and transparent way.

223

It must thus be said that the apparent prospects for automatic classification for library purposes are not very bright: appropriate methods and applications of classification have not been established. However, classification is a general requirement of information management; and as automatic classification has not been conclusively shown to be unhelpful compared with human classification, its longer term prospects, though uncertain, should be of interest to those concerned with information systems.

REFERENCES
1 For a fuller treatment, see Sparck Jones, K: 'Some thoughts on classification for retrieval'. *Journal of documentation,* 26, 1970, p 89-101.
2 Sneath, P H A and Sokal, R R: *Numerical taxonomy.* San Francisco, Freeman, 1973.
3 Stevens, M E: *Automatic indexing: a state of the art report.* Monograph 91, National Bureau of Standards, Washington D.C., 1965.
4 Stevens, M E, Heilprin, L and Giuliano, V E (Eds.): *Statistical association methods for mechanised documentation.* National Bureau of Standards, Washington D.C., 1965.
5 A detailed account of this research is given in Sparck Jones, K: *Automatic indexing 1974.* Computer Laboratory, University of Cambridge, 1974.
6 Dennis, S F: 'The design and testing of a fully automated indexing-searching system for documents consisting of expository text' in Schechter (Ed.): *Information retrieval—a critical view.* Washington D.C., Thompson, 1967.
7 Jones, P E *et al: Application of statistical association techniques to the NASA document collection.* A D Little Inc., Cambridge, Mass., 1968.
8 Curtice, R M and Jones, P E: *An operational interactive retrieval system.* A D Little Inc., Cambridge, Mass., 1969.
9 Salton, G and Lesk, M E: 'Computer evaluation of indexing and text processing'. *Journal of the ACM,* 15, 1968, p 8-36.
10 Lesk, M E: 'Word-word associations in document retrieval systems'. *American documentation,* 20, 1969, p 27-38.
11 Vaswani, P K T and Cameron, J B: *The National Physical Laboratory experiments in statistical word associations and their use in document indexing and retrieval.* National Physical Laboratory, Teddington, 1970.
12 Minker, J, Wilson, G A and Zimmerman, B H: 'An evaluation of query expansion by the addition of clustered terms for a document retrieval system'. *Information storage and retrieval,* 8, 1972, p 329-348.
13 Sparck Jones, K: *Automatic keyword classification for information retrieval.* London, Butterworths; Hamden, Conn, Archon Books, 1971.
14 Sparck Jones, K: 'Collection properties influencing automatic term classification performance'. *Information storage and retrieval,* 9, 1973, p 499-513.
15 Gotlieb, C C and Kumar, S: 'Semantic clustering of index terms'. *Journal of the ACM,* 15, 1968, p 493-513.
16 Salton, G (Ed.): *The SMART retrieval system: experiments in automatic document processing.* Englewood Cliffs, N.J., Prentice-Hall, 1971.
17 Litofsky, B: *Utility of automatic classification systems for information storage and retrieval.* Thesis, University of Pennsylvania, 1969.

18 van Rijsbergen, C J: 'Further experiments with hierarchic clustering in document retrieval'. *Information storage and retrieval,* 10, 1974, p 1-14.

19 van Rijsbergen, C J: *Information retrieval.* London, Butterworths, 1975.

20 Schiminovich, S: 'Automatic classification and retrieval of documents by means of a bibliographic pattern discovery algorithm'. *Information storage and retrieval,* 6, 1971, p 417-435.

21 Small, H and Griffith, B C: 'The structure of scientific literatures. I. Identifying and graphing specialities'. *Science studies,* 4, 1974, p 17-40.

22 Griffith, B C *et al:* 'The structure of scientific literatures. II. Towards a macro- and microstructure for science'. *Science studies,* 4, 1974, p 339-365.

23 Murray, D M: *Document retrieval based on clustered files.* Thesis, Cornell University, 1972.

24 Salton, G: 'Dynamic document processing'. *Communications of the ACM,* 15, 1972, p 658-668.

Dewey Decimal Classification

SARAH K VANN
Graduate School of Library Studies,
University of Hawaii

EDITOR'S INTRODUCTION: There is criticism, apparent or implied, elsewhere in this volume, of the most used of all the general classifications. However, it survives remarkably well and in the centenary year we depart from the general to special sequence of chapters to close this volume with a study of its achievements and prospects. Professor Vann was director of the survey in the '60s on the use of Dewey abroad and it is indicative of concern for librarian users that plans for Edition 19 cannot be finalized until comments from the more recent study of consumer views in North America have been fully analyzed. In updating the paper, the author has tried, as she explains in a letter to me, 'to bring into focus the remarkable vitality and resurgence of interest which is being manifested in (Dewey) as it enters its second century'.

Before his death, in 1931, when Melvil Dewey was writing of the 'Future of DC', he re-stated his requirements for classification as being:.
'To know where to put a book when it came up and then to know where to find it again whether next day or a century later'. (1)
That 'century later' date is a classificatory event of the '70s, for the year 1976 marks the one hundredth anniversary of the publication of a modest little pamphlet entitled, *A classification and subject index, for cataloging and arranging the books and pamphlets of a library.* (2) On that pamphlet, now considered the first edition of the Dewey Decimal Classification, devised by Melvil Dewey, the bibliographic lineage of succeeding editions is founded. During the centennial year the editions in use are edition 18 (full) and edition 10 (abridged) both of which attest to its durability.

While one may prognosticate about the prospects of Dewey in the '70s, therefore, the reality is that the pattern of growth which has both sustained and imperilled Dewey throughout the varying editions will

226

continue. Thus the '70s cannot be viewed as detached, but merely as the tenth decade in which the Classification flourishes.

Among the enduring characteristics of DDC have been its order of disciplines (subjects), its use of the universally known arabic notation, its decimal structure which permits intercalation of related concepts and varying levels of specificity, its sustained program of revising and updating, and its availability in full and abridged editions. Other characteristics which contribute to making Dewey viable during the '70s and later are:

1 Its pragmatic or realistic development now conjoined with an *a posteriori* molding of a philosophic design, notably purification of the concept of hierarchical subject relationships.

2 Its adaptability for use in libraries of various size and kinds because of its hierarchically expressive notation which permits varying degrees of inclusiveness and exclusiveness within its decimal structure.

3 Its adaptability both for conventional (manual) shelf or classed catalogue analysis and also, through its meaningful notation, for retrieval through mechanization and computerized systems.

4 Its thrust toward an international perspective both in depth of analysis and in adaptability of application.

5 Its endorsement and encouragement of translations.

6 Its use by central bibliographic services and the subsequent availability of classification numbers for specific titles.

Because the Dewey Decimal Classification is enduring, it is likewise vulnerable. Some consideration will be given, therefore, to the following which bear directly on its continuity: (1) 'integrity of notation' and 'integrity of hierarchical subject relationships'; (2) Changes in editions; Aftermath of Edition 15; Later Editions; (3) Dewey notation—its elongation; (4) centralized uses of Dewey; (5) Dewey use . . . Dewey users; (6) internationalizing Dewey within; (7) In the seventies . . . and beyond.

'Integrity of Notation' and 'Integrity of Hierarchical Subject Relationships'

Throughout the decades the *tables* (called *schedules* in edition 18) have reflected so clearly the basic structure of DDC and have remained so consistent that many titles, had they been classified in 1876, would be classified similarly in 1976. Such consistency does not imply inviolate notational meaning, but it does suggest the conflict that could polarize itself between 'maintaining integrity of notation' and 'keeping pace with

227

knowledge' or, more currently, 'maintaining integrity of hierarchical subject relationships' within the confines of the decimal tens.

The origin of the conflict is traceable to edition 2 (1885) wherein Melvil Dewey made what can only be considered excessive readjustments and changes despite his having stated in 1876, only nine years earlier, that the classification was 'unchangeable in its call numbers'. (3)

The revision in edition 2 formed the basis for change and extension which have become increasingly significant in recent editions. Those revisional techniques used by Dewey may be identified as:

1 Transferring parts of topics from one number to another.

2 Transferring whole topics completely.

3 Extending, through adding new headings or enlarging the scope of numbers.

4 Using the 'Divide-like' (now 'Add-to') principle to attain more specificity in subject analysis.

5 Devising special tables such as the 'Form divisions' (now called 'Standard subdivisions') which reflect a characteristic of the presentation of the content.

6 Using notation to the right of the decimal point for detailed aspects of subject, usually but not always hierarchical in relationships.

7 Furthering the mnemonic or fixed faceting concept, for example:

828, 838, 848, etc changed to *827, 837, 847, etc;*
829, 839, etc changed to *828, etc.* (4)

One revision, rarely cited, was Dewey's belated recognition of American literature as distinct from English literature. In separating the two, not only did he succumb to the priority or favoured nation concept, but he also abrogated the meaning of *810-819,* as outlined in 1876, and redesigned the division to represent American literature. Further, he transferred *in toto* the original analysis of *810-819* to the decimal expansion *808.1-808.9*

Having made extensive relocations and having experimented with most of the techniques even now used in revisional activities, Melvil Dewey assured his actual and potential users that the meanings of the numbers were 'settled'. (5) Equally important is that he also acknowledged that the numbers were 'not *likely* to be again altered' (italics mine). While there have been changes and additions since edition 2, it was not until edition 15 that such extensive alterations were made that the implications of the tradition of stability of notation were magnified. While no edition has extended its restructuring beyond that done at the divisional level *(810)* in edition 2, two techniques which involve substantial revision have been devised since 1885. These are: (1) use of alternate analysis such as,

228

for example, the alternate scheme for psychology based on *159.9* in edition 13; (2) use of a 'phoenix schedule' whereby a division is completely restructured, though the essential meaning of the division remains the same. Examples of the latter appear in edition 17 in *150* (Psychology) and in edition 18 in *340* (Law) and *510* (Mathematics).

The response to the conflict between integrity of notation and integrity of hierarchical subject relationships seems to have begun to lessen in intensity through recognition of the unavoidability of a reasonable compromise if the Classification is to be useful. That it had lessened by the time edition 18 was published in 1971 is evident for that edition simply states that 'the schedules are based on the principle of subject integrity' without attempting to justify that emphasis. Assurance is given, however, that re-use of vacated numbers is held 'to an absolute minimum' except for a 'phoenix' or a completely re-designed division.

Changes in Editions: Aftermath of Edition 15

A sustained pattern of revision, such as that of the Dewey Decimal Classification, invites in turn a continuing program of evaluation by critics and users. Widely divergent appraisals have been made throughout the years, an early one being that expressed at the conference of librarians in London, 1877. At that time the Classification was praised as being 'easy to be worked by the librarian, convenient for the reader, and thoroughly philosophical in principle'. (6) While all the criticisms have not been equally complimentary (7), it was not until edition 15 appeared in 1951 that the continuation of the Classification was in jeopardy. Its demise was assumed by the author of *Epitaph to a dead classification.* (8) It was found wanting by the profession generally, yet some members of the profession had been advocating since 1933 that a 'standard' edition be made available. It can be assumed that the implications involved in the preparation of such an edition were not anticipated, for when edition 15, known as the Standard (fifteenth) edition appeared, the 31,444 numbers in edition 14 had been reduced to a total of 4,621. (9) Not even the publication of the Standard (fifteenth) edition revised (1953) under the editorship *pro temps* of Dr Godfrey Dewey, son of Melvil Dewey, was sufficient to counter the unfavourable response to the reduction in the *tables* and to the *index*. Among the noteworthy accomplishments of the revision, nevertheless, was a 'completely restructured' (10) relative index which more than doubled the size of the drastically modified original effort.

Additional background information on the events leading to the publication of the Standard (fifteenth) edition and some of the consequences were vividly detailed in 1956 by Verner W Clapp, then chairman of the Decimal Classification editorial policy committee, in his *Progress towards the 16th edition of Dewey*. (11) Meanwhile it can simply be noted that the epitaph proved to be premature indeed! Nevertheless the miscalculation compelled changes in the editorial program and policies which had sufficed for the earlier editions.

Among the changes which have had a continuing impact on the development of DDC are:

1 Creating of the Decimal Classification editorial policy committee in 1955 as a joint committee of the Lake Placid Education Foundation and the American Library Association. (12) While the committee was entrusted originally with the responsibility for the editorial policy of DDC, after the publication of edition 17 in 1965, the scope of the responsibility was changed from 'control of the editorial policy of the Dewey Decimal Classification' to that of an 'advisory body, to make recommendations to Forest Press with respect to editorial policy for the Classification'. (13)

2 Transferring of the administration of the editorial office to the Library of Congress by the Forest Press under a contractual agreement whereby Forest Press assumed editorial costs. The transfer was effective on January 4, 1954. The endorsement by the Division of Cataloging and Classification of the American Library Association of the transfer was assured since the division, with the concurrence of the Forest Press, had requested in 1953 the Library of Congress to undertake the preparation of edition 16. (14)

3 Combining the Decimal Classification Section, Subject Cataloging Division, and the Dewey Decimal Classification Editorial Office, both at the Library of Congress, into a unified Decimal Classification Office (15), known since 1968 as the Decimal Classification Division. Such a merger has permitted the same staff both to edit and to apply the Classification practically through assigning DDC numbers to specific titles catalogued by the Library of Congress.

Edition 16

During the six years that elapsed before the publication of edition 16 there was a search for new directions, for specifications and for criteria. Mr Clapp in his *Progress towards the 16th edition of Dewey*, earlier cited, has recorded that search, the contributions of the special advisory committee on DC, created by the Division of Cataloging and Classification of the American Library Association, in 1955, and the assumption of
230

responsibility by the Decimal Classification Editorial Policy Committee with its decision to proceed with the criteria as revised in 1955.

Before the completion of edition 16, users of the Classification were informed of its new features by Benjamin A Custer, editor, in *A preview and report to the profession.* (16) In 1958, the appearance of edition 16 itself confirmed the survival of Dewey. It was the first edition to be published following the association of the Forest Press with the Decimal Classification Editorial Policy Committee and the Library of Congress. Whatever its strengths, its faults and limitations, many of which have been noted in reviews, edition 16 furthered a sense of proprietorship and renewed confidence in the durability and usefulness of the Classification. Long after the publication, the editor commented on this edition thus: 'Its public reception, and the experience of the Library's (*ie* the Library of Congress) Decimal Classification office staff in applying it to books, showed that it, like its predecessors, was still not ideal . . . and that substantial re-evaluations were in order'. (17)

Edition 17
Such a warning that 'substantial re-evaluations' had been made in edition 17 might well have alerted Dewey users to the fact that a crisis reminiscent to that of edition 15 might be imminent, particularly since something 'quite new' was promised. Some observations on the *tables* and *index* follow:
The tables: a major criterion which affected the revision of the *tables* was the 'renewed emphasis on subject integrity and relationships' with a concomitant de-emphasis on classification by 'attraction'. (18) Other decisions which contributed to the emphasis on hierarchical classification structure were:
1 Accepting a reasonable amount of relocation as inevitable.
2 Making the notation hierarchically expressive as far as reasonably possible.
3 Developing subjects from general, through general-special, to specific aspects.
4 Providing for division of topics by more than one principle.
   Among the innovative and bold changes were:
1 Creation of a whole new schedule for 150 (Psychology) wherein new meanings were assigned instantly to previously used notations and to which psychological topics from 130 were transferred.
2 Assigning new meanings to notation previously used.
3 Implementing a zero motif to achieve uniformity of subdivision

231

sequence through the decision that if one standard subdivision of a specific class required the use of two or three O's, then all standard subdivision
of that class would be assigned a similar O notation.

4 Re-designing the 'form divisions' into a 'standard subdivision table'
through freeing 04, re-locating collected essays and lectures to 08, and
expanding 02 to included all of 08 (except collections) as 'Miscellany'.

5 Expanding scope of analysis through increased opportunity for number building (edition 16 had 851 entries amenable to such expansion:
edition 17; 2,670 entries; edition 18; 3,389). (19)

6 Creating an 'area table' as an auxiliary; thereby identifying the 900's
more significantly as the discipline of history.

7 Experimenting with an 'Add to' rather than a 'Divide like' technique.

The index: In the 'preview' scant attention was given to the *Index* other
than for its being characterized as 'rational, limited, coordinated with
the tables, and truly relative' as well as 'completely new in conception
and execution'. (2)) While the editor warned that it would be impossible to classify directly from the *Index,* few of the reviewers confirmed
his expectation that 'the intelligent and thoughtful classifier will find it
far more rewarding than indexes to earlier editions'. (21)

Candidly negative expressions revived the spectre of edition 15.
R K Olding, of Australia, felt that the index was 'an appalling piece of
work and a travesty of his [*ie* Melvil Dewey's] *Relative index*' (22)
and Ruth Strout of the University of Chicago referred to it as an 'inadequate index'. (23) An amusing but equally devastating appraisal from
Frances Hinton of the Free Library of Philadelphia, concluded that the
Index 'seems to be designed not only to prevent the slothful from
attempting to use it to class a book directly, but effectively to discour-
age anyone from using it at all'. (24)

Such a response compelled the Editorial Policy Committee, which
originally had accepted the editor's new indexing scheme, to seek
remedial action. Subsequently the Forest Press, equally dismayed by
the rejection of the *Index* announced: 'In response to expressions from
cataloguers and the library profession in general, there is now in editorial
preparation a revision of the original index to edition 17. In general it
follows the pattern set by the index to edition 16. (25) When the
revised *Index* appeared in 1967, two of the reviewers of the original
Index were favourably impressed with it. One complimented it thus:
'The entries themselves, as well as the over-all pattern of entries, have been
greatly changed and, according to the editor, have been based almost

232

entirely upon the index to the sixteenth edition . . . What we have now seems to be a good, thorough, reasonable index with a straightforward approach'. (26) Another, a bit testily though astutely, rebuked librarians for not recognizing that 'When we try to index a universal classification scheme, we try to index infinity . . . So no Dewey index ever really did list everything. Dewey 17's second index embalms the old problem. Progress is two steps forward and one step back.' (27)

One wonders what might have been the consequences had there been a readiness for the *Index* through advance information. Would it have been more acceptable if the concept of upward referencing had been more nearly perfected before it was substituted for the conventional 'Relative index' of edition 16 of which there had been minimal criticism? What might have happened had the *Index* not been revised at all or so hastily? While the revision acknowledged a monumental and costly miscalculation, the Forest Press could have done nothing less than respond to the criticism because of its commitment to further the usefulness of the DDC. (28) Yet there must be recognition of the complexities of indexing infinity even in its relative aspects as thus far revealed and fragmented into the disciplinary structures of DDC. What seems certain is that the search for an amalgam of the traditional objective of containing an entry for every significant term and the emerging principle of upward references was contained in edition 18 and will continue, it can be anticipated, in editions beyond. (29)

Edition 18
The anxiety felt by users waiting for a new edition was assuaged, in part, by the advanced reporting, as was done for edition 17, in 'Dewey 18: a preview and a report to the profession' prepared by a member of the Decimal Classification Division of the Library of Congress, which proved to be informative, clear and direct. It contained no veiled promise of 'substantial re-evaluations'. Edition 18, published 1971, has had a seemingly sobering effect if viewed on the basis of reviews of it. Launched with the hope of the Decimal Classification Editorial Policy Committee that it would 'prove to be a happy combination of the high principles of edition 17 and ease of use of edition 16', it blended the principle and the practice skilfully. In three volumes, it has an increase in comparison with edition 17 for it accommodates 3,786 total entries and 719 entries with 'built-in expansion', exclusive of the use of the Table of Standard Subdivisions. Refinements of terminology, notes, and hierarchical relations within the schedules are evident. The 'Editor's Introduction' has been

re-written in an impressive but readable style despite the complexity of the topics discussed. Gone are the extremes of pedantry and coyness, the latter evidenced especially in use of the word 'drip' to convey a hierarchical characteristic. Instead the phrase, 'hierarchical force', is used to impart the meaning. Changes in terminology but not in intent are evident; among the new terms are 'citation order', 'Class here' and 'Class elsewhere' notes, and 'General Special' (3.371) which is 'reserved for special concepts that have general application thruout the regular subdivisions of certain specific disciplines and subjects.' Standard Subdivision *04* is to be used for such concepts appearing for the first time in edition 18. Explanations are offered, for example, for 'Comprehensive Works on Concepts in Centered Headings' (3.43) and for '*Add from schedules*' (3.3542).

Among the new features are (1) abandonment of 'divide-like' for which is substituted the more positive 'add' notes and (2) inclusion of two 'phoenix' divisions, as earlier noted, for 340 and 510. Other new features are a 'Glossary' and an 'Index to Preface, Editor's Introduction, and Glossary.' For those with historical interests, the following inclusions in edition 18 will have special appeal: (1) Dewey's portrait as a frontispiece, the original of which is at the Lake Placid Club; (2) an essay, 'Melvil Dewey', written by Godfrey, son of Dewey, in 1951; (3) 'Melvil Dewey's Introduction to Edition 12', dated Dec. 10, 1926.

The most comprehensive change, continuing an evolutionary trend, are the five additional auxiliary tables which are to be used with the *Sched Schedules* of edition 18. The tables (3-7) are:

3 Subdivisions of Individual Literatures
4 Subdivisions of Individual Languages
5 Racial, Ethnic, National Groups
6 Language
7 Persons

These tables permit more detailed analysis through a faceting technique, some parts of which were fixed within the schedules themselves, for example in the 400's and 800's, before they were patterned.

Specific directions for application accompany each table; however, Table 3 appears to be exceedingly complex in its design. Appended to the 800 schedule is a 'Table of Examples' which serves as a guide in building numbers and demonstrates the use of Table 3. Since the tables (except for Table I: Standard Subdivisions) are to be used only as directed in the schedules, it is likely that ensuing editions will extend applications of some of them, especially Table 5, to such subjects as Ethics
234

(172-179) and Culture and Cultural Processes (301.2), particularly with the current trend toward cultural enclaving rather than acculturating.

The index: The Index is designed to contain 'an entry for every significant term named in the schedules and tables, and with leads . . . to every aspect that is named or that is implied by an add note.' It reflects the manifest content of the schedules since it would not have been feasible to anticipate every topic likely to be written about or of all aspects of the topics actually included.

The Index revives the policy superimposed in the original index of edition 17 and minimized in its revision—the policy of demonstrating through upward cross referencing the hierarchical and faceted characteristics of the Classification. A practical motivation for the policy appears to be editorial concern lest the classifier ignore aspects of subjects not thus analyzed or rely on an index entry without further search. An example illustrating use of the Index from Matthews' essay (29a) follows:

Suppose the classifier has a book on how to arrange lilacs artistically. By using the original index of edition 17 he finds:

Lilacs *see* Loganiales

Upon turning to Loganiales, he finds the following:

Loganiales
    botany   583.74
    floriculture   635.93374

Thus he finds a relationship between the common and scientific names for lilacs; however, he also finds an incomplete number for floriculture and no number for the arrangement of lilacs. If he tries the revised index, he discovers the following entry:

Lilac
    botany   583.74
    floriculture   635.93374

This entry gives the complete number for floriculture but no number for the arrangement of lilacs. He then tries the scientific name and finds:

Loganiales   583.74

This search turns out to be a complete waste of time, since the only entry gives the botany number, which duplicates the information already found under lilacs. Upon using the index of edition 18 he finds under lilacs:

Lilacs *see* Loganiales

Under Loganiales he finds

Loganiales

botany	583.74
floriculture	635.93374
forestry	634.97374
med. aspects	
crop prod.	633.88374
gen. pharm	615.32374
toxicology	615.952374
vet. pharm.	636.089532374
toxicology	636.0895952374

other aspects see Plants

This time he finds a relationship between the common and
scientific names, complete entry numbers, no duplication of
information, and, although he finds no entry for the arrangement of lilacs, he does have a cross reference to plants, which
indicates new possibilities. The first entry under pot plants is:

arrangement
dec. arts   745.92

He thus finds a number for the artistic arrangement of plants,
which is also the correct number for the arrangement of lilacs
and which, as the index indicates by both term and number
being in boldface type, is subdivided in the schedules by flower
arrangements in containers, without containers, and other
similar topics (but not by kind of flowers).

(One might wonder if a classifier might not have reasoned immediately
that the arrangement of lilacs was a floral art and found in the index
the following entry:

Floral
Arts   745.92).

A question inviting further editorial consideration remains: Should
the index be used for the display in inverse pattern of the hierarchical
design of the Classification to aid in classificatory decision-making as
well as for its assumed primary purpose: quick entry into the schedules?

Abridged Edition 10

The remaining recent edition, the Abridged 10th (29b), abandoned the
premise upon which earlier editions were based—that they were abridge-
ments and that libraries could switch to the unabridged Dewey simply
by lengthening the class numbers previously used in the abridged. It is
therefore no longer an abridgement but an adaptation "addressed to the
236

thousands of general libraries that have no expectation of ever growing very big". While the implications of this fundamental change have not yet been measured, among them are these: (i) problems of near total reclassification should a collection exceed the potential of the unabridged; (ii) the possible bifurcation of policies and practices between the unabridged and the abridged; (iii) a trend towards the development of two neo-independent schemes.

Dewey's notation: its elongation

The long applauded traits of DDC, simplicity of notation and ease of recall, are being obscured as the Classification becomes increasingly complex. While such a trend seems inherent in a decimal structure, the elongation becomes visible in application more so than in the *Tables* themselves. While there had been criticism throughout the years, especially about the length of DDC numbers on Library of Congress cards, that criticism became intensified after the publication of edition 16. In 1962 for example, the editor had advised: 'If the numbers assigned by us . . . are too long to suit you, or if your collection in a given subject is small, do not hesitate to cut back judiciously'. (30)

Elongation of notation was magnified again as a result of the extensive revisions made in edition 17. The complexity of the notation was created in part by the zero syndrome, the increased emphasis on synthesis of notation, and expansions for new topics which, within a decimal scheme, tend to be lengthier than notation for obsolescent or less current topics. Meanwhile the Forest Press, aware of the continuing dissatisfaction with the notation, requested that some action be taken by the Decimal Classification Division in an effort to alleviate the vexing position.

That effort resulted in the policy of segmenting the DDC notation. Since 1967, Dewey numbers on Library of Congress cards, in its book catalogues, and on MARC tapes, appear in from one to three segments. The segmentation, shown by prime marks which are not part of the notation itself, identify for the user the varying levels at which the notation is meaningful. Since never more than three segments are indicated, the knowledgeable classifier will recognize that the third segment may consist occasionally of more than one synthetic element which could be further segmented if desired. While the use of segmentation results in loss of precision, it demonstrates a unique value of the hierarchical notation of DDC. (31) The following are examples of segmentation:

      301.3'64'071177595
      338.4'7'6555730942

658.8'09'65573
711 .3'094255
301.15'43'3012917492705694

The use of a shorter notation on the work being classified and the full on the shelflist or for automated retrieval polarizes the two purposes of a bibliographic classification: for arrangement of entities in a subject related order and for analysis of precise information retrievable through the traditional shelflist or the computer. To what extent the use of segmentation has lessened anxieties about the lengthening notation is not known, nor is it known how many libraries have used editions 17 or 18 to a full level of analysis. What does emerge, however, is the conflict between the pragmatic requirements of shelf classification wherein the length of the number bears, in the minds of many users, some relation to the width of the spine of a book (and now other formats being classified) and the intellectual challenge of bibliographic (content) classification with the potential for utmost specificity and multiple analyses.

While recognizing the complexity, the Editor has acknowledged that no deterrent has been found for the lengthening of notation which 'does not erode' the present notational pattern. (32) It might be asked, though, if it would be considered erosion if only two figures to the left of the decimal point (with decimal value) were used? Such notation could accommodate interdisciplinary topics, the solar system, and as yet undeveloped disciplines.

Despite the concern for the length of notation, it does appear as if the unabridged editions of Dewey will expand towards bibliographic fullness even though its daily application is limited largely to 'shelf' classification analysis. The survey on the use of the scheme in the United States and Canada should provide data on actual use of the fullness of Dewey, on the use of segmentation, and on tinkerings with notation within libraries. Its findings will offer guidance for possible new directions in edition 19 and beyond. (33)

Centralized uses of Dewey
Dewey numbers on Library of Congress cards

It was not until 1930, long after the Classification had been used and adapted judiciously, and perhaps not so judiciously, by hundreds of individual libraries, that DDC numbers were assigned to some of the titles being catalogued by the Library of Congress. Then as now, the goal was a program 'embracing practically all books in foreign languages as well as in English'. (34) The number of titles classified has varied since the

238

service began . . . from a high of ninety percent of all the cards prepared in fiscal year 1933/34, to a low of twenty four percent in 1965/66. (35) During the fiscal year 1968/69, the Decimal Classification Division classified 74,336 titles which is about one third of the total number of titles classified (200,373) by the Library of Congress itself. (36) By contrast to these figures which reflect the scope of DDC coverage, the editor estimated in 1965 that DDC numbers actually appeared on eighty percent of the cards being *sold* by the Library of Congress. (37) Though in the early '70s the percentage of titles classified in DDC as compared to the total cataloguing production of the Library of Congress reflected a downward trend, there has been a favorable reversal of it. (38) In 1973/74 the number of titles classified was 90,793, a percentage increase of 11.4 over the previous high for the '70s. These titles included nearly all English language titles cataloged by the Library and a selection of those in French and other Western languages. (39) The increase reflects not only the impact of the wide use of the MARC database but, more significantly, the recognition of the superior retrieval capacity through DDC in searching a broad topic via MARC.

Even with the present scope, practical advantages to the editorial process could be immeasurable, since the opportunity exists to develop future editions using the wisdom gained in the daily application of the current one. Among other policies for consideration or further study are these: (1) should alternative classification numbers be included? (2) should multiple analyses be made because of the retrieval capability of DDC notation as demonstrated through use of MARC? (3) should some form of book notation be adopted, not necessarily alphabetic order tables but perhaps the 'Biscoe time numbers' concept? (40) (Note: While the Editor's introduction to edition 18 identifies sources on the use and construction of book numbers, the Editor concludes that the use of book numbers on Library of Congress cards "has not been considered feasible").

As of 1971, DDC numbers on LC cards reflect any changes or developments which have been made in edition 18. According to the Decimal Classification Division, this edition in its prepublication form was adopted immediately in order to permit early use of new expansions such as those for mathematics, law, economics, nuclear physics, the biological and medical sciences, history and geography. (41) To the extent that DDC numbers were then included and continue to be included, the decisions of the Division are available through the printed card service, MARC tapes, and the book catalog program of the Congress Library. The Cataloguing in Publication plan, as implemented, also includes DDC numbers. (42)

DDC numbers from other sources within the US
Both the R R Bowker Company and the H W Wilson Company use the Dewey Classification, either in the full or abridged editions, in their bibliographic publications. Bowker uses Dewey in the *American book publishing record* and the *Publishers' weekly*; Wilson uses Dewey in its *Standard catalog series,* its *Book review digest,* and its catalogue card service. The *Booklist* of the American Library Association is one of the many selection guides, reading lists, special library lists, and bibliographies which have been arranged by Dewey or have had the DDC notation added to the entry.

There are now over fifty commercial processing firms which will classify by Dewey at the request of the consumer library. (43) Most centralized processing centres, for example, the Hawaii State Library Centralized Processing Center, either accept the DDC number on the LC card or adapt according to the tolerance level of consumer acceptance. With the increasing number of book catalogues from library systems, such as that of the Cooperative Library System (Ventura, California), more classification numbers are being made available.

Another source of DDC numbers is automated bibliographic information available through membership of such systems as the Ohio College Library Center (OCLC) which contains in its database not only MARC records but catalog data from member libraries. In 1976 the database held two million records in its on-line catalog, many of which included DDC numbers.

The users of any of these sources, however, must be warned that differences in decisions are likely to occur and that the nearest 'official' analysis presently available is that made by the Decimal Classification Division which appears printed on Congress' cards, MARC tape, or book catalogs.

DDC in other countries
The decision of the BNB to use edition 18 as of January 1971 for the beginning of its new five year cumulation was in itself a monumental achievement of the '70s. (44) As a consequence, libraries throughout the world which receive the BNB or the Library of Congress cards, its MARC tape, or book catalogs, will have available the DDC decisions from these two sources as models of analysis. International cooperation is strengthened in that the Decimal Classification Division of the Library of Congress considers the BNB decisions as authoritative, though each assigned BNB number is verified before its acceptance. Among other national

bibliographies which use Dewey at varying levels of expansion are these: *Australian national bibliography, Canadiana, the Ceylon (now Sri Lanka) national bibliography, the Indian national bibliography,* and *SANB South African national bibliography. Fichero bibliográfico Hispanoamericano,* published by the R R Bowker Company, is a record of books published in the Americas in the Spanish language and is in DDC classified arrangement. Through exchanges of information and views with the staffs of some of these publications or their organizations, the DC Division has developed a rapport through an understanding of their editorial policy and through progress towards standardized interpretation of the schedules. (45)

Each of these—and others not noted—contribute in a small way to the fulfilment of the concept of a world information network. In the attainment of such a network, the Dewey Decimal Classification will find itself increasingly involved as it enters its second century.

Dewey use . . . Dewey users

Far beyond the '70s, the scheme will continue to be introduced to an untold number of users and to students in schools of library science studies throughout the world. The rapidity of its adoption is evident when its near universal use is compared to Melvil Dewey's statement in 1931 that the Classification had been carried 'to 14,000 users in 20 nations'. (46) A general estimate of recent distribution figures is that in a period of four years edition 17 had wider distribution than did edition 16 in seven years (47) and that it is being used in libraries in approximately one hundred countries. Interest in acquiring edition 18 continues.

Once again it can be observed that such distribution reconfirms the appraisal made by E A Savage in 1946 that: 'No other book has had a more powerful influence upon library administration than this invention of Melvil Dewey . . . Puck-like, he put a girdle round the earth with his 'damned dots' . . . and with them American library methods were carried from Albany to the Antipodes.' (48)

Among the countries which have acquired copies of edition 17 and/or 18, in which English is a second or less used language, are Afghanistan, Argentina, Brazil, Denmark, Egypt, Ethiopia, Finland, India, Indonesia, Iran, Israel, Japan, Liberia, Mexico, Philippines, Poland, Sri Lanka, Thailand and Zambia. The classification continues to be used widely in nearly all the present and former British Commonwealth nations, extensively in Australia, Canada, Britain, India and Pakistan.

241

Translations

The use of Dewey is being extended through translations, many of which, in part or in whole, abridged/unabridged, have been made. Since there is no formal program of translation, the initiative thus far has been assumed by the translator and/or his sponsor. While such translations should be published with the permission of Forest Press as the copyright holder, it is likely that unauthorized translations occasionally appear. Among those that have been published, again in part or in whole, usually unabridged, with permission are those in Hebrew, Spanish, Thai and Vietnamese. A French translation of the unabridged DDC was published in 1975 through the collaboration of Forest Press with librarians in French-speaking Canada and in France. This helps make the classification more comprehensible to French-speaking nations throughout the world.

The translations themselves are uneven and are based on various editions of Dewey. They frequently include locally designed adaptations or expansions. Because of the increasing interest in translations and of the need for continuity in programs once begun, the Forest Press has assumed more positive direction of such programs. (49) Currently a Spanish translation of the unabridged edition is being sponsored by Forest Press. Such action will ensure some objectivity where divisive views are prevalent as well as encourage prompt completion.

Adaptations, etc

Numerous adaptations have been published either in English or in other languages, sometimes without authorization. Whatever the publishing pattern, a causal factor continues to be that the ten classes, while universal in scope are not yet analysed with a universal perspective. Thus the internationalizing of Dewey itself must be continued.

Within the United States

The '70s continue to see libraries adopting Dewey, abandoning it or remaining with it. No accurate record is kept, nor could one be kept by the Forest Press or the Decimal Classification Division as to such decisions made by individual libraries. Some, however, are learned through correspondence initiated by a library or through publicity given to them such as in Desmond Taylor's 'Classification trends in junior college libraries' (*College and research libraries*, v 29, September 1968, 351-356) or in A Robert Rogers' 'LC and BG: friendship without marriage'(*Library resources and technical services*, v 13, Winter 1969 47-61).

242

What is known, however, is that though there was a going away from—a flight from—Dewey in the United States, especially during the '60s, there has now been a decrease in its momentum. While many of the reasons for abandoning DDC may lie within the Classification itself, some of the contributing factors have been:

1 Failure of a library to accept changes in succeeding editions of Dewey and thereby vitiating the Classification and lessening its practical usefulness.

2 Irresistible lure of tinkering with Dewey because of its apparently simple structuring.

3 Relative absence of DDC numbers on Library of Congress cards in contrast to the inclusion of LC numbers plus specific book numbers.

4 Increase in cost of classification (as a result of 1, 2 and 3).

5 Concern over the lengthening notation of DDC.

6 Popular view that DDC was designed for the 'small' library without awareness of its scope with all mnemonic devices and synthetic notations repeated throughout.

7 Routine recommendations to reclassify frequently made by surveyors.

8 Escape route from past mistakes; perhaps a substitute for creative search for developing user services.

9 Sincere conviction that another classification was better designed and more appropriate.

During the '60s DDC was assailed openly and received negating publicity such as in the bibliography of reclassification compiled by Howard F McGaw which included thirty nine references. The compiler acknowledged his bias by advising his readers that 'If the annotations are slanted toward an abandonment of DC, this is due to the fact that in my case the decision has been made, the die cast, and my staff and I are committed to a professional life with LC'. (50) In 1966 an issue of *Library journal* had emblazoned on its cover the question: 'Is Dewey Dead?' and it included offerings for an anticipated obsequy. (51) In addition, several conferences on classification were held during the decade, one of which was *Problems in library classification: Dewey 17 and conversion,* sponsored by the School of Information and Library Studies, University of Wisconsin-Milwaukee. (52) At the time when continuing directions for instant flight from Dewey were not uncommon, two counter views—one cautionary, the other decisive—were expressed by representatives of the Library of Congress and of the University of Illinois.

243

From the Library of Congress

The anomalous position in which the Library of Congress was being thrust was little realized by the proponents of the adoption of its Classification. Not only has the Library of Congress never officially advocated the use of its own Classification, its responsibility for the Decimal Classification Division implies a commitment to the development of both. Consequently in 1967, William J Welsh, then Director of the Processing Department, took the extraordinary step of offering 'Considerations on the adoption of the Library of Congress Classification. (53). In it he brilliantly delineated the problems of the Classification, some of which were similar to those for which Dewey was being abandoned. He stressed particularly that the LC schedules were being revised constantly with the range of revision extending 'from the addition of a single class number to a considerable expansion of a topic or the insertion of a new section'. (54)

He warned of the literal use of LC numbers as they appear on LC cards which could result in separating materials on the same subject and he noted also that the *LC subject headings* were substituting as a general index for the entire classification. Having offered his authoritative appraisal, Mr Welsh demonstrated his impartiality by concluding: 'I trust it will be clear that the foregoing observations do not constitute an attempt to dissuade libraries from adopting LC classification; equally, they are not made to encourage or advocate its adoption. Rather I have considered it important to set forth as clearly as possible certain features of the schedules, and aspects of their development and use at the Library, that appear not to have been given full consideration in some of the decisions to adopt the classification. We are anxious that no misapprehensions enter into adoption or classification decisions that would affect those decisions adversely and so result in disappointment with the schedules and dissatisfaction with our services.' (55)

From the University of Illinois

Robert L Talmadge, Director of technical departments, announced at the 1967 *Conference on problems in library classification,* that the University of Illinois, after lengthy consideration of the factors involved, such as cost, time, interruption of user services, and possible impairment of faculty confidence, had decided to continue its use of DDC. Mr Talmadge made it clear that the decision had been based on pragmatic reasoning and not on the superior advantages of one classification over another. (56) Nevertheless, the decision confirms that the DDC,

244

considered by many as being for the 'small' library, had been weighed and not found excessively wanting in its applicability to a large collection of library resources.

That a library with a collection of four million volumes had reached such a decision introduced a sobering dimension at a time when small institutions such as Albion College (Michigan) and Antioch College (Ohio) were deciding otherwise. (57) Among other academic libraries which have made decisions to remain with Dewey are: Bowling Green State University (Ohio), Duke University, University of Florida, University of Minnesota, Northwestern University, and Oklahoma State University; among public libraries, Denver and Brooklyn Public Libraries.

While libraries must and will continue to evaluate the advantages/ disadvantages of change, the decision making process has become more rational and deliberate in the '70s than in the '60s.

Internationalizing Dewey within
The widespread use of Dewey has magnified increasingly the unequal development of the ten classes which historically have been analysed more thoroughly for Western than for other cultural concepts. Such growth was simply pragmatic, reflecting the strengths of collections primarily in American libraries. However, because libraries in other countries have tended also to collect resources first which reflect their own culture— religion, language, literature, economy, history—it has long seemed imperative that as DDC became more internationally used it became more internationally useful.

As early as 1895 Melvil Dewey had recognized the uneven pattern of development. In that year, in acknowledging Paul Otlet's request that the newly organized Institut International de Bibliographie be permitted to make the Decimal Classification the basis of its analysis, he added: 'We shall be very glad to have the suggestions from you as to what would best meet European needs, and we shall willingly undertake the task of enlarging those departments to any desired extent. You will know that the classification has grown very irregularly, being enlarged not symmetrically but here and there as demand rose.' (58)

Throughout the years adaptations have been made by individuals 'here and there' or by libraries rather than by the editorial staff of DDC. One of the early adaptations designed to meet the needs of a different cultural environment was that of Mukand Lal, assistant librarian of the University of the Panjab. His expansion of 954 (history of India) was included in the *Panjab library primer,* written in 1915, by Asa Don Dickinson, librarian of the University of the Panjab. (59) Mr Dickinson noted also that the University Library had, in manuscript, elaborations for 290 (ethnic and other religions), 495 (Eastern Asiatic languages), and 891.2 (Sanskrit).

A new internationalism permeates the development of the schedules themselves as shown when British librarians, including the staff of the *British National Bibliography,* assumed responsibility for developing new schedules subject to guidance "and review of the Decimal Classification Division". The first result of this cooperative effort was the schedule for the new local administrative divisions of the United Kingdom, officially effective as of April 1974 onwards. (60)

Problems in use of DDC (outside the US)
Many years later, in response to criticisms of edition 16, published in 1958, which warned of continuing inadequacies both for libraries in the United States and abroad, the Forest Press, with the cooperation of the American Library Association, the Council on Library Resources, and the Asia Foundation, sponsored a survey on the use of Dewey abroad. (61)

While emphasis in the survey was to be on problems relating to the applicability of DDC in cultures other than Western, it was assumed from the beginning that any improvement would be welcomed by those libraries in the United States and elsewhere which were acquiring an increasing number of imprints from all over the world.

The findings of the survey, completed in 1964, were transmitted to the Forest Press and the Decimal Classification Division of the Library of Congress for study and appropriate action. The report was accompanied by recommendations and by supporting evidence both of the classificatory interest in many countries and of the continuing experimentations in adapting, expanding, and translatinv Dewey. (62) All who cooperated in the data gathering were later informed that: 'Some of the changes either had been anticipated or, as of this date, have been incorporated into the seventeenth edition. Many of the suggestions, however, are so complex and so encompassing that they will require extensive analysis before they can be evaluated fully. Thus not only the seventeenth, but succeeding editions will reflect the findings of the survey.' (63) Since the completion of this survey, additional comments have been received and evaluated by the Editorial Office.

Edition 17 (64)
As anticipated, edition 17 was by far more international than earlier editions. Not only did it include additions and expansions, it introduced for the first time an artificial digit. The expansions, some occurring
246

belatedly in the very areas identified by Mr Dickinson, were made in 181.04-181.09 (Philosophy based on specific religions); 294.3 (Buddhism), 294.5 (Hinduism), 296 (Judaism), and 297 (Islam). In the 800's historical periods for many literatures, including 'colonial' literatures, were added and in the 900's history periods for nearly every country, not so detailed perhaps as might be desirable as the literature itself multiplies . . . but a beginning. The new *Area table* with its detailed entries for regions, ethnic and religious groups, hemisphere and space, permitted for the first time more refined analysis of content.

Through the use of the artificial digit, which could be, for example, the letter of an alphabet, a symbol, or an asterisk, each without meaning other than preferential intent, it was possible to secure primary placement or precedence for the literature of/about a nation or a culture. Throughout the *Tables* carefully worded directions appear offering the option, through use of the artificial digit, to place local literature first in a sequence (examples may be found at 030 and 420-429. Similar use of the artificial digit was proposed for use with the *Area table* also. De-emphasis on the United States was implied at 353 where, if preferred, the section could be used for a national government other than the United States.

While the editor's 'introduction' acknowledged that edition 17 reflected some of the early results of the survey, a recognition of the need for further internationalizing was also expressed thus: 'It is the editors' and publishers' earnest hope that the DDC of the future will be made continuously more and more useful for librarians of Europe, Asia, Africa, and the Pacific, as well as for those of America'. (65) That such a hope has not been regarded lightly can be seen in the following advice offered during a 1968 Seminar on Librarianship as a Profession in the Philippines: 'Philippine librarians might want to wait for the eighteenth edition before making drastic changes, because it promises to include the results of the Vann-Seely report on the use of DDC around the world'. (66)

Because expectations which exceed realistic fulfilment could have diminished the actual developments that characterized edition 18, it should be noted that the editor stated in edition 17: 'It may be expected that edition 18 will reflect . . . more detailed study of the results of the 1964 survey of DC use abroad'. (67)

Edition 18
In fulfilling that expectation, edition 18 continues the plan for reducing the Western emphasis of the Classification by adding new or extending older subjects. (68) Also in response to requests from librarians and

scholars who were dissatisfied with the geographic entity of area 91-92 (Malay Archipelago), a major relocation has been made. The geographic notations for Indonesia, the Philippines, and the Malaysian parts of Borneo and Brunei have been transferred to Area 59, thereby identifying these areas more significantly as part of Asia. Edition 18 further introduces for the first time in its 'principle of usefulness' a flexibility of notation beyond the use of artificial digits to the *use of established numbers with unofficial meanings.* (69) In some instances the use of artificial digits as suggested in edition 17 has been supplemented by an alternative proposal in edition 18. Examples illustrating the two techniques for insuring preferential classification of local literature follow:

Technique	Example (From *Dewey Decimal Classification edition 18*)
	810-890 Literatures of specific languages
Use of artificial digit:	Arrange as below; but, if it is desired to give local emphasis and a shorter number to a specific literature, place it first by use of a letter or other symbol, *eg,* literature of Arabic language 8A0 (preceding 810), for which base number is 8A
	810 *American literature in English
Use of established numbers with unofficial meanings:	(If it is desired to give local emphasis and a shorter number to a specific literature, *eg,* Afrikaans literature, it is optional to class it here; in that case class American literature in English at 820) or (If it is desired to give local emphasis and more and shorter numbers to a specific religion, *eg,* Buddhism, it is optional to class it here and its sources in 220; in which case class Bible and Christianity in 298) (70)

Thus in the '70s DDC endorses flexibility of notation as an internationalizing technique. This flexibility is to be 'controlled' through the inclusion of notes telling where to class subjects displaced. How long the 'official' Dewey will remain official in use, therefore, is highly speculative until further study is made. It can be assumed, however, that the use of the basic text both by the *British national bibliography* and the Decimal Classification Division of the Library of Congress will continue to insure authoritative interpretation of notation.

248

Meanwhile, answers to the following questions could anticipate to some extent the trend toward further internationalizing:

1 Is there a plan for the development of a compressed analysis for a displaced subject for example, an analysis of Christianity in 298?

2 Is a special supplement to be prepared with the flexible notations and analyses both for the pre-emptive and displaced subjects?

3 Has adequate attention been given to varying concepts of 'disciplines' in cultures which differ from the West?

4 Has there been consultation with authorities in the countries or of cultures concerned in order to insure accuracy and acceptance of pre-emptive and other analyses?

5 Are pre-emptive analyses being prepared for such areas as 329, 340, 350 and 610?

6 Will representation on the Decimal Classification editorial policy committee be extended beyond its present scope? (71)

7 Is a guide being prepared for international usage?

Should a guide be prepared, it might well include directions relating to the use of Dewey for the classified catalogue not for shelf analysis, to author or book identification numbers, to suggestions for expanding for local needs and for classification of subjects not yet included in the *Schedules,* to the creation of local index/indexes within the structural design of the official *Index.* Such a guide would be regarded as a supplement to the editor's 'introduction' which becomes increasingly a complex and informative guide for the general use of DDC.

In 1976 at least one international conference is to be held for the furthering of the global usefulness of the DDC in its second century: a European seminar, sponsored by the Forest Press in association with the Library Association.

In the Seventies . . . and beyond

Among the events in honor of the date, 1876, sponsored by Forest Press, were the issue of a facsimile reprint of the first edition, *A Classification and Subject Index for Cataloguing and Arranging the Books and Pamphlets of a Library*, conferences held at the University of Illinois and by the (British) Library Association's Cataloguing & Indexing Group; and the anticipated publication of the history of the Dewey Decimal Classification by John Phillip Comaromi, based on his doctoral dissertation, University of Michigan, 1969. As the classification enters its second century, it must be recognised that the DDC, long exposed to public view and expectations, can never be satisfactory to all or be proclaimed 'ideal'.

Nevertheless it will continue to be used. Its format may differ; its publication program may vary, for the computer offers promise for a meaningful and continuous pattern of updating, revision, and availability. It will continue—at least for a few more decades—to be the identifiable Dewey it has long been.

It seems also that the Decimal Classification editorial policy, with its heritage of pragmatism and its commitment to usefulness, can never be unrestrainedly *avant garde* without impunity. While this penalizes creativity in editorial policy it has contributed to the durability of DDC. Sometimes the policies appear imitative of other classifications; sometimes, as if cyclically progressive. For example, edition 18, following the successful experimentation in edition 17 with the *Areas table,* has revived the emphasis on auxiliary tables inversely patterned after those included in edition 13 and edition 14. (72) If the Classification dies, therefore, it will be a demise self-imposed, for the elements of destruction lie in its unique relationship with its users. By Melvil Dewey's 'Deed of gift', executed as of October 31, 1924, its destiny was thus transferred to its users: 'All receits or royalties from the sales of the various editions of the Decimal Classification herinabove referd to shal be spent under direction of the Foundation Executiv Board for editing, revising, bringing out needed special editions and making them known, thus making the sistem more widely useful without allowing it ever to be a source of personal profit beyond necessary expenses and reasonable salaries for actual work'. (73)

Should those three bodies entrusted with the Decimal Classification, The Forest Press (74), the Decimal Classification Editorial Policy Committee, and the Library of Congress, falter or fail in seeking continually to make the 'sistem more widely useful' and should its users throughout the world reject it, there would be no further need of it. Such an eventuality seems distant, for the Classification in the '70s seems remarkably vital, adaptive, and enduring. It is no longer earth-bound. Long ago Dewey mused: 'I think of the earth as launched into space and as if it were a great ship'. Had he lived long enough to see the publication of editions 18 and 19, he would have witnessed the launching of his system into space for a new dimension has now been added through the 'Areas' Table -99 Extraterrestial worlds; Worlds other than Man's Earth. It is an auspicious omen!

Towards Edition 19

Users are advised to write to Richard B Sealock, Executive Director, Forest Press, 85 Watervliet Avenue, Albany, New York, USA, 12206, for information concerning plans for this edition. See also DC & (Dewey Decimal Classification Additions, Notes and Decisions, v. 2 - 1971 -)for decisions affecting edition 19.

REFERENCES

1 Dewey, Melvil: 'Future of DC, 11 March 31'. (Included on a mimeograph leaf entitled, 'Dr Melvil Dewey's statement on American library needs and DC's dependence upon supplying them'.nd)

2 Dewey, Melvil: *A classification and subject index for cataloging and arranging the books and pamphlets of a library.* Amherst, Mass, 1876.

3 US Office of Education: *Public libraries in the United States of America . . .* Special Report. Washington, Govt Print Off, 1876, p 641.

4 Dewey, Melvil: *Decimal classification and relativ index for arranging, cataloging and indexing public and private libraries, and for pamflets, clippings, notes, scrap books, index rerums, etc.* 2nd ed, rev & greatly enl. Boston Library Bureau, 1885, pp 32-33.

5 *Ibid*, p 32.

6 Conference of librarians, London, 1877. 'Proceedings'. *Library journal*, v 2, January-February 1878, p 270.

7 See comments following the publication of edition 13, for example: Schofield, E B 'The future of "Dewey" '. *Library Association record*, vol 3, August 1933, pp 245-250.

8 Eaton, Thelma: 'Epitaph to a dead classification'. *Library association record*, vol 57, November 1955, pp 428-430.

9 The figures are those quoted in Clapp, Verner W: 'Progress towards the sixteenth edition of Dewey'. *Journal of cataloging and classification*, vol 12, October 1956, p 199. On p 207, footnote 45, Mr Clapp notes that 'Dr Godfrey Dewey reaches the figures of 28,570 and 4,661 respectively'.

10 Dewey, Melvil: *Dewey decimal classification & relative index.* Devised by Melvil Dewey. Standard (15th) ed., rev. Lake Placid Club, Essex County, NY, Forest Press Inc, 1952, p iii.

11 Clapp, Verner W: 'Progress towards the sixteenth edition of Dewey'. *Journal of cataloguing and classification*, vol 12, October 1956, pp 196-208; *Library Association record*, vol 58, June 1956, pp 207-215.

12 The creation of the Decimal Classification editorial policy committee involved a restructuring of the Decimal Classification committee which had been created in 1937 by the Lake Placid Club Education Foundation 'to have control of the management and editorial policy' of the Classification to include representation by the American Library Association. As early as 1933 the American Library Association had created a special 'Committee on Cooperation with the Lake Placid Club (education foundation) on Decimal Classification with Margaret Mann as chairman. For additional information, see Clapp, Verner W 'DCC editorial policy committee'. *Library journal*, vol 81, January 15, 1956, p 155. See also Benjamin A Custer: 'Dewey Decimal Classification'. *Encyclopedia of Library and Information Science.* New York, Marcel Dekker, c1972, vol 7, pp 128-142.

13 *Dewey Decimal Classification additions, notes and decisions,* vol 2, Spring 1971, p 23.
Recommendations from the Decimal Classification Editorial Policy Committee, when accepted by Forest Press, become the official editorial policy.

14 Clapp, Verner W: 'Progress towards the sixteenth edition of Dewey'. *Journal of cataloging and classification,* vol 12, October 1956, p 202.

15 *Decimal Classification additions, notes and decisions,* vol 1, January 1959, p 1.

16 Custer, Benjamin A: 'Dewey 16: a preview and report to the profession'. *Library resources and technical services,* vol 1, Fall 1957, pp 165-179; *Wilson library bulletin,* vol 32, November 1957, pp 197-204.

17 Custer, Benjamin A: 'Dewey 17: a preview and report to the profession'. *Library Association record,* vol 67, March 1965, p 79.
Also published in *Indian librarian,* vol 19, March 1965, pp 191-197; *Wilson library bulletin,* vol 39, March 1965, pp 555-559 (title varies slightly).

18 According to the editor, 'Classification by attraction' implies classifying a given subject only where it is named, for example, the inclusion in *296* of works on the sociology of the Jews. Custer, Benjamin A: 'Dewey 17: a preview and report to the profession'. *Library Association record,* vol 67, March 1965, p 79.

19 Figure of 3,389 furnished by Forest Press Inc.

20 Custer, Benjamin A: 'Dewey 17: a preview and report to the profession'. *Library Association record,* vol 67, March 1965, p 82.

21 *Ibid.*

22 'Dewey decimal classification edition 17': (review by) R K Olding. *Australian library journal,* vol 14, December 1965, p 206.

23 'Dewey decimal classification, edition 17': (review by) Ruth Strout Carnovsky, *Library quarterly,* vol 36, April 1966, p 158.

24 'Dewey decimal classification, edition 17': (review by) Frances Hinton. *Library resources and technical services,* vol 10, Summer 1966, p 396.

25 *Dewey decimal classification additions, notes, and decisions,* vol 2, Spring 1967, p 1.

26 'Dewey Decimal classification, edition 17, revised index' (review by) Ruth Strout Carnovsky. *Library quarterly,* vol 38, July 1968, pp 272-273.

27 'Dewey decimal classification, edition 17, revised index'. Dunkin, Paul: 'New Wine Made Old Again'. *Library journal,* vol 93, May 1, 1968, p 1876.

28 The Forest Press, Inc, acknowledged its obligation specifically by distributing the *Revised index* free to those who had acquired the original *Index* volume to edition 17.

29 Another indexing approach to the DDC has been made by the *British national bibliography* which has abandoned its chain indexing technique because of the difficulty of using it with Dewey. The new system is called PRECIS (Preserved Content Indexing System). *LC information bulletin,* vol 30, March 25, 1971, p 176.
a. Matthews, Winton E: 'Dewey 18: a preview and a report to the profession'. *Wilson library bulletin,* vol 45, February 1971, pp 572-577.
b. Dewey, Melvil: *Abridged Dewey Decimal Classification and Relative Index.* Devised by Melvil Dewey. Ed. 10. Lake Placid Club, NY, Forest Press, Inc., of Lake Placid Club Education Foundation, 1971.
For a reviews, see:
Chan, Lois Mai: 'The tenth abridged Dewey Decimal Classification " . . . and children's room/school library collections".' *School Library Journal,* vol 20, September 15, 1973: 38-43.

30 *Dewey decimal classification additions, notes, and decisions,* vol 1, June/December 1962, p 3.

31 US Library of Congress. Processing Department: *Cataloging service bulletin 78*, December 1966.
32 Custer, Benjamin A: 'Dewey decimal classification: past, present, future', in *Progress in library science, 1966*. Edited by Robert L Collison. London, Butterworths; Hamden, Conn, Archon Books, 1966, p 46.
33 Letter from Richard B Sealock, Executive Director, Forest Press, February 5, 1976.
34 Memorandum from David J Haykin, in charge of American Library Association Office for Decimal Classification Numbers on Library of Congress Cards, Library of Congress, p 1. (Undated but can be dated on basis of internal evidence as after April 1, 1930, and before August 1, 1930).
35 McKinlay, John: 'More on DC numbers on LC cards: quantity and quality'. *Library resources and technical services*, vol 14, Fall 1970, p 518.
36 US Library of Congress: *Annual report of the librarian for the fiscal year ending June 30, 1969*. Washington, 1970, p 107.
37 Custer, Benjamin A: 'In the Mail'. *Library resources and technical services*, vol 9, Spring 1965, p 212.
   Response, with statistical data, to 'Statement on types of classification available to new academic libraries'. *Library resources and technical services*, vol 9, Winter 1965, pp 104-111.
38 Custer, Benjamin A: 'Reply to John McKinlay'. *Library resources and technical services*, vol 14 Fall 1970, p 527.
39 US Library of Congress: *Annual report of the librarian of Congress for the fiscal year ending June 30, 1974*. Washington, 1975, p 23. Consult succeeding reports for later statistics.
40 'Biscoe time numbers,' designed by W S Biscoe, provides for the arrangement of books by years (date of publication or year of copyright). The scheme has been included in several early editions of DDC, for example, in *Decimal classification and relativ index*. edition 13. Memorial ed. Lake Placid Club, Essex County, NY, Forest Press, 1932, p 1643.
41 US Library of Congress: Processing Department. *Cataloging service bulletin 95*, November 1970.
42 Welsh, William J: 'Report on Library of Congress plans for cataloging in publication'. *Library resources and technical services*, vol 15, Winter 1971, p 25. An example appears in edition 18 of Dewey.
   For background information on 'Cataloguing in publication', *see* in the same issue of LRTS the following:
   Clapp, Verner W: 'CIP in mid-1970'. pp 12-23.
   Wheeler, J L: 'Why we must have CIP'. p 6-12.
43 Westby, Barbara M: 'Commercial processing firms: a directory'. *Library resources and technical services*, vol 13, Spring 1969, pp 209-286.
44 Permission for prepublication use of edition 18 was granted to *British national bibliography*. *Dewey Decimal Classification additions, notes, and decisions*, v 2, Spring 1971, 11. *See also* US Library of Congress, Processing Department: *Cataloging service bulletin 95*, November 1970.
45 US Library of Congress: *Annual report of the librarian of Congress for the fiscal year ending June 30, 1974*. Washington, 1975, p 23.
46 Dewey, Melvil: '80th birthday letter 10 December 31.' p 3.
47 Interview with Benjamin A Custer, August 31, 1970. More specific data may be secured from Forest Press Inc, 85 Watervliet Avenue, Albany, New York, 12206, USA.
48 Savage, Ernest A: *Manual of book classification and display for public libraries*, London, Allen & Unwin, 1946, p 67.

49 Inquiries concerning translations should be addressed to Richard B Sealock, Executive Director, Forest Press Inc, at address given in footnote 47.

50 McGaw, Howard F: 'Reclassification: a bibliography'. *Library resources and technical services,* vol 9, Fall 1968, p 483.

51 *See* the following for example:
Evans, G Edward: 'Dewey: necessity or luxury; a study of the practical economics involved in continuing Dewey vs converting to LC'. *Library journal,* vol 91, September 15, 1966, pp 4038-4046.
Taylor, Desmond: 'Is Dewey dead?' *Library journal,* vol 91, September 15, 1966, pp 4035-4046.

52 *Problems in library classification: Dewey 17 and conversion:* Papers presented at a two-phase conference held at the University of Wisconsin-Milwaukee, School of Library & Information Science, November 1966 and May 1967. Edited by Theodore Samore. New York, Bowker (c 1968) (Library and information science studies, no 1).

53 Welsh, William J: 'Considerations on the adoption of the Library of Congress Classification'. *Library resources and technical services,* vol 11, Summer 1967, pp 345-353.

54 *Ibid,* p 348.

55 *Ibid,* p 352.

56 Talmadge, Robert L: 'One library's case against conversion', in *Problems in library classification: Dewey 17 and conversion. Op cit,* p 66.

57 Gaines, James E: 'Reclassification in the libraries of the Great Lakes Colleges Association'. *College and research libraries,* vol 29, July 1968, pp 292-296.

58 Letter to Paul Otlet from Melvil Dewey, 21 June 1895, p 1.

59 Dickinson, Asa Don: *The Panjab library primer.* Lahore, University of Panjab, 1916, pp 35-36. *Mr Dickinson* is credited with having introduced the Decimal Classification into India and Pakistan.

60 US Library of Congress: *Annual report of the librarian of Congress for the fiscal year ending June 30, 1975.* Washington: 1975, p 23. Consult succeeding reports for additional information.

61 Vann, Sarah K:'Dewey abroad: the field survey of 1964'. *Library resources and technical services,* vol 11, Winter 1967, pp 61-71; 'Dewey abroad'. *Wilson library bulletin,* vol 39, March 1965, pp 550-554.

62 Field survey of Dewey Decimal Classification (DDC) use abroad. *Final report.* Prepared for the Steering Committee, Edwin B Colburn, Chairman, by Sarah K Vann, New York, 1965 (limited circulation).

63 Letter, dated August 15, 1964, mailed to about one hundred persons by the director of the field survey.

64 Dewey, Melvil: *Dewey Decimal Classification and relative index.* Devised by Melvil Dewey. Edition 17. Lake Placid Club, NY, Forest Press Inc of Lake Placid Club Education Foundation, 1965. 2 vols. Vol 2 (revised): auxiliary tables; revised relative index. Lake Placid Club, NY, Forest Press Inc of Lake Placid Club Education Foundation, 1967.

65 *Ibid,* 'Editor's introduction', vol 1, p 56.

66 Chambers, Elizabeth: 'New trends in cataloging and classification', in *Librarianship as a profession in the Philippines.* Proceedings of the first regional seminar of college and university librarians, Visayas and Mindanao Area. Edited by Gorgonio D Siega and Eliseo P Bañas. Dumaguete City. Silliman University, 1969, p 61.

67 Dewey, Melvil: *Dewey Decimal Classification and relative index.* Edition 17. 'Editor's introduction', v1, p 58.

254

68 Dewey, Melvil: *Dewey Decimal Classification and Relative Index.* Devised by Melvil Dewey. Edition 18. Lake Placid Club, NY, Forest Press, Inc, of Lake Placid Club Education Foundation, 1971, 3 vols.

69 *Ibid,* vol 2, p 1497.

70 *Ibid,* vol 2, p 1497; 540.

71 Membership is appointive. Nominations for appointments alternate annually between the American Library Association and Forest Press. Consult issues of *Dewey Decimal Classification Additions and Notes* for identification of members of the Decimal Classification Editorial Policy Committee.

72 In edition 13, five tables were developed:

Table 1   Geographic divisions
Table 2   Common subdivisions (plus an index)
Table 3   Languages
Table 4   Philological divisions
Table 5   Literatures

Dewey, Melvil: *Decimal classification and relativ index.* Edition 13, rev and enl Memorial ed Lake Placid Club, Essex Co, NY, Forest Press, 1932, pp 1625-1642.

In edition 14, the following tables were included:

Table 1   Geographic divisions
Table 2   Uniform subdivisions (plus and index)
Table 3   Languages and literatures
Table 4   Philological divisions

Dewey, Melvil: *Decimal classification and relativ index.* Edition 14, rev and enl Lake Placid Club, Essex Co, NY, Forest Press Inc 1942, pp 1876-1892.

73 Dewey, Melvil: 'MD deed of gift preferd stock, October 31, 1924', p 4, 'Indenture made, executed and delivered at Lake Placid Club, Essec County, NY, October 31, 1924, by and between Melvil Dewey . . . and Lake Placid Club Education Foundation'.

74 The Forest Press Inc was created by the Lake Placid Club Education Foundation as a non-profit subsidiary. To it has been delegated the responsibility for editorial policy development, publication, and distribution of the *Dewey Decimal Classification.* The President of Forest Press in 1976 is Mr John A Humphry, Assistant Commissioner for Libraries, State Education Department, University of the State of New York.

For background information on the Forest Press, see *Dewey Decimal Classification additions, notes and decisions,* vol 2, Spring 1971, pp 1-22, and subsequent issues. See also 'The Dewey Decimal Classification: History, ownership, Editorial and Publishing Arrangements,' signed 'Forest Press, Inc.,' and dated March 9, 1971, Edition 18, pp 3-5.

Index

This index excludes references made to individuals or organizations in bibliographies at the end of each paper. References to individual general classification schemes have normally been indexed only when they appear in chapters other than the one devoted to the scheme in question. Alphabetization is on the 'all-through' principle.

256

Bliss Classification Association
25, 28, 48
Bulletin 28, 49
Blue, B J 203
Boreal Institute 106
Bowker, R R Co. 240, 241
Bradford, S C 101
Branch libraries and classification 18
Brevity of notation *see* Notation
British Library 20
British National Bibliography
46, 48, 126,159, 186,
246, 248
British Society for International
Bibliography 101
British Standards Institution 101
British technology index 126
Broad classification 17
Broad system of ordering (BSC)
21-22, 109-110, 115, 159
Broughton, V 28
Brown, W S 202
Brown's Subject Classification
44, 172
Browsing 16, 20, 57
Butcher, P 126

Canons of classification 53
applied to LC 82ff
Carmichael, J J 203
Case Western Reserve
University 149
Cataloguing and classification
use studies 22
Cataloguing in publication 239
Centralized (national) classification 17, 21, 22, 238-240
Chain indexing 94-97, 166
Chemical abstracts 199

Chemical titles 131
Citation order
BC 30, 32-33
CC 64-65, 70-72
idea of standardized 15, 164-
166, 179ff
need for neutrality re subject
fields 185
Clapp, V 230
Classification Research Group 11,
32, 39, 102, 158-159, 175,
186
Classified catalogue 21, 96
Cleverdon, C W 147
Cliques and clumps 212
Coates, E J 7, 95, 125-126
College and university library
classification 17, 244-245
Colon Classification 159, 160
and BC 42
and UDC 102
and mechanized retrieval 203
vocabulary compared with
TEST 135ff
Comaromi, J P 249
Comfort, A 174
Common entities 40
Common isolates 73
Compound subjects 56
Computers *see* Mechanized
retrieval
Comte, A 27
Consensus 26
Cosati classification 202
Coward, R E 162
Cranfield project *see* Aslib
Cross references 123
Cuadra, C 195, 198, 201
Curtice, R M 218, 220
Custer, B A 231

Cutter, C A 83, 124
  numbers 88

Dahlberg, I 21
Daily, J E 91, 93
Decimal Classification 20, 22, 38
  and BC 49
  and CC 53, 76
  and LC 82
  and UDC 102
  mechanized retrieval 203
  vocabulary compared with
    TEST 135ff
Defense Documentation Center
    202
Dennis, S F 218
Depth classification (CC) 77-78
Detail (in BC) 29, 31
Detroit Public Library 18
Dewey, G 229, 234
Dice's coefficient 212
Dickinson, A D 245
Disadvantages of classification
    13-16
  in information retrieval 155-
    156
Disciplines 15, 26, 40, 42-43,
    165
Documentation Research &
    Training Centre 77, 78, 159
Document clustering 216, 221
Dubuc, R 105
Duyvis, F Donker 101
Dynamic classification 222

Einstein, A 102
Empty and emptying digits
    51, 62
Engineers Joint Council
    Thesaurus see TEST

Epsilon project 142
Esdaile, A 9
Excerpta medica 131

Faceted classification 12, 15,
    28ff, 58ff, 83, 125, 127,
    145-146, 152
  in revised BC 29, 31, 39
  in CC 58-60, 64-65
  in LC 85ff
  and UDC 102
  see also Freely faceted
    classification
Fairthorne, R A 159, 177
Farradane, J 41, 126, 144, 150,
    171, 181
Fiction classification 18
FID *see* International Federation
    of Documentation
Fill, K 101
Form classes 84-85
Foskett, A C 82, 115, 161, 168,
    172
Foskett, D J 10, 11, 12, 110, 174
Frank, O 101
Freely faceted classification 65,
    178, 192-194
Freeman, R R 105, 106

Gardin, J C 168
General-special concept
  in DDC 234
  in LC 84
Geography, treatment of in BC 43
GIBUS 203
Gonzalez, R F 183
Gotlieb, C C 220
Gradation principle 13, 27, 39, 84
Guiding, value of 23
Gupta, B S S 203

Macmillan, C 183
Main classes 165-167
Main subjects 55, 65-68
Mann, M 91
MARC tapes 17, 48, 89, 97, 102,
      161-162, 186, 192, 203,
      205, 237ff
Marosi, A 110
Martel, C 85, 87
Matter isolates 51, 71
Matthews, W E 235
Mayne, A J 13
Mechanized retrieval and
      classification 100, 161-
      162, 167
   and UDC 101, 105-106, 203
Medlars 152
Mentefacts 172
Mercury system 202
Meta-language 192
Metcalfe, J 93, 119
Mills, J 81-82, 91, 102
Minimum vocabulary 145
Minker, J 218
Mnemonics 63, 89
Moss, R 16
Murray, D M 222

National Bureau of Standards,
      USA 201
National Cancer Institute 204
National Library of Medicine 204
National Technical Information
      Service 201
Neelameghan, A 72, 82, 192
Newton, I 102, 173
North London Polytechnic 28
Notation
   brevity 14, 28, 164-165
   hierarchical 14, 35, 51, 165

   hospitality 47, 74, 89
   mnemonics 63, 89
   retroactive 34-35, 38
   the notation of schemes is discussed
   in appropriate chapters.
Nuclear science abstracts 198,
      202, 205

Ohio College Library Center
      database 240
Oklahoma Dept of Libraries 203
Olding, R K 232
Ostwald, W 27
Otlet, P 101, 245

Palmer, B I 12
Parallel classification 14
Partitioning 149, 198, 221
Perreault, J 20
Pettee, J 93
Phase relations 84
Phenomena 40, 44-45
Phoenix schedules (DDC) 229,
      234
Planes of work in classification
      54
PMEST categories. 58, 166, 181
P notes (UDC) 107
Pollard, A F 101
Porphyry, tree of 13
Post coordinate indexing 13,
      90, 144ff
Precis indexing 20, 48, 103,
      151, 159-160, 175-177,
      185-192
Precision ratio 145
Predictability of new BC 30, 49
Prevost, M 93
Psychological barriers to use of
      shelf classification 14

260

261